ONTARIO SCENE

ONTARIO SCENE

JAMES SCOTT

TORONTO
THE RYERSON PRESS

Unless otherwise credited, all photos are Courtesy of the Ontario Department of Tourism and Information.

For Fred

Good companion on many a journey

PRINTED AND BOUND IN CANADA BY THE RYERSON PRESS, TORONTO

Contents

Illustrations

ONTARIO SCENE

CHAPTER ONE

The Salad Bowl

Ontario is a province. It is one of the ten provinces which along with what are presently called The Northwest Territories make up the nation known as Canada. Most Canadians assume that they know what a province is, and perhaps at one time they did but when they try to explain this political and geographic entity to our closest neighbours—the citizens of the United States of America—they find themselves in difficulty. In trying to extricate themselves from this dilemma they resort to comparisons, and comparisons are usually inaccurate and often dangerous. A citizen of Ontario attempting to try to explain a province to an American is likely to say it is something like a state. In a vague, very vague, way this is an explanation but it really doesn't tell the whole story.

Canadians themselves have difficulty in comprehending the nature of a province. In the hundred years which have elapsed since the original four provinces (and Ontario which was then known as Upper Canada was one of them) joined together to form what has been known as "Canada" ever since, a substantial section of the Canadian intelligentsia has devoted its time and brain-power to attempting to explain just exactly what a province is. Judging by our present state of confusion on the matter their efforts have not brought either very much sweet-

1

ness or light up to now. Perhaps the best way to explain a province is to say that it is a geographically defined area whose inhabitants are certain beyond any question that the part they inhabit is the most desirable place in the world and that the inhabitants are of a superior culture, morality, sagacity and, most important of all, can make more money faster than anybody else in the country.

Provinces, being what they are then, inevitably exhibit strongly marked physical and cultural characteristics. Being a native of Ontario and true to the definition which I have just outlined, this book is going to attempt to show that the characteristics of Ontario, if not always laudable, are at least interesting and, of course—writing with a strong bias—much more interesting than any other part of Canada.

One of the most interesting characteristics of my province and which we will see exhibited in almost everything it does is the fact that the majority of its citizens—and this includes a vast number of recent arrivals whose ethnic origins are not from the British Isles—are either WASPS (white Anglo-Saxon Protestants) or else people who have accepted the standards of this group. For a hundred and fifty years Ontarians have resolutely cultivated this image and with equal resolution have blandly turned their backs on either the facts of history or of the present day. This is a facility which requires considerable mental ingenuity and in Ontario we are very good at it.

THE FRENCH BACKGROUND

For example, this province which extends from the Arctic fringes of James Bay and Hudson Bay up to the 60°N latitude down to its southernmost tip—Pelee Point just slightly below 40°N latitude—comprises a land area of some 334,000 square miles which in the beginning, at the time of the white man's arrival, was completely covered by forest, hardwood in the south and various species of evergreen in the north, and the first white visitors were all of French extraction. As far as is known the first white man who came to Ontario and decided he would like to stay there was Etienne Brulé whose sole biographer, J. H. Cranston, dubbed him "The Immortal

Scoundrel." Curious isn't it, that the first person who decided that Ontario would be a good place to live (apart from the Indians who had been there for quite some time) should be considered a scoundrel? Undoubtedly he was, but so have been a great number of gentry whose names now occupy prominent places in our carefully edited history textbooks.

As a matter of fact, Brulé's real disgrace was not what he did but rather that he was caught at it. He was a hearty young chap who came out with Samuel de Champlain, the "Father of New France," on his second voyage in 1608. At that time Brulé was sixteen years old. Two years later, Champlain was still in what was then called New France, and Brulé had become greatly intrigued by the Indians and wanted to go back with them to their hunting grounds and find out how they lived. The Indians were hesitant because they were afraid something might happen to the young Frenchman and invite reprisals from the French but finally an agreement was reached whereby a young Indian would go to France with Champlain and Brulé would remain, as he wished, with the Indians. He never returned to France. One way of putting it would be to say he had gone native. Another, and more romantic interpretation would be that this vital and imaginative young fellow was the first of many, many thousands, indeed millions, who from that time on came to this new land, were captivated by its grandeur and its challenge and decided to make it home.

Whatever the reasons, Brulé was undoubtedly the first white man who roamed through almost every section of Ontario, got to know its geography, its perils, its ambiguous attraction and, above all, the fatal lure of its great beauty. From time to time, as Champlain continued other voyages of exploration into the Ontario section Brulé would meet his former French companion but he always stayed with the Indians. It was here he came a cropper. Some of the Indian maidens undoubtedly were a joy to behold and Brulé was a young man who savoured all the delights of vigorous youth. Although the records are not explicit, he seduced one too many and his luck ran out with the result that his Indian brothers drew and quartered him and then ate him and, it is assumed, a good time was had by all with the exception of the unfortunate Brulé.

So much then for the first white man in Ontario. Undoubtedly by nature he was an adventurer but equally certain it is that the very nature of the country in which he found himself challenged his spirit and he responded to it with vigour, if not good judgment. Curiously enough, Ontario to this day elicits this response from a great number of people who live there and from those who are continuing to come to Ontario in increasing numbers every year. Fortunately, most of them at least work out their energy in ways less offensive to the piously moral environment of the province. Or, at least, not too many of them are caught at it.

What today is called the "French Fact" in the neighbouring province of Quebec is not restricted to the isolated example of Etienne Brulé. The French were a fact in Ontario for a long time in its earliest years. The first permanent white settlement in Ontario was established on the shores of Georgian Bay by Jesuit missionaries who, but not for the same reasons as applied to Etienne Brulé, were ultimately massacred. As we wander through the province we shall come upon their story and the reconstruction of their settlement. Similarly the first military installation in Ontario was French. It was established by Count de Frontenac, called after him and located where the present city of Kingston now stands. The first voyages of exploration were carried on by Frenchmen, notably by Sieur de La Salle. Niagara Falls was first seen by a Frenchman called Lamotte and a Récollet friar by the name of Hennepin. Father Hennepin wrote the first white man's description of the Falls:

Betwixt the lakes Ontario and Erie there is a vast and prodigious cadence of water which falls down after a surprising and astonishing manner insomuch that the universe does not afford its parallel. 'Tis true Italy and Suedeland boast of some such things but we may well say that they are but sorry patterns when compared to this of which we now speak . . . This wonderful downfall is compounded of two great cross sections of water and two falls with an isle sloping along the middle of it. The waters which fall from this vast height do foam and boil after the most hideous manner imaginable, making an outrageous noise, more terrible than thunder; for when the wind blows from off the south their dismal roaring may be heard about fifteen leagues off.

The French did not confine themselves to what is generally known as Southern Ontario. In fact most of them were more familiar with that vast territory to the north which even today is very sparsely populated. The reason for this was that the French in their hunger for fine pelts of fur raced over what were in those times unbelievable distances in order to contact and trade with the Indians of the Northwest. These adventurers quickly mastered the art of handling what one of them called "that miraculous invention, the birch bark canoe." Starting from the major trading post, which was Montreal, they proceeded up the Ottawa River to the site of present-day Mattawa, crossed what was known as the Grand Portage into Lake Nipissing and down the French River into Georgian Bay and then on up into the Lakehead and beyond. Long before the British had ceased their preoccupation with clearing the land and settling Southern Ontario and then heading northwards, the French had been there, knew it well and travelled through the perilous country with ease. Today in Northern Ontario there are many French-speaking Canadians but they are not the descendants of the original fur traders.

The historical background of Ontario, then, is undoubtedly French in its earliest times. The question is, what happened? How did it come about that this province made a complete about-face and became what it is today, through the efforts of a completely different people, largely drawn, in the beginning, from the British Isles? To find the answer we have to journey into every corner of the province, see what it is and try to find out how it became the way it is and, happily, this is not a dull intellectual exercise. It is a journey, or series of journeys, where there is something interesting to see and, even more important, something interesting to think about wherever we go.

THE COUNTRY AND THE CLIMATE

Certainly coming into Ontario today, until one gets well up into the north country, there is little to suggest the rugged wilderness which was its primeval state. In Southern Ontario there is some of the richest and most fertile land in the world.

At its best moments—just on the edge of summer—its undulating countryside, dotted with prosperous cities and towns, is rich and varied. One of my friends who makes regular pilgrimages through the beautiful countryside has called it "The Salad Bowl" and she is right. There is a freshness and a crispness and a tastiness about Ontario which is most appetizing.

It was not always like this. It certainly was not like this when the French were there; no more was it like this when the first real settlers came into its vast forest. These people did not come seeking beauty. They came for a thoroughly practical reason. Almost all of them were having a hard time in their native lands and the lure of cheap, or in some cases free, land in the new world was the magnet which drew them into Ontario. Most of them expected to have a hard time and they did.

I think of one story about a band of four men trudging along what was little more than a blazed trail through unknown territory, walking over forty miles to the place where their land holding was to be found. Each carried a pack on his back with the supplies which would have to do them through a long, hard Canadian winter—a longer and harder winter than any them could possibly imagine. Besides their supplies their only equipment were muskets and axes but one of them, a young man from Scotland, carefully carried his violin. The saga of the axe and the fiddle is typical of those pioneer days, and one of them reminiscing at the age of ninety-seven is on record as saying he was not sure whether the axe or the fiddle was more important in their survival. In purely utilitarian terms the axe of course was essential but these men, separated from their families, were three thousand miles from home. Despondency and despair were as serious enemies as nature itself and when these black moods came upon them it was the lilting strains of the old familiar Scottish airs which restored their spirits and gave them the courage to carry on. Today, the same combination applies. Even my dentist, who perhaps represents as unpleasant an experience as modern man is called upon to face, plays soothing music while he goes about his fiendish business.

It is not easy, looking at Ontario today, to identify it with what is was one hundred and fifty years ago. When I was a student at Harvard I made a friend who had the standard conception of the average American about Canada. For him it was one vast hunting ground with little in the way of the civilization of cities, largely covered with woods, its streams loaded with fish and it was the ideal place for an outdoor holiday. In vain I tried to tell him that one had to go many, many miles north to get even close to this. He didn't believe me so I asked him to come to see for himself. He arrived with complete camping equipment and every latest gadget known to civilized man for conquering the wilderness. He was a little baffled and, in fact, I think a little disappointed to find that he had travelled all the way from Pennsylvania on excellent paved roads to my house and that the cities where he stopped were virtually indistinguishable from those of his native state. Nevertheless, an illusion dies hard and he was still convinced that an hour's drive in the right direction would take us into some kind of sportsman's outdoor paradise.

As we talked and made plans for our trip, a beguiling thought was forming in my mind, something I had often thought about but never had had the courage to try out alone. I told my friend something about the early days and what they were like until his interest was really aroused, then came the clincher: I suggested that we try the same thing, that is that we go well up into Northern Ontario into as remote a region as we could find, leave his fancy utensils behind, take a canoe and with only basic supplies see how we would make out in the true wilderness for a week. He agreed and with considerable foreboding on my part we actually did set out to perform the experiment.

We drove to Sudbury, still on paved road all the way, much to his surprise, and then farther and farther north until we found a rather dilapidated establishment which rented canoes for fishermen. We had no map and only two packs—mostly clothes, mosquito repellent (that was cheating a bit) and basic food—salted bacon, pork, flour, oatmeal, etc. True to old tradition I even had a well sharpened axe. We had no tent. We set off bravely. The weather was fair, the stream we followed sparkling clear and fast running and soon we came to a little rapids which we had to portage. A little later we reached a lake and it seemed indeed as if we had left all civilization behind us and there we were, two intrepid young adventurers precariously re-living the past of our ancestors, excited and challenged by the fact that here indeed was nature in the raw and that to survive we would have to subdue it.

Well it's a long story. During the period we were there we caught exactly three fish large enough to feed us and one of them was wormy. The lean-to shelter which I had read about and thought I knew how to build proved to be absolutely useless when a wild and terrifying thunderstorm and downpour of rain struck us on our second night. If it had not been for the bottle of good Canadian rye whisky we had been far-sighted enough to bring along with us we would have packed up right then.

By this time we were beginning to worry about food and although we had brought along some firearms there just plain wasn't anything to shoot. Over the lake each night (we had camped on a small island) the crazy laugh of the loon mocked us. By the middle of the fourth day the storm clouds were gathering again and we decided to leave. Paddling at a frantic pace across the lake the two outdoorsmen got lost, missed the river which we had taken on coming to the lake and after some exploring for two or three miles along the shore suddenly came upon a very civilized little village complete with pub, general store and an assortment of tourists. All the time we thought we had been living in splendid isolation we were not more than about four miles from this little paradise. We spent the night there, savoured every minute of civilization, hiked a ride back to where we had left our car and headed to "The Salad Bowl" where my friend discovered Toronto, decided it was as good as Philadelphia any day and spent a wonderful week on the town.

In the four days which I had spent outdoors virtually naked, my already deep tan had become almost mahogany and while we were enjoying the delights of Toronto we were asked to a party to meet a rather famous British writer. In those days I was a well-brought-up child and the next day I phoned my hostess to thank her for a pleasant evening.

"But my dear," she said, "You absolutely *made* my party. My guest said that ever since she has come to Canada she has been looking forward to meeting a real North American Indian and you are the first one she encountered!"

I have never tried to be a pioneer since nor have I ever again been mistaken for a North American Indian.

The British as well as the Americans still carry some strange misconceptions about this province of ours.

A couple of years ago returning by car from a trip to Florida I was caught in a violent blizzard in the mountains just outside of Harrisburg and was benighted for a day and a half. As I waited for them to clear the roads of the tremendous snowfall I kept thinking of my old friend who, amongst other things, was convinced that once winter comes all of Canada, including Ontario, is snow-bound for at least six months. The temptation was too great and I had to phone him to tell him that the Pennsylvania winter had entrapped me for a longer period of time than any snowfall I had ever experienced in Ontario. He didn't believe me of course. He swore I was calling from Toronto!

It is a fact, however, that we do have a wide range of climate in Ontario and, to some extent, it does influence our way of life. The normal course of business is not interfered with but the climate does determine the kind of recreation which we enjoy in this province. For me this is great because it gives us a wide variety of things to do.

It is fairly commonplace in Ontario (in the Southern section at least) to hear old-timers say, "The winters ain't what they used to be." Broadly interpreted this means that they don't think we get as much snow. The Meteorological Offices will prove this is wrong. The only difference is that we now have highly sophisticated equipment to remove it from our roads and traffic moves with almost the same ease as during the summer months. But we still have plenty of winter to provide all the opportunities for winter sports which have characterized the life of this province. As we continue our journey we shall see the ski slopes, the arenas and rinks but we will not see many cutters or bobsleds except in the museums. The roads are kept too clear for their general use any more. Each season brings its own particular type of recreation and we will look at them all and find out where to go as we explore Ontario.

The variability of the climate is really one of the province's greatest assets. For one thing it determines the wide range of vegetation which is to be found here. Every time I spend a considerable stretch in southern latitudes I find I am getting a little tired of palm trees and start yearning for the sight of a big, solid elm or maple even though it be in the middle of winter, completely defoliated. In the south even when the grass is green it somehow doesn't have the alive greenness of my lawn after it has been cut for the first time for that season. I long for the sight of the rich, greasy, black loam turned over at the first plowing in the spring and I savour the moment when the first tulips and daffodils thrust their way through the cold ground with their promise of beautiful bloom in a few weeks. Perhaps variety is indeed the spice of life and if this be so then there is no place which by its very nature provides a more spicy environment for man than this province.

Generally speaking no season lasts too long. If we have had a really tough winter and have reached the point where we are just about ready to pack it in, suddenly there comes a balmy March day and we know that spring is not far behind. Our climate is such that it is always a bit tantalizing and it certainly makes life more interesting. After warm summers we have the autumn which many people consider to be our most spectacular season. Now colour runs riot. The flaming reds, oranges, yellows, often contrasted sharply against a thicket of evergreen almost seem to explode before the eyes and generate a peculiar kind of excitement in the native of Ontario. The leaves fall, people rake them up and burn them and one of the most pleasant aromas in the world is that which comes from a bonfire of dried Ontario leaves. The corn is ready then too and this is the season of corn roasts and the good fellowship which inevitably develops around an open fire. Even a wild winter gale, when one is snug inside, creates a feeling of pleasant well being.

In short there is no time of year when it is not good to visit Ontario. The environment is inevitably interesting and, as we shall see, there are plenty of things to do and see as well as a variable and delightful atmosphere to savour.

ONTARIO "CHARACTERS"

And then there are the people. No matter where one rambles in Ontario, if he takes the time he will come upon as amusing, irritating, and delightful "characters" as can be found anywhere in the world. They exist in the small towns, along the country roads and in our huge cities.

In Toronto, until a few years ago, it was a commonplace sight on Bay Street (the financial centre of Canada) to see a horsedrawn carriage or phaeton (depending on the weather) transporting two dignified old ladies bedecked and beplumed in the styles of the Edwardian era. With a fine disregard for the killer instincts of the average Toronto driver, the top-hatted coachman, sitting straight on his box, would thread his way through the maze of traffic as the ladies went about their business as if nothing had changed in seventy-five years. As they made their way back to their mid-town mansion, a virtual replica of the Victorian era, they would pass a little shop on Yonge Street run by another determined old girl who resolutely refused to accept change. In her shop she carried a complete line of carefully horded clothes of another day— high-button shoes, corsettes, lisle stockings, voluminous petti-coats, hundreds of boxes of fancy buttons, and a mad assort-ment of everything from ostrich plumes to bustles. She had many visitors drawn by curiosity but, to my knowledge, no customers. On every side were fancy tailor shops, all-night record shops blaring forth the frantic rhythms of the rock age, large department stores, expensive jewellery stores and all the adjuncts of mercantilism in the affluent society, but the old girl remained untouched by it all.

In the towns there is always an assortment of characters. Sometimes they are but the butt of practical jokers; sometimes they are just remarkable sturdy individuals firmly set in their own ideas and not ready to give an inch to anything. I think of a friend of mine in a small and very quiet Lake Huron resort. He operated what was called—inevitably—The Ritz

Hotel. The Ritz was a frame structure of many turrets, iron grills and fancy porches. One fine summer evening as my wife and I were strolling down the main street near the hotel we saw billows of smoke pouring from the vicinity of the chimney. When we arrived on the scene my friend Tom—the ideal prototype of an innkeeper, bald, red of face, genial of expression and immense in girth—was standing outside his hostelry carefully contemplating the smoke.

"Your chimney is on fire, Tom!" I shouted.

Tom accepted this with complete equanimity. "It was on fire this afternoon too," he said.

At this point the whole roof burst into flames and for the first time Tom was moved to action. "Save the bar!" he shouted. By this time a considerable crew had been attracted and without any question whatsoever, despite the fact that there was a good deal of valuable equipment in the hotel, to a man they devoted their strength to pulling out the magnificent mahogany bar which had graced the Ritz ever since it had first been built around 1885. Tom himself, with admirable single-mindedness of purpose, rescued his favourite rocking-chair, set it across the road well away from the now wildly burning building, and sat down to contemplate what had happened. It burned, literally, to the ground. Outside of a few odds and ends only the bar and Tom's rocking-chair had been rescued and he was well content, but not so his wife. As the fire diminished she began buttonholing everyone in sight, asking them if they had seen her laundry bag, the one that was hanging on a peg behind the kitchen door. She explained with considerable urgency that this was the place where she kept all the receipts for the total summer's business. "You can't trust banks you know," she said, expecting complete understanding from everyone. And believe it or not, in a pile of odds and ends which had been thrown out at some point during the fire, the laundry bag was found. The last I saw of the hotelkeeper and his wife they were carefully counting the money and agreeing with each other that a laundry bag behind the kitchen door was indeed a much safer place than any bank in Ontario.

And so it goes. Every town is full of such stories but it is not really the eccentrics who have created the climate of present-day Ontario. To understand the myriad things which are to be seen and enjoyed in this province it is necessary to have some slight comprehension of the people who made it this way.

HERE COME THE BRITISH!

While the French undoubtedly were the first white people in the province, largely due to the Iroquois who had been sworn enemies of the French ever since Champlain had taken the side of the Algonquins and then the Hurons against them, the French settlements never really took root in Ontario and there is no continuous French settlement in the province. It was after the Peace of Paris, signed in 1763, that all the French-held lands in North America became British. Little of the action occurred in Ontario save at Fort Niagara and the uprising of the Indian chief, Pontiac. The significant thing for our narrative is that the French, who were not really very vigorous colonizers were succeeded by the British who, at this point, really did not want the French holdings in North America at all and showed similar disinterest in opening up this rich country. It is fair to say that no one — French or English—had any concept of the potential which existed in what is now Ontario or had any interest in finding out about it. It was the American Revolution which produced the first major change.

When the war between Britain and the thirteen colonies was lost, through dull generalship, political ineptitude and an obtuse king, there were many British in North America both in the army and amongst the settlers who had little faith in the future of what was to become the United States and little desire to remain there. Many of them had been active antagonists of the republicans and quite justifiably felt that they were going to have a rough time if they stayed. In Britain there was some stirring of conscience over these people and, with vast tracts of land under British control north of the 49th parallel, it seemed a good idea to offer this group, which was known as "The United Empire Loyalists", free land. A great many from the New England States found their way into the Maritime Provinces; others mostly from Pennsylvania and upper New York State came to Ontario and constituted the first substantial band of colonizers in the province. Much has been written about these so-called Loyalists. In actual fact far from all of them were heroes dedicated to the crown and imperial sceptre regardless of the cost. For example, several thousand were mercenary troops, not British at all but Hessians and the British government decided it would be cheaper to give them free land in Canada than to try to bring them back to Europe. A large number of others were simply people who realized that the areas they were living in in the United States were becoming over-populated, that land was getting very valuable and who saw in their "loyalty" a chance to get large holdings of excellent new land. They were wise in the ways of pioneering and for them this was a practical rather than a patriotic opportunity. True enough, there were distinguished leaders who had fought valiantly against the revolution but they were in the minority.

Once in Canada, and this includes what is now Ontario, an interesting phenomenon occurred. Safely on their good land and with clear title to it they could afford the luxury of noble sentiments and thus began a myth carefully cultivated to this day. One of the favourite places picked for settlement was along the Bay of Quinte, lovely country and good land. Here the predominant population was Hessian and they gave their settlements names such as Adolphustown—hardly a fine old Anglo-Saxon name but then the British king himself was hardly a fine old Anglo-Saxon either. But now they busily set about proving that they were British to the core. They were the group which, without too much substantial help from Britain, had the virtue to stand up and fight for (and remember many of them were paid for it) all the traditional British values which were being torn down by an ill-bred rabble led by highly ambitious men who, in this definition, were the founders of the United States. In terms of active colonization and opening up the land, the contribution of the Loyalists is relatively insignificant but like does attract like. The next group of any size which came into Ontario was made up largely of retired army officers, half-pay officers and men and a strange group of pretentious people who somehow got the idea that in Ontario they would have an opportunity to live like the gentry they never were back in Great Britain. Most of these people settled in what is still called Eastern Ontario, that is the half of the southernmost part of the province extending eastward from Toronto to the Ottawa River. They straggled out a bit to the west along the coastline as far as Niagara but the great portion of what is the richest part of Ontario — Western Ontario—attracted no interest whatever.

When the time came for the first governmental structure to be set up under the first Governor, John Graves Simcoe, it was comprised of sixteen men, ten of whom came from Eastern Ontario and the remaining six from the Niagara Peninsula. The legislators took haphazard passes at setting up some kind of responsible government but the population was so small and so scattered that for the next thirty years the province limped along with very little progress in terms of expansion and development.

On the other hand it deeply confirmed the attitude which had already begun with the United Empire Loyalists. Many offices carrying considerable prestige with them were created and in this period an official class sprang up which left its mark on Ontario almost up to the present day. Taken out of the context of extreme provincialism, what went on in Ontario in those years is really high comedy or low burlesque. For example Governor Simcoe in 1794 in the middle of the woods which is now part of Toronto built a primitive rectangular log house 30′ x 50′ with a façade which was a crude approximation of a Greek temple and this rough hewn building he called Castle Frank. Later, an honest-to-goodness castle of the same name was built in Toronto but the pretensions of the governor are an indicator of how almost the whole population was behaving in Upper Canada as Ontario was known at that time. Anybody of any consequence whatsoever had some kind of official title. Elegant carriages were imported, or a little later, built locally to transport the would-be gentry over virtually non-existent roads. Upper Canada was filled with administrators with high-sounding titles.

This intriguing façade was shored up considerably by the church—The Church of England, of course. Part of the posture of being British to the core, included the concept of a state church, a prospect by no means unappealing to the Anglican clergy in Upper Canada. Despite the fact that even in this lightly populated area there were Methodist circuit-riders, Presbyterian missionaries, and a wide variety of other Protestant sects as well as Roman Catholics, "The Group" firmly believed that they could brush all this activity aside and make the Church of England the state church of Upper Canada just as it was in England itself. As the years went on officialdom at all levels became inextricably tied in with the Anglican clergy and further reinforced the gentry-in-the-back-woods concept of living which pervaded Upper Canada.

Because this way of life was not suited to the realities of pioneering, sooner or later it had to be challenged and it was with ultimate success, but a residue of this kind of thinking exists in Ontario even today as we shall see when we start to attend some of the functions which mark the Ontario social calendar.

THE PIOUS PIONEERS TAKE OVER

The identifiable challenge came in the form of a charade of a rebellion in 1837 led in Ontario by William Lyon Mackenzie, grandfather of one of Canada's greatest Prime Ministers, William Lyon Mackenzie King.

The rebellion was lost but the things which it stood for gradually gained support as the population increased and a different kind of settler moved into the province, especially into the neglected Western Ontario area. They began to come after the War of 1812-1814 was over. As hard times and shifting ownership of land made the lot of the British peasant farmer increasingly difficult within the next forty years migration to Ontario increased at an astonishing rate. Now the majority of the population was made up of a different kind of settler. These were in a sense desperate men, men who had nothing to lose and everything to gain if they took cheap land, cleared it, cultivated it, harvested their crops from the extremely fertile soil and gradually established themselves in positions of prosperity and influence. This is exactly what they did and they formed the nucleus of the Reform Party which ultimately challenged the administration group which had come to be known as The Family Compact. It was a very tough and long-drawn-out battle. Those in power and authority were not willing to relinquish it readily; those now in the majority and, as they felt, suffering from a narrow-minded and snobbish minority were equally determined to assert their rights and gain power. The struggle see-sawed back and forward over the years and, in a sense, it is not over yet.

While the new settlers were not much interested or attracted to the way of living practised by the backwoods aristocracy, they did develop their own particular brand of provincialism. While effectively destroying any possibility of a state church they substituted their own rather rigid forms of religion and for many years in Ontario the church, regardless of its denomination, was a major influence in the life of the province, its towns and agricultural communities. These people who had survived only through hard physical labour accepted this as a primary virtue. Reacting against the frippery of the Upper Canadian aristocracy, they over-emphasized a plain way of life. In short, a rigid kind of puritanism with all its unique imbalance of virtues now marched side by side with the Anglophiles.

In these two groups can be found the origins of what Ontario has become today. Looked at in the perspective of history, it is something of a miracle that today's Ontario is the thrusting and exciting place which it, in fact, is. What the traveller has to remember is that what you find here today is relatively new. In a sense it is a spectacular and sometimes violent reaction against a kind of smugness which blanketed this province for almost one hundred years.

On the other hand, that century of solemn piety, narrow morality, conservative business practices and cautious idealism was probably very necessary in order that today's swinging Ontario could be built on a strong and firm foundation. There is a great deal in our past for which we ought to be grateful and which it is easy to admire. Wherever we go on this particular journey, we will be assailed by the past and the present—so widely different in character—living side by side and in considerable harmony.

As we move through this province we will find people, architecture, customs and ways of doing business which will sometimes irritate but more often interest the traveller. We are back to a very old proposition: one cannot get the full value out of what he experiences as he travels unless he has some comprehension of the past which led to the present.

Throughout Ontario, for example, you can find truly wretched, ugly buildings along every highway and at every crossroads. Plain, gaunt frame structures which were maybe churches, schools or public halls. To look at them is almost to shudder and to think "What sterile and unimaginative people have made this land." But, as we have seen, that is only one side of the story. These are the physical manifestations of those plain folk who in their struggle for a viable economy (and encouraged by their reaction to the Family Compact) deliberately, and it would seem with some kind of perverted enjoyment, built the plainest, starkest public buildings they could conceive. The other side of the coin is the fact that, while the style of living was not just mediocre but in many cases unnecessarily dull, it did produce a reservoir of wealth on which it has now become possible to build this province to its present stature and greatness. And of course there is the exception. Not quite so easily found but, in every town in any part of the province one will come upon the antithesis of the plain style. Here a beautifully proportioned house, a magnificent church, a beautiful town hall. These too represent the other stream which has been here from the beginning of British rule.

ONTARIO IS NOW

Now, of course, Ontario is striking out on its own and the two old adversaries have been melded into one. This in itself was not enough. Ontario still attracts more immigrants than any other part of Canada and these, now in vast numbers in this province, have been the leaven which has created an impressive ferment and which has given Ontario a broad outlook, a sensitivity to what is going on all over the world and with its wealth, its firmly rooted institutions, both cultural and financial, it has been in a unique position to take advantage of this new kind of thinking.

The Ontario which I have explored over many years and which is always worth seeing again is a fascinating amalgam of its stodgy past and its activist present. Understood this way, this makes for good looking and it makes for good experiences, the kind which are appreciated best if the traveller has time to pause, contemplate and perhaps think a bit about the basic implications which underlie whatever it is that has caught his interest.

As a veteran explorer of my own province, one who has never tired of the infinite and interesting variety of my homeland, I inevitably start any journey by moving only a few miles away from home.

When I was a boy our Presbyterian Sundays were rather grim. We were not allowed to look at the comics; I was forbidden to ride my bicycle; I even had to shine my shoes ready for church on Saturday night (all this was fairly typical of a good deal of Ontario even twenty-five years ago). We went to church and Sunday school but that did not fill the entire day. With some kind of intricate rationalization we reached the point where it was considered to be morally acceptable to drive through the countryside on a Sunday afternoon. To make it more interesting we worked out a plan. Our objective was to travel over every road in my native county—Huron County. We kept a map, marked it with pins and each Sunday worked out our itinerary. At the time it was not particularly exciting but many years later, when I was undertaking to write a history of the settlement of Huron County, I was astonished to discover how much I had absorbed from those Sunday drives. I still drive through my local area and now I have many points of reference. I can see the changes and often I marvel at them. Travel has become something which I now experience in depth and it seems to me that this is the right way to do it.

Since those early years I have travelled in many parts of the world and have tried it both ways—the quick, organized tour where you return home with two hundred slides and can hardly remember the ten minute stop you had when you took twenty pictures or, on the other hand, the infinitely more rewarding method of choosing a spot which looks interesting, a subject which is intriguing, and then spending lots of time seeing more, observing more closely, and gradually absorbing the feel of the area.

The same thing applies to armchair travel. Basically it is fun but underneath it one hopes he will emerge with a little deeper comprehension of how his fellow man has lived, lives now and is going to live.

Another permitted Sunday diversion in my youth was a walk in the woods. In my part of the county we still have substantial stands, wisely kept intact by the early settlers as they cleared the land, made up of the deciduous trees common to this part of the world with a large predominance of hard and soft maple. Even today, a walk in the woods is a soothing and pleasant experience and if one goes in the spring he will still find an abundance of wild flowers of which by far the most plentiful is the trillium. The trillium is an almost virginal-looking three petalled flower. It is usually white and because it grows with such profusion throughout all of Southern Ontario it has been chosen as the floral emblem of the province.

It is a somewhat curious choice. In the first place, it does not take kindly to domestication. From time to time all my life I have attempted to transplant trilliums from the woods to my garden. Sometimes they would grow for a while but never did they proliferate vigorously and they require almost constant attention. The trillium indeed is truly a wild flower. It is hard to believe that whoever it was who chose this as the emblem of this province did so because it was hard to reduce to orderly cultivation. Unconsciously perhaps we do things that are wiser than we know. I am firmly convinced that Ontario's people are far from the staid, contained and tractable citizens some of our legislators seem to think we are. As we explore the province we will see, time and time again, evidences that the trillium is indeed a proper symbol for

Ontario and that the wild ones, quietly and unobtrusively but stubbornly, resist the imposition of an outside system of order.

It is appropriate too that the trillium grows in the woods. Over two-thirds of this province is still woodland albeit mostly in the north country. All of the province was woodland in the beginning. Our origins then lie in the wilderness and later on we shall see how the Ontario folk subdued it and the ingenuity which they brought to bear in order to achieve their purpose and, of course, at the same time make money. But, from the arrival of the first white man at least, the simple and beautiful trillium was nestled along the ground in the midst of the wilderness. Prolific and defying extinction, it not only represents nature but nature at its best and gentlest. A lot of this has been translated into the facts of Ontario life. The trillium may not be the most flamboyant floral emblem in the world but for anyone living in Ontario it has a wealth and depth of meaning, a kind of meaning which, hopefully, would get to every visitor who seeks to explore this contradictory, sometimes irritating, always exciting and very hard-headed province.

CHAPTER TWO

The
Thoroughly Enjoyable Death Wish

The Ontario Department of Tourism and Information lists over two hundred historic sites and museums in a readily available brochure. Most of these two hundred are indeed museums of various kinds ranging from artifacts of the pioneer period to mining and the development of other similar industries. Also included are a few of Ontario's most imposing monuments, some early churches and houses as well as a few very distinctive ancient public buildings. These interesting spots are located in every corner of the province and generally are easily accessible.

The interesting thing about this proliferation of collections of material from the past is not so much their great number and wide variety as the fact that most of them have come into being within the last generation. Especially since the end of World War II, the whole of Ontario has been on a search-for-the-past kick. This bears a little investigating.

When I was a boy growing up in a Scottish-Canadian community I can well remember that I actually felt it was a disgrace that neither my parents nor my grandparents had been born in Scotland. Actually, I am a sixth-generation Canadian and somehow—I haven't any clues as to where I got the idea—in my youth I was firmly convinced that this made me

Trilliums, Floral Emblem of Ontario

Ste-Marie among the Hurons, Midland

Upper Canada Village, near Morrisburg
Fanshawe Park Pioneer Village, near London

an inferior sort of citizen. It would be easy enough to say that this was merely a personal manifestation of a colonial complex which Canadians are supposed to have had and, to some extent, still have. Our writers and social analysts worry at this one constantly, and undoubtedly there is some truth in it but surely it is far from the whole story. In Ontario at least, and I suspect to a lesser extent in all the other provinces, we have developed recently a very strong identification with the past, not the past of our ancestors in some foreign clime overseas but the past of our immediate ancestors who settled and built the province. This is an intriguing phenomenon and in my travels I keep looking for some kind of indicators which may give me some enlightenment beyond the broad generalizations of our social scientists.

One thing has emerged which both puzzles and fascinates me. In the scores of museums of any respectable size one of the prize exhibits is a horse-drawn hearse and usually ranged around it are a variety of coffins ranging from very small ones for those who have died in infancy up to reasonably elaborate ones of the pioneer era. Inevitably as I make a tour through such a museum the spot where the hearse with its attendant coffins is located has a group of almost hypnotized onlookers. Now here is something to ponder indeed.

I doubt that any psychologist has examined this particular and peculiar behaviour pattern amongst the people of Ontario but if they were to I am sure the phrase "death wish" would quickly be bandied about. Well we all are going to die some day and some people more than others do indeed have a preoccupation with death and all the elaborate and illogical trappings with which our civilization has surrounded it. In my own town, for example, we have several old ladies and a couple of idle old gentlemen who never miss a funeral. In some way which a layman like myself does not quite comprehend this is a highly-rated form of entertainment for them and, better still, in a Scottish community like mine, it doesn't cost a cent. In my district there are also families which pay at least weekly visits to the local graveyard. Some of them go to inspect the graves of loved ones of their family and perhaps put some flowers there but—and I have checked this out—a

good number of them go merely to wander around the cemetery. This too is free entertainment. There are a large number
of Ontario people who actually enjoy going to a funeral parlor
where some corpse is "laid out" and who take considerable
delight in checking out the flowers, examining the possible
cost of the coffin and, best of all, shedding a few tears. On the
basis of this highly unscientific personal research I am convinced that a large number of people thoroughly enjoy the
paraphernalia which surrounds death and, if I am going to
continue my armchair analysis further, it is because they can
look at these objects and unconsciously say to themselves I am
not there yet.

Broadening this reaction I am convinced that this is the
real attraction for most people when they look at all relics of
the past. When you stand in a pioneer museum if, say, you are
a farmer you can spend a considerable amount of enjoyable
time looking at primitive hay rakes, flails for threshing and
several other hundred equally clumsy items and your real
enjoyment will derive from the fact that back on your own
farm you have the modern and sophisticated equivalents—all
extremely labour saving—and unconsciously the reaction must
be pleasurable. Ideally this is not what museums are supposed
to do to people but I think it is very likely that this is really
what museums do. The theory, of course, is that when one
goes to a museum he relives history—usually local history.
This is often a component of the museum visitor's experience
but I am highly sceptical that it is the strongest or basic reaction. Man, being what he is, gets some of his highest
pleasure from being what he thinks the other fellow is not.

In any event, regardless of motivation, most people like to
go to museums primarily not to be instructed but to derive
enjoyment. Ontario has plenty of such places to satisfy both
general and special needs.

UPPER CANADA VILLAGE

Because Eastern Ontario was settled first—and therefore its
history goes back farther than any other part of the province
—some of the best places of this sort to visit are to be found

in this area. And here it might be well to digress to point out that it is not difficult to get almost anywhere in Ontario and especially in Southern Ontario.

This province is particularly fortunate in that it now has a double-laned throughway which runs from Windsor on the west to the utmost eastern extremity. As has been the custom with the present provincial government, major roads such as this bear the names of party heroes and this highway which is designated as Highway 401 also carries the name of two great early Canadian Conservatives—Sir John A. Macdonald and Etienne Cartier, hence the Macdonald-Cartier Freeway. And it is important to note that it is indeed a freeway if not necessarily a Tory one. There are no tolls on this magnificent road. It is easy to reach Highway 401 from any United States border crossing point in Southern Ontario. Those farthest away from it, that is in the Niagara Peninsula, have their own double-laned freeway which is called the Queen Elizabeth Way (it was named before the Conservative Party took office in Ontario). For side trips almost all the connecting highways are in excellent condition and there are few places in North America with a better system of roads than Ontario.

So it is easy to get to Eastern Ontario, no matter where your starting point may be, and then you can explore to your heart's content museums going back to the earliest days of white settlement. And most important you can visit the pioneer village which is by far the most outstanding in the province, Upper Canada Village, near the site of a battlefield in the War 1812-1814. This battlefield known as Crysler's Farm has now been made into an attractive park. The combination of the pioneer village and all the recreational facilities included in Crysler's Farm Battlefield Park makes this one of the most attractive places for the historically-minded traveller. It can also be reached by water and there are good docking facilities on the St. Lawrence River side of this elaborate tourist development. Not being a warlike people, we are a little short on battlefields and the Crysler's Farm site does not represent any epoch-shattering moment in Canadian history. It was indeed the scene of an engagement where, if our side is to be believed, eight hundred sturdy Ontario militiamen defeated four thousand United States regulars. This may or may not be but the fact is that the Crysler's Farm episode was only a small part of that curious see-saw battle which raged mostly along the waterways (the St. Lawrence, Lake Ontario and Lake Erie) during the war. From time to time we have attempted to create some military heroes in Ontario but they don't seem to have taken on very well. Rather, it is something to our credit that no visitor to Upper Canada Village is going to be in any way irritated by the kind of jingoism which is found in almost every country in the western world and is happily and conspicuously absent in this province. Crysler's Farm wasn't bad, it has turned out to be an excellent site for a park, and it is best to let it go at that.

Upper Canada Village, however, is another story. It is administered by the St. Lawrence Parks Commission and what has been done here has been done very well. Upper Canada Village has only been in operation a few years and, up to this time, represents the finest achievement of the people of Ontario as they have become conscious of their past and started doing something about it.

Look out for the first sight of the village. It is enclosed and one has to pay a minimal entrance fee at the gate. So far so good but also look out for the souvenir shop at the exit—very good of its kind, with most of the stock authentic goods actually made in the village, which tourists are supposed to find irresistible. I have been to Upper Canada Village many times and I have resisted everything, even a penny folder of matches up to this point. But once past this totem of North American materialism and commercialization you move into another world, an authentic world of life as it developed in the earliest years of settlement in Eastern Ontario. To savour it fully and see the multitude of interesting things with which the village abounds takes at least half a day and, curiously, most of the people who come to the village (even those dedicated to covering as many miles possible in as short a time possible) are trapped by its easy-going charm and very few people hurry through. Were it not for the visitors in their gay summer clothing you could easily swear that the clock had been moved back a hundred and fifty years.

The way of life which Upper Canada Village reflects is indeed unique to Eastern Ontario and the kind of reconstructed villages which are now starting to spring up in Western Ontario are noticeably different. In terms of Ontario's evolution from a colonial attitude to democratic and responsible government, the way of life exemplified in Upper Canada Village may be deplored but its charm and grace cannot be gainsaid. The overall impression is imposing. In the centre stands open pasture land where cattle and oxen feed, dirt roads wind with apparently no fixed plan linking together the various facets of life at the turn of the nineteenth century in colonial Ontario. The village has its own population, men and women dressed in the costumes of the period and going about the business of the period—stripping logs for the sawmill which actually operates, operating the two inns, the sexton of the Anglican Church busily keeping it in order, the men in the stables looking after the horses and, right on time, the arrival of the stage coach. Everything seems real in Upper Canada Village. When you go into a stable it smells of horses because horses are still kept there and, similarly, when you walk along the dirt roads you keep a wary eye out for horse droppings because horses actually travel these roads.

In order to have a vivid picture of what the first type of settled life in Ontario was it is worth while looking rather closely at Upper Canada Village because all of it is here. The most imposing building in the village is Crysler Hall which is as close to a manor house as one will find anywhere in Ontario. Built by the son of the Crysler on whose farm the battle was fought, Colonel John Pliny Crysler, it is built of brick with a central square and two wings ornamented on the front, with gracious Doric columns rising the full height of the house. A circular driveway curves to the front door and the grounds are laid out in a formal garden. This kind of thing was in the mind of many a settler and we shall see some more examples of it as we move along, but the lord-of-the-manor concept is alien to Ontario even though it could flourish sporadically in the early days. Not quite so imposing but equally representative of the urge to be "gentry" is the French-Robertson House which was first built in 1784. Jeremiah

French was a United Empire Loyalist and, typically enough, even when he first settled he refused to build a log cabin but insisted upon a house built with unbaked clay brick which gradually grew in size to its present somewhat imposing proportions. Ultimately Jeremiah French became a member of the Legislative Council and married his daughter off to George Robertson, a wealthy merchant who further added to the house. The house is filled with excellent examples of fine furniture imported from England and equally attractive examples of early Canadian cabinet-making. The wallpaper is the original wallpaper printed before 1820 in England and hangs on the drawing-room walls. There is also a large stable with quarters for a groom and stablemen included.

Next down the scale is the pastor's house which one might have expected to have been for a rector of the Church of England but, remembering the many Germans who were numbered among the United Empire Loyalists, this is the home of a Lutheran pastor, the Reverend William Sharts. It is interesting, however, to discover that the early pattern was not really much disturbed, because a few years later two of the Lutheran pastors in the area went over to the Church of England. The doctor's house, in this case that of Dr. Keogh, is smaller but still a very considerable cut above the usual dwelling of the times. In terms of historical interest virtually an entire chapter on pioneer medicine is illustrated in this house with its waiting-room, consulting-room and a very complete assortment of instruments and drugs which a pioneer doctor used. From the doctor to the schoolmaster there is a noticeable drop. The schoolmaster's house is plain though sturdy. His living quarters are somewhat cramped and the upstairs attic used for pupils who boarded with him indicates the limited nature of education available in those days. The downstairs classroom could not hold more than a dozen pupils. In that era in Ontario, education was for the rich and was counted as a privilege. The schoolmaster himself was accepted but grudgingly; he was underpaid and did not quite rate amongst the true gentry—the large landowners, preferably of U. E. L. stock, the clergy, and the wealthy merchants and particularly those who had sought and gained public office.

There is a sharp distinction between these graceful homes and those which represent the sort of dwelling in which the true settler lived. The village contains excellent examples of the various types of farmhouses which developed as settlement progressed. There is a good settler's log cabin and log barn, a most primitive dwelling which will bring vividly to mind the situation which the average pioneer, without advantage of land grants, military or civil prestige or wealth, had to endure. There is also an example of a hired man's house. A hired man came later but he was given short shrift, and long after the proprietor of the farm had moved to more commodious quarters he was still living in a log structure although of considerably larger proportions than the original settler's cabin.

The McDiarmid House which is in the village is a typical farm house which came after the pioneering period. It is still stark, unornamented, of unpainted clapboard. Here you see women actually in the act of spinning, churning and doing all the other back-breaking chores of a farm wife. The smokehouse is there as well.

The third phase of farm dwelling is also represented in the village in the Louck's Farmhouse. The Loucks again were of German descent and did well in Upper Canada. Their dwelling represents what a hard-working and thrifty farmer could achieve. It is not pretentious but it is commodious, built of field stone, and while its architecture may not say gentility it certainly does say stability. Inside are many evidences of the ingenuity of the early Canadian, including a complicated heating system from stoves rather than open fires, a dumb-waiter to carry food from the cold storage of the basement up to the cupboard in the kitchen, a sewing machine, kerosene lamps instead of candles, etc. Once again when one visits this house one will see women in period costume busily going about the chores of that long ago era.

The real social centre of an early village was the tavern. In Upper Canada Village there are two. First, there is Cook's Tavern built by Michael Cook who obtained his inn license in 1804. The tavern served as a resting-place for immigrants coming up the St. Lawrence River on their way west. Cook too was a Loyalist of German descent. For an inn of that vintage Cook's Tavern is remarkably well equipped. In Western Ontario the taverns were little more than rude log shelters but at Cook's there was a dining-room, a well equipped kitchen, a small room for ladies, a barroom of course, and the Cooks' private sitting room. Upstairs there was a gracious ballroom which also served as a community hall for political meetings and was where the first courts were held. When the small number of bedrooms were filled the ballroom also doubled as a dormitory. The second hotel was Willard's, originally built in 1795 by Daniel Myers, again of German descent. The name was changed from Myers to Willard's in 1830. This inn is more typical than Cook's. There is no ballroom, it is much more utilitarian in its layout and it has a double balcony running across the front, a very typical feature of Upper Canadian inns. This inn is in operation in Upper Canada Village today and the traveller can have either afternoon tea, cold lunches or steak dinners. These meals are greatly enhanced by the fact that a bake house adjoins Willard's Hotel and fresh bread is made daily, using the utensils of the early days.

Upper Canada Village has two churches, the variation in their architecture, reflecting the position of the church at that time. Christ Church (Church of England) is a well built frame building in the Gothic tradition. Originally it had no chancel but one was eventually added. While its interior is austere it is graceful and makes an imposing place of worship in the context of the rough-hewn pioneer days. Providence Church by contrast is an extremely simple small log church, bare and uncomfortable inside with the high pulpit being the only impressive piece of furnishing in the building. This rather mean structure was little more than a nod of compromise to the fact that even in the earliest days there was a heavy proportion of settlers who were not of the Church of England persuasion. The church was used by all other Protestant denominations as the need arose. It is said that it got its name from the fact that the poor settlers, determined to have a church other than Anglican, in their strained circumstances found it very difficult to raise any money to provide for its erection but were encouraged by an old lady known as "Granny Good" who assured them that "Providence would provide." Apparently she was right, and the church was built and so named.

It is interesting that there is only one general store in Upper Canada Village and it was operated by the lord of the manor, Colonel John Crysler, and must have been a virtual gold mine. Here business was carried on in typical Upper Canadian fashion. Furs were bartered, potash and pearl ash were traded for merchandise. What money was in circulation could be either pounds, shillings and pence, United States dollars, or Spanish dollars. It was not until 1865 that the Canadian dollar was considered to be a respectable currency. Today the store is well stocked with items typical of one hundred to one hundred and fifty years ago, including dry-goods, bonnets, tools and patent medicines. Two other typical enterprises are also represented in the village in a cabinetmaker's shop and, of course, the blacksmith's shop.

There are three industries in Upper Canada Village, all of them true to the period. There is a woollen mill, the Asselstine Factory, where one can see the entire process of textile manufacturing being carried on—carding, combing, washing, drying, dyeing, spinning and weaving. The second enterprise is the sawmill where again a water-driven saw turns great logs into planking. Finally, there is the cheese factory, a replica of the first cheddar cheese factory known to exist in Glengarry County. The factory is in operation and samples of its products can be bought in the village.

To make the picture complete the military must also be represented. There is a small guardhouse and a replica of the blockhouse which was originally at Point Henry near Kingston. There is a telegraph atop the timber blockhouse typical of those erected along the St. Lawrence during the war of 1812. This is not a telegraph in the modern sense of the word but rather a mast and yardarm on which various signals could be flown. The way messages were transmitted was for a cannon to be fired to attract the attention of the next "telegraph" station along the river which would then, using a telescope, read the message strung out by the signal flags on the mast and yardarm. At night, in case of emergency, signalling was done by rockets. In the military complex there is also a small steep-roofed frame house which was the home of the Commandant. The one in the village was actually the Commandant's house in Kingston and was moved from there where it served during the regime of the first Governor of Upper Canada, Colonel John Graves Simcoe.

In this area also there is a replica of an early lock. This kind of construction was used all along the St. Lawrence in the earliest days where the rapids made navigation impossible. Close by the lock is a shed containing the *Marguerite*, a typical St. Lawrence bateau, the kind of vessel in which huge numbers of settlers were transported from Montreal into Upper Canada. The bateau was both hazardous and uncomfortable and was succeeded by various types of sailing- and then steam-vessels as navigation down the St. Lawrence and into Lake Ontario developed. Some indication of this development can be found in a naval museum which also adjoins the village. It consists mainly of bits and pieces of equipment used on early ships and models and pictures and plans of ships. There is one other museum, a vast building containing all types of horse-drawn vehicles—pony carts, wagons, sleighs, buggies of all descriptions, surreys, coaches, phaetons and, of course, the inevitable hearse.

On my last visit to Upper Canada Village one of my companions was what is generally known as a young swinger—with tight corduroy pants, tangerine shirt, sideburns, the lot. As we went through the collection of vehicles I bided my time and hoped to check my "death wish" theory. Sure enough, the vehicle which caught his eye, and held him entranced was the hearse. I probed carefully and the answer I got was, "It's cool, man. It's way, way out." The only other vehicle which caught his attention was a bright red racing sleigh, trim, sleek with such beautifully streamlined form that one could almost see it moving at breakneck speed over the ice of an early Canadian winter. "That," said my young friend, "must have been the sports car of those days. It's real kicky." And so it is.

Here then in Upper Canada Village can be found a thoroughly rewarding experience for almost any visitor. From a purely aesthetic point of view, some of the finer homes and Christ Church are a delight to the eye; for those interested in early manufacturing methods the various primitive factories are as authentic as can be found anywhere in North America. Almost everybody will succumb to the slow pace and the atmosphere of peace (despite the hundreds of tourists who visit the place every day) which pervades the village.

Most important of all, for those interested in how we have developed and what we are today, is the total message of the village which represents the first phase of settlement to be found in Ontario. Here is the transplanted class system of Great Britain and the meanness of the average settler in striking contrast, giving promise that in this new land, which all regarded as an opportunity, the old ways would not survive, as indeed they did not. Here we see the attempts to establish values which were alien to a province which, even though it did go through a period of smugness, has emerged vital, thrusting and insatiable in its desire to develop and its almost uncontrollable urge to move faster and faster in what indeed is a very fast age.

Move outside the boundaries of the village to the park with its marina, golf course, swimming facilities, and campsites and you will see the Ontarian of today with all his sophisticated equipment for comfort carried in his inevitable automobile, his urge not to waste a minute in his pursuit for enjoyment and underlying it all his fascination for the past and, deeper down still, his intimation of his own mortality which, with his strong instinct for survival, he turns into something enjoyable.

THE MUSEUMS OF EASTERN ONTARIO

There are other places where one can explore the thoroughly enjoyable death wish, Eastern Ontario style, but none of them as complete and few of them, even as individual items, are as good as one can find in Upper Canada Village. The museum craze of course is strong in Eastern Ontario and a large number of centres have some kind of old building or collection of bits and pieces of old artifacts which do indeed hold considerable interest. My two favourite museums are those which set out to revive the feeling of the pioneer era and suddenly, interjected into them, is a collection quite inexplicably out of keeping with the original purpose. One of these is at Almonte, a small town only a few miles from Canada's capital—Ottawa. This museum is called "the Mill of Kintail, Canadian Arts and Pioneer Museum." It is housed in an excellent example of a fine old stone gristmill which was built in 1830 by a Scottish immigrant called John Baird. It contains the usual assortment of pioneer items but you can see those in lots of other places. With a thrift which I am sure the original Scottish proprietor of the mill would have approved, this particular project has been made to serve two purposes. In addition to being a pioneer museum it is dedicated in part as a memorial to one of Canada's great surgeons who also happened to be an extremely good sculptor, Dr. Robert Tait McKenzie. The McKenzie sculptures are almost in the Greek tradition; they are as classic as anything which has ever been produced by a Canadian artist and many of them are both exciting and beautiful, and here in Almonte there are some seventy examples of Dr. McKenzie's work including three of his most famous—"The Sprinter," "The Boxer," and "The Athlete." Were it not for the McKenzie sculptures I doubt that I would bother very much with the Mill of Kintail but Almonte is a pleasant run from Upper Canada Village and certainly anyone who is going to visit Canada's capital ought to make the slight detour necessary to go through Almonte.

As for the nation's capital, in terms of museums it is singularly arid and uninspiring. In a way the treatment of the National Museum of Canada, which is at the corner of McLeod and Metcalfe Streets, represents the curious ambivalence of the nation itself which, in essence, is simply that despite the British North America Act we are still not exactly sure, in many areas, what belongs to the provinces and what belongs to the country as a whole. You can see this very plainly in the National Museum where they have stuck pretty well to the past of the Indians and the Eskimos and what they have of that is not very exciting. It is badly arranged and generally imparts an atmosphere of mustiness and neglect. To be fair there is some rationale at least for the approach if not for the performance. Local history is best handled in the locality where it has actually occurred and since various regions do represent quite significant distinctions it would be a gargantuan task to assemble them all for the whole of Canada.

My second favourite museum because it holds a surprise is the Hastings County Museum located in Belleville which again is just off Highway 401. It is located in the old County Registry Office and again has the usual hodge-podge of pieces relating to the history of the area. The unexpected is to be found in the Coutrey Collection which has nothing to do with pioneer life whatsoever but is an interesting if not first-rate collection of European and Oriental furniture and paintings. We do not have very much of this in Ontario and it is well worth a stop in Belleville.

Just before one arrives at Belleville it is interesting to take a side trip from Trenton through Prince Edward County (which is almost an island) down to its tip to the town of Picton, a pleasant town with some fine old buildings still reasonably intact and also the landing point for the Glenora Ferry which will carry you, car and all, across an inlet from the Bay of Quinte to a road which runs along the bay through a series of very old Loyalist towns such as Bath and Adolphustown. At Adolphustown one can visit the Loyalist Memorial Church (Anglican despite the fact that most of the settlers were Lutherans) and a little farther on at nearby Hay Bay there is the oldest Methodist Meeting House in Ontario, built in 1792 and still intact. At Adolphustown is a Loyalist Museum which purports to illustrate the story of the Loyalist immigration into Ontario and the contributions they made to its early development. Because of the way the United Empire Loyalists ultimately organized themselves into a group which strove mightily to prove that they were not only of superior patriotism but of superior lineage one must take the Adolphustown Empire Loyalist Museum with a grain of salt but, having done that, it is worth a visit. And in any event, the drive is one of my favourites, one of the most restful and one of the most beautiful. The Bay of Quinte area is still not spoiled by a rampant resort complex which has invaded a good number of our most pleasant places in Ontario. While you may not find all the comforts of modern motel living very readily available they are only a few miles away and the trip along the Bath Road is a relaxing experience.

Another museum which has a unique feature is to be found in Cornwall which is farther east along Highway 401 than Upper Canada Village. The United Counties Museum in Cornwall is in the "Wood House," a fine old stone building. Once again there are the usual household articles, furniture, clothing, maps, documents, implements, etc. of the early days, but what intrigues me is the installation of electrical equipment which was orginally designed for the Stormont Mill by Thomas Edison. To get the full value of the Edison exhibit one should also take time to visit the fabulous hydro-electric generating plant just west of Cornwall which was part of the St. Lawrence Seaway development. Slick and modern, it is designed to attract and impress visitors. The view of the installations is magnificent and in the rotunda there is a huge and, at one time controversial, mural done by one of Canada's finest contemporary artists—Harold Towne.

There are other museums of varying degrees of quality and interest and they are worth a visit if the death wish is urgent that day and the traveller has a bit of time. In Eastern Ontario these include the Arnprior District Museum which is just nicely under way and is going to concentrate on the early French explorers, the fur trade and the development of lumbering which was very important in that area. Arnprior is west of Ottawa. In the same area there is the Blockhouse Museum at Merrickville. This is one of the original blockhouses built by Colonel John By for the defence of the Rideau Canal which he built and whose name was the original of Canada's capital, now Ottawa but formerly Bytown. In the same area is the Champlain Trail Museum at Pembroke, housed in two old buildings—one a schoolhouse which concentrates on pioneer settlement and early lumbering and the second a log cabin furnished in mid-nineteenth-century style. Back down along the St. Lawrence River at Dunvegan which is about thirty-five miles east of Cornwall, there is the Glengarry Museum, a log building containing pioneer memorabilia. There is the Gananoque Museum again with Indian and pioneer artifacts. At

Grafton there is the Barnum House Museum which is one of the finest examples of Neo-classic architecture in Ontario and has been refurnished to represent the home of a nineteenth-century country gentleman. All these places are along or immediately off Highway 401 as is Napanee where the Lennox and Addington Historical Museum is located in the County Memorial Building—Indian and pioneer life again. In Oshawa which is only some thirty miles east of Toronto off Highway 401 there is a Canadian Cabin Museum, a settler's cabin of the 1830's authentically restored, and the Henry House Museum, an attractive old home with displays of agricultural tools and household objects of the mid-nineteenth century. Since Oshawa is also one of the major centres of automobile production in Canada there is a Canadian Automobile Museum there where some forty vintage cars illustrate the story of Canada's contribution to the development of the automobile in North America. This is one of the best vintage car exhibits to be found in Ontario.

NIAGARA PENINSULA MUSEUMS

Like the land along Eastern Lake Ontario and the St. Lawrence River, the Niagara Peninsula also traces its beginning of settlement back to the American Revolution. As early as 1779 it too had been designated as an area which would be suitable to receive the Loyalists fleeing from the United States. In 1782 sixteen families, consisting of eighty-three persons (one of whom was a slave) were settled on the west side of the Niagara River. One of these families was the Secords— two brothers, Peter and James, a name which will figure in a romantic story when we come along to the military history of the province. By the end of the war the number had increased to forty-six families and on this nucleus early settlement was based. Although the period was the same, and there was a similar combination of the military, the official and the Loyalists, settlement in the Niagara Peninsula, while it, too, often aspired to elegance, never became so hidebound by colonial tradition or as smug as in the early years in the settled part of Eastern Ontario. The answer is probably due to the fact that these were indeed turbulent years on the peninsula and the fighting, particularly during the War of 1812-1814 was much more real and in earnest than any other part of Ontario. Here the battle lines see-sawed back and forth and the settlers lived in an atmosphere of uncertainty over a longer period of time than those of any other part of Ontario. As we shall see later, Ontario as a whole really knows very little about war at first hand but the early settlers of the Niagara Peninsula are the exception. Although there was considerable devastation during the hard early years, in the long run it undoubtedly made for a more progressive and adventuresome outlook. This, coupled with the fact that the peninsula has peculiarly rich soil, a very moderate climate and is sometimes known as Ontario's "Banana Belt," has resulted in its becoming today a densely populated district, a very beautiful area and perhaps that part of Ontario least tied to the apron strings of the past.

Just the same the old enjoyable death wish still operates although it marches side by side with some of the most ingenious tourist traps which modern man has yet been able to contrive.

Perhaps the contrast is best illustrated by the fact that there are no reconstructed pioneer villages in the Niagara Peninsula. Instead there is Niagara-on-the-Lake, onetime capital of Upper Canada. Niagara-on-the-Lake is one of the earliest towns of the district. Here one will find the best collection of the neo-classic architecture of the period that exists anywhere in Ontario. The difference is that these buildings are still largely in use, the houses occupied and the town still goes about its business ornamented and enriched by these fine homes, stores and public buildings of the past. It is possible to visit at least one of these houses—the McFarland House which is situated on the beautiful Niagara Parkway just outside Niagara-on-the-Lake, a fine old brick house built in 1800 and furnished in the style of the era. And of course there is a historical museum; indeed it is the oldest museum building in Ontario. Its contents are devoted almost exclusively to relating the exciting history of the Niagara area in its formative years and it is well worth a visit.

The City of Niagara Falls proper and its immediate vicinity

is Ontario's—and perhaps Canada's—most famous tourist attraction and amongst its many adjuncts for tempting the traveller are a wide assortment of museums. The Niagara Falls Museum which is located near the Rainbow Bridge is large, consisting of four floors of historical material and displays. It is a very comprehensive collection revealing the nature of the peninsula's past. The Potvin Museum is in Queen Victoria Park and has an international reputation. It is a collection of wood carvings of astonishing ingenuity and skill including twenty-two scenes carved by hand with a pocket knife. Anyone interested in wood carving ought to see this one. There is also an antique auto museum with a collection of over fifty vintage cars, displayed in period settings and situated near the Falls. There is also the Crown Jewels Exhibit, housed in Table Rock House also adjacent to the Horseshoe Falls. The collection here is over ninety items, mostly replicas of crowns, jewelled swords, orbs, sceptres, the gold anointing spoon—all part of the traditional regalia of a British coronation. Then there are a couple of special museums for the honeymooners and tourists. There is a Ripley Museum —based on Robert L. "Believe it or not" Ripley's long-time newspaper feature of odd and unusual and quite often unbelievable events. Another museum of this ilk is Louis Tussaud's English Wax Museum based on the famous Tussaud Museums in Great Britain. Here one finds life-sized and usually lifelike reproductions of the world's most famous and infamous people.

Other points for those seeking to recreate the past include the Beaver Dam Church, built in 1832 and one of the oldest Methodist meeting-houses in Ontario, the Dundas Historical Society Museum which has one of the best collections of Indian artifacts in the province as well as an excellent exhibit of old china and glass. The Lundy's Lane Historical Museum is a fairly standard example of a miscellaneous collection of everything from Indian and military relics to pioneer utensils and tools. At the town of Queenston there is Mackenzie's Printing House where in 1824 William Lyon Mackenzie, "The Little Rebel", first published his controversial newspaper, the *Colonial Advocate*. Later he moved publication to Toronto.

In St. Catharines there is the Mountain Mills Museum which is a reconstructed grist mill at De Cew Falls and the St. Catharines Historical Museum which is housed in the former Merriton Town Hall which was moved to the city. This museum has just begun. At Stoney Creek, the site of a decisive battle in 1813, there is Gage House, also known as Stoney Creek Museum; this is another miscellaneous collection.

Finally in the City of Hamilton at the beginning of the Niagara Escarpment is Dundurn Castle, built by Sir Allan Napier MacNab, a renowned businessman and statesman. It has been beautifully and authentically restored and is now open to the public. Ontario is rather short on castles and Dundurn as it now stands is perhaps the best and most authentic example of how the successful but colonial-minded leader in Upper Canada sought to reproduce the glory and the grandeur of the British aristocracy. Sir Allan MacNab was a colourful fellow in his own right. Beginning his career as a rather effervescent Tory lawyer in Hamilton he became curiously embroiled in a minor riot which occurred in that city in 1829 when a group of amateur politicians paraded an effigy of the newly-appointed governor—Sir John Colborne—in the streets of Hamilton. The sensitive government at Toronto attempted to prove that the Reform Party was responsible for this outrageous disrespect for the representative of the Crown. Among the witnesses summoned was MacNab who, although he was on the side of the government, did not like the tone of the examining lawyers and refused to answer questions with the result that he was charged with contempt and committed to York jail where he remained for ten days. He quickly turned this to his advantage, assumed the role of the misunderstood martyr and the next year was elected to the Legislature to represent Wentworth County, thus beginning a political career which ended with him as Premier of the United Canadas and secured him a baronetcy. In the castle which he built to provide tangible evidence of his success and importance there is much to interest the visitor. Even the brewery, located in the basement of the house, has been restored with complete authenticity. Indeed every corner of Dundurn Castle is now perhaps the most faithful reproduction of this kind of structure in Canada. In addition to this, each evening at dusk during the summer months a production called "Son et Lumière," featuring spectacular colour and stereophonic sound, provides a most enjoyable and unique interlude.

The real difference between the museums of Eastern Canada and those of the Niagara Peninsula is that the best ones are for real. Well done as many of the museums of Eastern Ontario are, one still cannot but have the impression that they are precisely what they actually are—that is reproductions, reconstructions and a synthetic combination of buildings moved from various places to make a unit. But Niagara-on-the-Lake and such places as Dundurn Castle are where they have been from the beginning and are still in good order. One gets the feeling that the colonial period in the Niagara Peninsula became absorbed into the rhythm of its progressive march to the modern period. There is less of the death wish here, less of a feeling that one is deliberately going into a mortuary to view the remains, regardless of how interesting those remains might be. In the Niagara Peninsula, somehow, the past has blended into the present much more successfully.

PIONEER MUSEUMS, WESTERN ONTARIO STYLE

In Western Ontario the remains of the past tell still another story. Although it was slow to start, comparatively speaking, Western Ontario is so rich and the nature of the settlers who came to it was so aggressive that the pace of settlement far surpassed that of any other part of the province. It is in Western Ontario that one finds the source of the thrust for progress, the ruthless drive for success which characterizes the province generally. People do make the difference and the difference between the settlers of Eastern Ontario and Western Ontario was substantial.

True enough, as we shall see, the various land settlement schemes and companies attracted a certain small percentage of would-be backwoods aristocracy but their rule was never strong and their days short-lived. Primarily Western Ontario was settled by people who had to make it or else. The great

settlement period here, as elsewhere in the province, was
between 1820 and 1880 but the difference was that those who
came to Western Ontario had an absolutely clear field in which
to work. And the one thing which characterized them to an
almost frightening degree was their capacity to work. Perhaps
never at any time or in any other place in Canada has work
been exalted to the extent of those early pioneer days. And
by work what is meant is hard physical labour. The average
settler worked steadily throughout all the daylight hours with
virtually no respite. Almost none of them had any money.
They had land which had to be cleared and made productive
as soon as possible so they could raise their families. Their
ambition was almost unlimited. Almost all of them came with
a driving compulsion not just to survive or even just to survive
comfortably but to build a land of the future which would
provide their descendants with a way of life infinitely better
than anything which they themselves had known.

Since these were essentially a simple and unsophisticated
people they were largely incapable of making a blueprint for
what this kind of better life would be. They were completely
open to outside forces and in their struggle for improvement
were much stronger on the negatives than on the positives.
For example, most of them had suffered under the class system
of Great Britain and this was one thing which they definitely
knew they did not want in the new land they were creating in
Western Ontario. What to put in its place was, and indeed up
to the present is still, something of a dilemma for the native
of Western Ontario but, although they did not realize it and
perhaps still do not, the most attractive model seems to have
been the one which emerged in the spectacular material
success achieved south of the border in the United States of
America. Most Canadians and certainly most inhabitants of
Western Ontario would deny this but I have yet to find any
researcher, historian or social scientist who can pinpoint
specifically the values which motivated the early settlers in
Western Ontario or which presently drive its inhabitants
towards some still undefined goal. Many people will admit to
an admiration for things American. Even more will say that
there is definitely a difference between a Canadian and an

American. When pressed neither one of these groups can provide very specific documentation for their position. But broadly speaking, the pattern of life as it is found in Western Ontario today is remarkably close to that which is found in the nearby states such as upper New York, Ohio or Michigan.

There is no doubt that the primary drive underlying the settlement of Western Ontario was to achieve material comfort and material possessions and, along with this, freedom of government as represented in the "rep. by pop." concept of democratic procedure. Somewhere, hovering in the background, was the fact of the British monarchy, the one thing which the people in Western Ontario do not share with their immediate American neighbours. This is a curious mystique not very well understood or defined but definitely in existence. It has always been there.

When William Lyon Mackenzie was starting his rebellion he found his Commander-in-Chief in Western Ontario in what is now Huron County in the person of a Dutch nobleman called Colonel Anthony Van Egmond. Van Egmond was popular in the primitive settlement that existed in the Huron Tract at that time and although most of the settlers (but not officialdom) thoroughly sympathized with him there was not one man from the district who volunteered to join his forces. Perhaps the explanation lies in an old letter which I uncovered many years ago. It was written by a Scottish settler, who lived only a few miles from Van Egmond, to his son who was in Scotland. He explained in some detail the troubles of the times and Van Egmond's role in it. He indicated that he thought Van Egmond's cause was right but he added "I could never take up arms against the Crown." The force of this mystique is one which Canadian political scientists either have avoided or, perhaps, it just plain baffles them. It was there from the beginning and, in ways often hard to understand, it still expresses itself. Only a few years ago when finally Canada got around to getting its own official flag one of the major pockets of resistance to it was in Western Ontario. This area which had provided so many doughty fighters against British colonialism, by the same token deeply resented adopting any

kind of symbolism which seemed to ignore the monarchical tie.
   In Western Ontario this peculiar attachment to the institution of the monarchy is just about the only consistent tie with
the past which has remained throughout the history of the
area since its first settlement. With virtually no significant
exceptions (the Talbot Settlement along Lake Erie is one
which proves the rule) there were no pretensions to the lord-
of-the-manor style of living in early Western Ontario or, as it
was then, Canada West. Even John Galt, the founder and first
superintendent of the largest independent land company ever
to be formed in this country—The Canada Company—while
building himself a rather commodious dwelling in Guelph
which he called The Priory (in design very much like John
Graves Simcoe's Castle Frank) really had no dreams of setting himself up as an aristocrat amongst the peasants. His
dream was to make the fertility of Western Ontario available
on equal terms to all and especially to the poor and distressed
of the British Isles. He firmly believed that out of such people
could be built a strong nation and he was one of the first men
in British North America to conceive the idea of a confederation which would ultimately produce a nation from sea to sea.
Although Galt only lasted a few years himself, his assessment
was quite correct.
   The settlers did come. They worked like that most industrious of all North American animals and the one which has
become a symbol for Canada—the beaver. They were successful. In less than fifty years as a result of their industry and
thrift what was almost entirely untouched bushland had been
transformed into hundreds of square miles of well cultivated,
well kept and thriving farms serviced by a myriad of prosperous villages, towns and small cities. In that fifty years
Western Ontario had far outstripped Eastern Ontario in commercial importance. The basis for their success was agriculture. The land was much richer than in the eastern part of
the province and perhaps the settlers were more industrious.
As the land became increasingly productive and its products
far surpassed local needs and achieved a strong export position all the service industries followed. In quick succession
the lean-to shanty which was the usual habitation of the

settler in his first year gave way to the log cabin, the clapboard house and in a great number of cases huge, ornate brick farm houses of proportions which even today surprise the traveller. There is not a road through Western Ontario where one cannot see these houses of fifteen or twenty rooms, solid, ornate and impressive and, curiously enough for such an industrious people, not very practical. In a half a century the rugged pioneer had established himself, achieved a high level of prosperity and settled into a solid and sometimes smug position.

The impetus of such speedy settlement and development left little time for any preoccupation with the past and literally no desire to preserve any remembrance of time past. For the average Western Ontario citizen the past was something which had to be got through in order to reach the desired goal of solid affluent living. The result is that Western Ontario has far fewer buildings and other mementoes of pioneer days than either the Niagara Peninsula or Eastern Ontario and this despite the fact that it was settled later.

And then, within the last fifteen years, the reaction set in. The old enjoyable death wish began to operate; having reached a plateau of affluence the Western Ontario citizen finally felt it was safe to enjoy a nostalgic look backwards. In these past fifteen years, with customary diligence, Western Ontario, like the rest of the province, has seen a mushroom-like growth of museums, restored villages, etc. Like Eastern Ontario, they have had to be assembled. Artifacts have had to be sought out and many men have devoted many years searching for them. Where restored pioneer villages are found the buildings have to be brought together often from considerable distances away. But they are all there now and some of them are well worth looking at.

The restoration of the pioneer settlement era in Western Ontario looked at overall is more stark, more crude, less graceful than one will find in other parts of the province. It is a true reflection of the harshness of pioneer life and the little time which the average settler devoted to graceful living in the early years. There are some exceptions of course but the plain style is the rule. If one includes Toronto (and really it is an area by itself) there are three major restorations of pioneer villages in the western half of Ontario, none of them yet complete but all of them of substantial proportions. Of these, while it is not the largest, my favourite is Doon Pioneer Village immediately north of Doon which can be reached at cut-off 34 on Highway 401.

The site consists of fifty-five acres and has the usual museum packed with pioneer implements and artifacts. It includes a general store which is one of its best features, a Lutheran Church (this was an area heavily settled by Germans), a blacksmith's shop, a printer's shop and several early houses. Typical of the approach to the past in Western Ontario, a little bit of everything is thrown in. For example at Doon there is a 1911 steam locomotive — hardly a pioneer article — but interesting enough in its own right. There is also one of the first automobiles produced in Canada which stands side by side with a Conestoga wagon. This latter is indeed true to the period and since a great number of the settlers came into this area from Pennsylvania this is the vehicle which transported most of them. And if you think the death wish has been neglected, there is not just a hearse in Doon Village but they recently brought in a whole cemetery!

Just north of London, Ontario, is an even more ambitious, but for some reason or other less convincing, pioneer village located at Fanshawe. It is intended to be an authentic reproduction of a typical crossroads community of the pre-railway era and includes several log cabins and barns, a blacksmith's shop, a weaver's establishment, a carriage maker's shop, general store and an early Presbyterian Church. It also has an Orange Hall, a feature which recalls a very important influence in the development of Canada.

While relatively few could be United Empire Loyalists, anybody with a colonial complex, dedicated to loyalty to the motherland above all else, could become an Orangeman. This organization or lodge, for many decades dominated the political scene throughout Ontario and particularly in Western Ontario. It is commonly believed to have been the first really potent lodge organization in the province but this is not so. Actually the first—and rather curiously, considering the drinking habits of the province which we will examine later—the Knights of Temperance were originally the strongest lodge organization in Western Ontario. They were largely responsible for the origin and development of the temperance movement which ultimately led to prohibition. But the Orange Lodge was broader in its scope. It was dedicated to the proposition that the best thing for Ontario and for Canada was the British connection. Its credo was simple — one crown, one flag, one language. The crown was the British monarchy; the flag was the Union Jack and the language was English. It responded enthusiastically to Sir John A. Macdonald's famous cry "A British subject I was born; a British subject I will die."

As it developed in power it became the backbone of the Conservative party as it was constituted through the nineteenth century. Its membership tended to break down upon religious lines with the majority belonging either to the Church of England or the Methodist Churches. The arch-enemies who were members of the Reform or, later, the Liberal party were usually Presbyterians and Roman Catholics. To celebrate the Battle of the Boyne when the Irish were driven out of Ulster by William of Orange (the origin of the name of the order) these lodges would gather in central locations on the 12th of July and have gargantuan and impressive parades headed always by the leader of the lodge who was to represent "King Billy" and who always rode a white horse. These parades still exist in Ontario but in the modern atmosphere of the province the Orange Order is a declining institution, the parades are neither as numerous nor as impressive as they were even twenty-five years ago and their political influence is nothing like it was in its heyday.

At one time when the capital of Ontario, Toronto, was known as "Tory Toronto" it was impossible for anyone except a Conservative to be elected mayor and equally impossible for a candidate even though he were a Conservative, to win an election without the support of the Orange Order. All this is now changed and Toronto's last two mayors have been Jewish although the city does not have a particularly large Jewish population. The journalistic organ of the order was the old Toronto *Telegram* which, in keeping with the times, no longer has any such identification but it was intimately connected with the last real kick of the declining influence of the order. Some thirty years ago the municipal politicians in Toronto found themselves in an awkward position. There was no suitable or willing Conservative Orangeman who wanted to be mayor. The story goes that the editor of the *Telegram*, facing this dreadful crisis, walked into the city room, cast his eye over the reporters sitting there, fastened upon one who was prominent in the Orange Order and, pointing his finger at him, said, "You are going to be the next mayor of Toronto." He was; and he was also the last ever elected through the powerful pressure group of Orangemen which even then was beginning to fail noticeably. It is, therefore, well worth having an Orange Hall in a pioneer village in Western Ontario and when one contemplates it he can recall the days of glory of that order, and, perhaps, meditate on the reasons for its decline and fall.

The third pioneer village is at Rockton which is on Highway 22 just north of Highway 8 and is called Westfield Pioneer Village. At the present time there are thirteen buildings on the site and there is a well organized expansion program. It is designed to display the story of rural community life in Canada West and, while it is not as good as the other two, it is worth a visit.

Finally there is Black Creek Pioneer Village in the northern section of Metro Toronto, half a mile east of Highway 400 on Steeles Avenue. This is a good one and more artful than the others. There are attendants here to add authenticity to this simulated nineteenth-century village. It has a representative variety of houses and barns, stores, a church and a school. Because it is close to Ontario's largest city it will be the easiest for many a traveller to visit and he will not feel he has wasted his time.

In addition to the pioneer villages there are of course an ever-increasing number of pioneer museums. My own favourite almost has to be the one which is located in my home county—Huron. The museum is in Goderich and is called the Huron County Pioneer Museum. Leaving prejudice aside, it has one of the largest and most variegated collections of pioneer artifacts to be found anywhere in Ontario and the way it came into being is fairly typical of all such projects in this province.

In the early 1950's the citizens of Huron County, in common with their counterparts throughout Western Ontario, began to be aware of the mysterious tug back to the past which we now have the time to enjoy. For many years prior to this, a Huron County antiquarian called Herb Neill had been collecting odds and ends of the pioneer era and taking them around to the local fall fairs. Through a series of negotiations between Neill and the Huron County Council it was decided to absorb his collection, make him the curator and thus set up the nucleus of the present museum which was located in a rather attractive but no longer used public school in Goderich.

Almost every local museum has its life blood in a few dedicated people firmly committed and giving generously of their time to the difficult business of collecting more and more suitable material for the museum. Herb Neill was such a person himself. A few other local citizens joined him, and their efforts have resulted in an impressive success. The Huron County Pioneer Museum as it presently stands probably has a wider range of Upper Canadian pioneer artifacts than any other in the province. Because of limitations of space which have plagued it from the beginning (no one—as usual—had any idea, when it was begun, that there was so much important and relevant material around) and a not very concentrated effort at organization, the museum requires considerable time to absorb its full value. It literally has a bit of everything from our pioneer past. There are, as is common in this type of Ontario museum, some odds and ends of Indian relics but these one can afford to ignore. The real value of this museum is that there is hardly any implement used by the Ontario pioneer which cannot be found here.

This, it seems to me, is the real message of our pioneer museums. As one will find at Goderich and in the many others throughout the province, within their own terms of reference our ancestors were just as ingenious in their time as we like to think we are today. Man is still a species which survives by

using its brain power to create new tools and gadgets and by
the time he reached the nineteenth century, and again found
himself in a wilderness situation, he put this power to work
not just borrowing from the accumulated knowledge of the
British Isles and Europe from whence most of the pioneers
came, but creating a wide range of new implements required
by the unique and peculiar situation of Upper Canada in the
settlement period. Basically all these museums stress the same
point: man's astonishing capacity to create an implement or
machine to meet any recognizable need.

Apart from the impressive and wide-ranging displays of
implements used in the harvesting of crops and in the pioneer
household, the Goderich museum impressively displays the
development of motive power from the horse to the tractor
to the locomotive; both the milling process and the various
methods used for processing salt are extremely well illustrated
in this museum. There are also some somewhat irrelevant,
but nevertheless interesting, displays which really do not have
a great deal to do with Upper Canadian pioneer life such as,
through the use of models, an elaborate display showing how
time was told throughout the world including such unlikely
places as Egypt and China!

Another similar pioneer museum in Western Ontario which
is worth mentioning is the Haldimand Historical Society
Museum located at Cayuga which in addition to pioneer
material contains some Indian relics, military equipment and
natural history exhibits. One of the most interesting features
of this particular museum is the place where it is housed—the
fine old County Court House. In Chatham one can find the
Chatham-Kent Museum; in Elora (near Guelph) the Welling-
ton County Museum; in Grand Bend (one of Ontario's most
popular summer resorts) the Eisenbach Museum, a complex
of five buildings; in Dundas, the Dundas Historical Society
Museum which has one of the best Indian collections and also
an unusually fine exhibit of old china and glass. At Midhurst,
five miles north of Barrie on Highway 26, is the Simcoe
County Museum; in Owen Sound on the shores of Georgian
Bay the County of Grey and Owen Sound Museum which is
just nicely getting under way; in St. Thomas just south of

London is the Elgin County Pioneer Museum and at Shelburne, the Dufferin County Historical Museum. The Bruce County Museum is to be found in Southampton, another popular Lake Huron resort area. At the border at Windsor, the Hiram Walker Historical Museum is located in one of the finest old houses of the district built by Colonel François Baby shortly before the War of 1812; and in Woodstock the Oxford Museum is built in one of the best examples of municipal architecture to be found in Upper Canada, the old City Hall.

Well, there they are and many more besides. Outside of the obvious relish which North Americans seem to have developed for the "dead" past it is not too easy to understand just why we have so many pioneer museums in Ontario and, perhaps equally baffling, why they are of unfailing interest to tens of thousands of people every year. If one wants to talk about "Tourist attractions," the records of any of the longer-established museums in Ontario provide without question proof that people flock to them in inexplicable numbers. Not long ago, still attempting to ferret out the underlying meaning of this phenomenon I took a visitor from Portugal to see two or three museums within a radius of fifty miles of my home. Antonio is a very bright, intelligent man who had been sent over by his very rich family to learn something about North American business methods.

With courteous punctiliousness, he examined in detail many large assortments of strange implements and tools. Some he recognized; others were completely baffling, but he was always eager to find out how they were used. As we approached our third museum he said "I know enough. Let's go home."

Driving back, his first query was "Why are there no pictures?" I explained to him that we had something which we called "Art Galleries" where one could find pictures. "These too are in fine old historical buildings?" he asked, and I had to explain that usually we built special places for our art galleries to make sure that the lighting was correct and the paintings could be displayed to best advantage.

We drove in silence for some time as Antonio pondered this. "Ah, I see!" said Antonio, "This is the organization man

I have been hearing about. You put each facet of your life
and your past into a special compartment, is that not so?"

I had never thought of it in quite this way but when one
attempts to catalogue the things to see and the things to do
in Ontario it becomes all too apparent that this is precisely
how we go about it.

So let the traveller beware. There is virtually no place in
the entire province where one can go and find good examples
of our past and present locked together.

The museums, the good ones and the not so good, are only
a chapter of the Ontario story. But a very significant chapter.
What the pioneer museums really confirm is that Ontario was
settled by and has developed from a group of original settlers
who, despite a wide variety of racial origins, shared one important characteristic. As a group, the Ontario pioneers represent
a highly skilled technology. It is commonplace in this province to say that it had its origins in agriculture and this is
true but the success of the agricultural phase of Ontario life
was based on technology. This is the story which every pioneer
museum confirms beyond any shadow of doubt.

Certainly the land was fertile but it was covered with a
heavy growth of trees and every pioneer museum will show
the wide variety of axes and saws which were developed to
clear the land. From there one can follow in any good museum
the evolution and refinement of special tools and implements
which were developed by ingenious minds to meet the special
needs of successful settlement in this province. Many of them
are unique to Ontario; many more are adapted for better use
in this particular setting. From the very beginning, the rich
agricultural industry which provided the basis for other growth
and development depended upon the creation and skilful use
of tools. There is nothing new in this since the entire human
species has survived by learning to use tools effectively. The
difference in Ontario lies in the fact that the settlers were
much more sophisticated and advanced in the ways in which
they created the implements they required. In this way they
are the counterparts of our American cousins and, perhaps,
this is why the industrial section of Ontario today is closer to
the technological situation of the U.S.A. than to any other

part of the world. We have preserved other valuable and different traditions but in the area of survival the citizen of Ontario is definitely a North American and this is the story which all the museums tell.

Now we have the answer to the highly enjoyable death wish. We can go back to the dead past and say that our present machine-dominated society had its roots in the earliest settlers who came to the province. These men and women survived. The message of the museums — and it may be a dangerous one—is that as long as we continue to advance technologically we too will survive.

The tangible affirmation of Ontario's technological orientation is our choice of a project to commemorate Canada's 100 years as a nation. Ontario decided to build The Centennial Centre of Science and Technology, a twenty-two million dollar, split-level cluster of three buildings, presenting the achievements of science and technology and emphasizing the expanding horizons of the future.

Magnificently planned, broad in scope, and set up so that the visitor both participates and learns, the Centre is almost a cathedral of science and technology. Located in Scarborough (part of Metro Toronto) on a twenty-acre site, with ready access to several major expressways, it opens in 1969. It is a total experience and will be surrounded by recreational facilities operable the year round. It will also keep abreast of new developments—with fifteen to twenty per cent of the exhibits changed every year.

Here is the message of the museums updated to tomorrow —a beautifully executed showplace with deeper dimensions of learning and experience. It is certain to become one of our most visited "showplaces."

If this were the total story, the more humanistic and humane development of our civilization might very well be alarming, perhaps even despairing, for Ontario. Happily, it is only one part of our story but rightly or wrongly one of the most significant parts.

CHAPTER THREE

Of Battles Long (Very Long) Ago

Implicit in the struggle for survival is the fact of war. Here, Ontario has a history which is both reassuring and comic. The plain fact is that in Ontario we have had virtually no experience with real war. The most spectacular engagement was over three hundred years ago (before there were hardly any white men here at all) when the Iroquois descended upon their ancient enemies, the Hurons, and massacred them to extinction. Other than that, rebellions and wars in Ontario have been little more than skirmishes.

With the exception of our one and only total war which after all only involved Indians and, from some people's point of view at least, therefore doesn't count, what battles have been fought in Ontario have all been in the cause of preserving some sort of establishment or another. Even in the Indian wars when the white man was involved to any real extent it was in defence of the Church.

White man's involvement in war in Ontario began with the French explorer, Champlain. Perhaps, with the possible exception of political scientists, the academic game of second-guessing is played harder and more consistently by historians than any other group of intellectuals. According to most of

ort Henry, near Kingston

Firing Guns at Fort Henry

Officers' Quarters,
Fort Penetanguishene

Dundurn Castle, Hamilton   Pioneer Church, St. Thoma

St. Andrews Presbyterian Church, Niagara-on-the-Lake

Antique Shop and Guest House, Brockville

ighthouse, Kincardine

Mennonites, Elmira

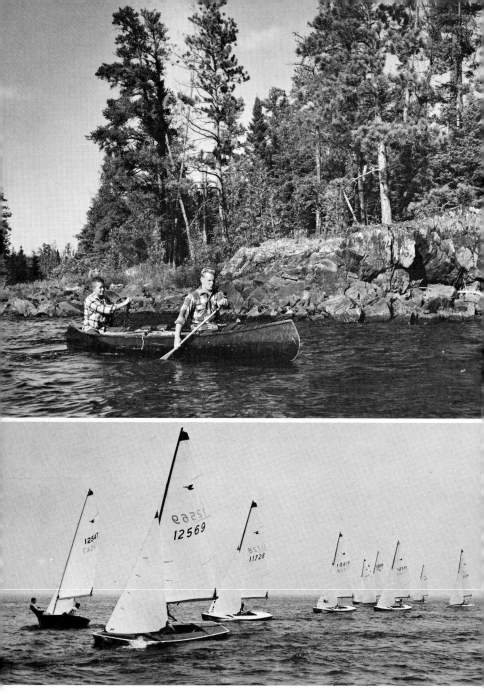

Canoeing, Quetico Provincial Park
Start of Race, Snipe Sailing, Lake Ontario, Oakville

the historians (second-guessing two or three centuries after the event) this intrepid adventurer, Samuel de Champlain, made a dreadful mistake producing even more dreadful results. The territory through which the French conducted the major part of their trade as they pushed ever westward in search of more and richer pelts of fine Canadian fur, was occupied in the east by the Algonquins and farther west by the Huron tribe. The arch enemies of the Hurons were the fierce Iroquois and, without going into the ramifications of the various tribes, or "nations" as they are sometimes called, it is enough to say that long before the arrival of the Frenchman these two major groups had been feuding. When Champlain came along he carried with him an instrument of war never before seen by the Indian warriors—a musket. The Alonquins, who saw it first, were mightily impressed by the performance of this firearm as contrasted to the flint-headed arrow and the tomahawk. Almost immediately they were urging Champlain to join them in an attack upon the Mohawks which he did on July 29, 1609, with spectacular results. This was the great mistake according to the historians because, from that time on, the Iroquois were the implacable enemies of the French and, as we shall see, with disastrous results.

Seen in perspective, if this were a mistake at all it was not much of a one. Champlain had to do business with the Hurons and the Algonquins and sooner or later would have had to use his resources to protect them and the now-beginning-to-flourish fur trade. On the other hand the British had a similar obligation to the Iroquois and ultimately they would have provided firearms for this group, as indeed they soon did. At best Champlain may have hurried up a development, which in any case, was inevitable.

So much for the historical background. It is merely the backdrop which explains why we came to have our best and most interesting example of both how sixteenth-century Indians lived and how isolated white men who came into their settlements set about establishing themselves.

Champlain's intervention with his terrifying and effective firearms did not come with no strings attached. In the wake of their awed gratitude, he quickly drove a bargain. Along with the insatiable greed of the French explorers for the beautiful fur pelts of the Indian hunters was a more noble motivation. To the Frenchman, the Indian was a pagan savage. True enough, he brought great wealth through the fur trade but in the strongly Catholic France of that day the Church too had a powerful voice. From the point of view of the Church, the redman was a soul to be saved. At every turn pressures were brought to bear upon officialdom by the Church to get missionaries who would bring the gospel to the Indians. Now, Champlain saw an opportunity and in return for his acting on behalf of the Indians he secured their permission and guarantee for safe passage for some Roman Catholic missionaries. First these were representatives of the Récollet Order, and later of the Jesuit.

Both these orders moved into territory in Ontario which is called Huronia, a region lying roughly between Lakes Simcoe and Couchiching and Georgian Bay. The name derives from the fact that this was the chief territory of the Huron Indians. Under the Récollet Fathers missions were established throughout Huronia up until 1620 and after that time very vigorous activities were carried on by the Jesuits and, indeed, by the 1640's there were more French living in Huronia than in any other single place in North America except the immediate Montreal and Quebec areas.

HURONIA EXCAVATIONS

For anyone interested in Indian ways, customs and above all in how they actually lived, Huronia is one of the best places in North America to go. A tremendous amount of accurate archeological research has been accomplished in the Georgian Bay area, largely under experts from two of Ontario's best universities—the University of Toronto and the University of Western Ontario. For the layman it is always something of a miracle that the trained archeologist can actually dig up the past. A few years ago I spent a period of time with just such a party of researchers.

This particular group emanated from the University of Western Ontario and was under the direction of Dr. Wilfrid Jury. Dr. Jury himself is a somewhat remarkable man. Ontario-born, of pioneer stock, he seems to have been uniquely endowed with an instinct for putting himself into the past. It is uncanny to watch him as almost before your eyes he stops thinking like a white man and, in one part of his brain at least, would seem to be a Huron Indian.

The day I arrived I finally tracked Dr. Jury and his party down in a section not far away from Midland and Georgian Bay in what looked to me like a somewhat neglected raspberry patch. Always patient, always ready to share his enthusiasm and explain what he was about, Wilf Jury said to me, "We've been rambling around this area for quite a while now and I think maybe we have found a place where we'll find the remains of a Huron Indian village."

I looked at this fellow in amazement. I am no stranger to the Ontario countryside and for the life of me I could not understand how anybody could pick a particular piece of ground, seemingly quite undistinguishable from similar territory within a radius of many, many miles and say, "I think the remains of an Indian village might be here." So I asked Jury why he thought so. Now came the thing which has baffled more than one of the more academic archeologists. "It looks like the kind of place a Huron might build a village," Jury said. I kept pressing him: Why did it look like this kind of place? Why would a Huron build here? I have to confess I never did get a very convincing answer from Jury. It was more something he felt in his bones, or sensed with a mind which had a different kind of equipment than most men can claim. The upshot of it all was, "Well we're going to dig here and you'll see."

And so Jury's crew got down to work. Pointing, for no good reason which I could understand, to a specific spot Jury had them clear away the underbrush and then mark it off roughly in two-foot squares. Now began what at first seemed to be almost a silly exercise.

Jury's crew comprised a somewhat motley collection: amateur archeologists of all sizes, descriptions and ages; some university students specializing in archeology; some high school students who had been bitten by this particular kind of bug. Male and female it was obvious they all had been carefully instructed in how to go about their somewhat baffling and, to me, frustrating business. With infinite care each member of the crew, assigned to his own four square feet for exploration, began carefully scraping away on the surface of the ground gradually, very gradually, working down slowly, inch by quarter inch, and carefully sifting almost every grain of the sandy soil looking for something which at that time I could not even possibly guess the nature of.

The work seemed to be unending and for the life of me I could not understand how anybody would get any kick out of carefully scraping away at four square feet of soil and sifting it through his fingers. Then a triumphant shout and Jury who had been ranging back and forth amongst his crew hurried over to take a look.

There, in a square of light sandy soil was an irregular circle, approximately three to four inches in diameter, much darker than the rest of the soil and clearly delineated.

"I knew it!" Jury shouted and pointed it out to me.

"You knew what?" I asked skeptically.

"That there *was* an Indian village here," Jury cried triumphantly.

So I looked at the dark spot in the earth. "That's an Indian village?" I asked skeptically and perhaps a little nastily.

"It is post mould, the remains of a pole that was part of an Indian structure," Jury said. "From the size of it I guess that this might have been the longhouse. We'll find out soon."

Now came the application of knowledge to instinct. People like Jury know at exactly what intervals the poles which made up the framework for an Indian longhouse were set. At the proper distance from the remains of the first discovery, Jury drew a circle and now his crew, again carefully and painstakingly scraping away at the dirt, once more set to work.

It takes a long time to work in this way but what I was beginning now to recognize as the almost inevitable triumphant call came once more. The remains of a second post were discovered somewhere along the circle. Then the third, then the fourth and by this time Jury and his educated companions knew they had indeed discovered the longhouse of a Huron Indian village.

Somewhere at this point, for reasons quite obscure to a layman like myself, Jury detached half his crew and, after some careful pacing put them to work in a quite different area.

By now a little more respectful, I asked politely, "What's this all about?"

With the same genial patience, Jury explained that, like all other peoples of the earth, the Hurons were creatures of habit. With variations, of course, they tended to build their villages very much alike. The place where they would do their cooking was almost always set in approximately the same relationship to the longhouse which, of course, was the main structure of the village.

"We were lucky to come upon the longhouse first," Jury explained. "When you've got that you can pretty well tell where the other buildings would be. What I'm looking for now is the kitchen middens because that is the place where you find the greatest concentrations of artifacts."

Naturally the archeologist was right. Before a week was out I was down on my knees under the boiling hot Ontario summer sun, scraping along with the best of them, infected by this curious and stubborn virus which gets into the system when you find that through your own efforts you are actually making contact with the past. By this time the outlines of several Indian structures were uncovered and the kitchen middens thoroughly investigated were yielding up a wide variety of valuable and illuminating fragments of Indian pottery, etc.

For the first time in my life I felt I had actually gone back through the centuries and touched a real thing. All the old and usually fantastic childhood concepts of the Indian were replaced by genuine belief in their existence. As the outlines of the village gradually became more clear and the remnants

of their way of life were extracted from the soil Indians became people, honest to goodness people who, long before any
white man had ever touched Ontario soil, had established
their own way of life, their own pattern for survival, and had
lived, men, women and children in a special structure as meaningful to them as ours is to us today.

It is a rare privilege to participate in such a "thing." But
anyone can see the result of Jury's labours. In Little Lake
Park in Midland there is a full scale replica of a typical seven-
teenth-century Huron Village, surrounded by palisades, lined
with firing platforms, filled with log houses, food storage pits,
drying scaffolds, etc. In my experience this is one of the best
reconstructions of Indian life to be found anywhere. It is a
place to visit and touch the past. It is a place to reflect, for the
Hurons, as we have already noted, became extinct not because
they could not survive in the wilderness but because of war.

STE-MARIE AMONG THE HURONS

Not far from Midland there is another magnificent reconstruction—this time telling the story of the first white men in
Huronia. The explorers, adventurers and traders of France
who occasionally touched this part of Ontario never made any
attempt at permanent settlement. This was the work of the
missionaries, and Huronia was the place where they concentrated their efforts. Particularly under the Jesuits many mission
stations were established with their capital at what became
known as Ste-Marie among the Hurons. The same careful
excavation process was carried out by enthusiastic archeologists under professional direction—first by the Royal Ontario
Museum and later by the University of Western Ontario. So
painstaking has been the work that to visit Ste-Marie among
the Hurons is, again, to step back into an almost incredible
past.

The construction of Ste-Marie was begun in the summer
of 1639 and it was far enough advanced to be ready for partial
occupancy by the following autumn. However before we take
a look at what was created it is worthwhile, after travelling
two miles out of the town of Midland, to take a hard look at

the site which the Jesuit Fathers chose for their headquarters. If nothing else, these men were completely realistic about their situation. They had reconciled themselves to the fact that the unremitting warfare waged by the Iroquois against the Hurons since Champlain's venture almost thirty years previously was not likely to abate. Their headquarters was located deliberately as far away from the Six Nations as possible—a hundred and fifty miles from the nearest, the Senecas, and two hundred and fifty miles from those farthest away, the Mohawks. Because of this remoteness Ste-Marie was spared the many periodic raids which harassed other mission stations, and when the final and ultimate battle was waged it remained the last bastion of the missionaries' defence. No skilled military commander could have picked a better spot.

Ste-Marie was built on the east bank of the river Wye just a mile from its mouth at a point which was always much too deep to ford. In this way it had, on one side, a natural line of defence in the deep river which also provided ready access into Georgian Bay and open water if the mission had to be abandoned. Immediately to the north of the site there was a high hill, a perfect sentry post. On this hill today stands the world famous Martyrs' Shrine which in itself is well worth a visit. Between the hill and the river the land was flat, perfect for construction purposes. The original fortifications were stone bastions surrounded by a heavy palisade. Gradually within these protecting walls an elaborate settlement was developed containing Ontario's first hospital and pharmacy, its first permanent Christian cemetery, and the first artificial lock waterway to be discovered in North America. Gradually a complex of buildings was developed to fulfil the many functions which were described in his annual report by the Rev. Paul Ragueneau, Superior of the Huron Mission, in 1648:

This house is a resort for the whole country, where Christians find a hospital in their sickness, a refuge in the height of alarms, and a hospice when they come to visit us.
During the past year we have reckoned over three thousand persons of whom we have given shelter . . . sometimes within a fortnight six to seven hundred Christians; and as a rule three

meals to each one. This does not include a larger number who incessantly come hither to pass the whole day, and to whom we also give charity; so that, in a strange country, we feed those who themselves should supply us with the necessities of life.

And yet, as one wanders through the chapel, the "European Residence," the stables and the hospital, one becomes aware of the fact that the human tendency to discrimination was practised in this first white man's settlement. There is a sharp demarcation between the territory where the white man lived and where the Indians lived and a sharp differentiation between the type of accommodation for the two races. And note also, Father Ragueneau's definition of those who were welcome: they had to be Christians. More understandably, they also had to be *friendly* Indians.

Because war did come. It never actually touched Fort Ste. Marie but in 1649 as the Iroquois, with their bloodlust up, ravaged the entire area of Huronia, this time determined that once and for all their troubles and enemies would be eliminated, all of the outpost missions fell until the remaining Fathers decided that discretion was the better part of valour and on their heavily laden barges took the escape route down the river Wye into Georgian Bay to Christian Island where they attempted to set up a second Ste-Marie. Once again their position appeared to be ultimately untenable and the next year they departed for Quebec taking with them a handful of Huron Indian converts.

But before the white man's first attempt to settle in the wilderness reached its point of defeat, acts of heroism and martyrdom were performed which have become woven into the fabric of the history of Ontario. By far the most spectacular of these was the martyrdom of two Jesuit Fathers at one of the outpost missions—Ste. Ignace. Almost every Canadian schoolboy knows the story of Fathers Lalemant and Brébeuf. Their story has been told many times; their martyrdom is commemorated in the Midland Shrine; and they have been incorporated into the literature of Canada by the poet who comes closest to being our laureate—the late E. J. Pratt. As is the way with great poets, in one of Ned Pratt's great narrative poems, *Brébeuf and His Brethren,* the significance of the restoration of Ste-Marie among the Hurons is brought into proper perspective:

> The years as they turn have ripened the martyr's seed,
> And the ashes of Ste. Ignace are glowing afresh.
> The trails, having frayed the threads of the cassocks, sank
> Under the mould of the centuries, under fern
> And briar and fungus—there in due time to blossom
> Into the highways that lead to the crest of the hill
> Which havened both shepherd and flock in the day of their
>   trial.
> For out of the torch of Ragueneau's ruins the candles
> Are burning today in the chancel of Sainte Marie.*

This is the feeling which assails the visitor as he moves into Huronia, the scene of the bloodiest battles ever fought in Ontario. At the time, it must have seemed to the remnant of retreating French Fathers that savagery had triumphed. In fact after this time no further organized attempt was ever made on the part of the French to settle any part of Ontario. When the British moved northward from the Thirteen Colonies to seize the French-held lands in North America the battles were fought in Quebec. There was nothing to fight for in Ontario.

But as the poet Pratt saw it, the ultimate victory went to the white man and his faith. In the reconstruction of both the Huron Village and Ste-Marie among the Hurons there is a rare treat for any visitor. There are few places in North America where one can find such authentic reproduction of the way of life of both the Indian and the white man in the wilderness, restored with such careful and honest attention to historic detail. Here again is a spot in Ontario not to be visited casually but toured leisurely and as an extra bonus it is in one of the finest resort areas in the province. Here too the countryside is salad green and the facilities for visitors are excellent. It is easily accessible by either car or pleasure craft. Immediately adjacent to Ste-

*From *Collected Poems* by E. J. Pratt, by permission of his Estate and The Macmillan Company of Canada Limited.

Marie among the Hurons is Ste. Marie Park, a thirty-acre picnic ground open throughout all the daylight hours providing barbecues, fuel, log-house-style shelters and docks on the Wye River for pleasure boats.

Huronia today is, among other things, one of Ontario's great pleasure grounds but its focal point is Ste-Marie where the ultimate message can be found.

THE EARLY BRITISH FORTS

While the French were desperately attempting to hold their part of North America against the British onslaughts during the 1750's, they did essay two or three rallying points in Ontario. None of them represent any great battles, nor does anything remain to be seen of these skirmishes today. In 1756 a certain Captain Bouchot was sent to Niagara to construct a fortress of proportions which were completely unrealistic in view of the fact that he was defending territory which was devoid of any population except Indians. Similarly the fortifications at Fort Rouillé, on the site of present-day Toronto, were strengthened again to defend virtually unsettled country. At Kingston a fort had been established in 1684 which was to have been blown up six years later but under orders of the new Governor of New France—Count Frontenac—was retained and remained fortified until it was captured by Colonel Bradstreet in 1758. For any evidence of these battles one has to go to history books.

In the mopping-up operations after the fall of Quebec City, the most spectacular incident was the battle plan conceived and attempted not by the French but by the Indians under Pontiac who, in 1763, launched simultaneous attacks upon twelve British posts along the western frontier including Detroit and Michilimackinac. These battles were fought across the border and not in Ontario but as a result of Pontiac's intransigency, Colonel Bradstreet, now a General, decided to organize a retaliatory expedition in 1764. Part of the plan called for the erection of a fort on Lake Erie just at the entrance to the Niagara River which connects it with Lake Ontario. In its original form Fort Erie was merely an enclosure composed of four bastions with connecting walls. Within were log barracks, officers' quarters and a storehouse as well as a parade ground. No glorious military feats were performed during the life of the original fort. In 1804 orders were received to rebuild it but it was not completed when it was attacked by forty-five hundred Americans on July 3, 1814. Since there were only one hundred and eighty British soldiers within the fort, but contrary to romantic legend, the Americans encountered little resistance. Six weeks later another British force under Lt.-Col. Drummond attempted to retake the fort and got control of the northeast bastion but in this gallant expedition the British accidentally ignited their own supplies of powder and blew themselves up. With the settlement of the war in the offing, the Americans decided to abandon the fort in November of the same year and they destroyed what the British had left behind. Today the work of restoration has been completed. This is not the most colourful of the restored forts in Ontario but it has the longest history. It is well worth taking a look at and since it is in the Niagara Region, one of the best tourist areas in the province, it is easily reached. It is also valuable because it offers a contrast to the more elaborate kind of forts which were also involved in the War of 1812-1814.

The nearest of these is Fort George which was built between 1796 and 1799 by the first Governor of Upper Canada, John Graves Simcoe. Simcoe had strong military instincts and a great fear of the newly-created United States of America. The Niagara frontier was obviously a very vulnerable spot and Fort George was designed to be the principal British post in the area. While it was clear that Simcoe was right both in his distrust of the Americans who attempted to take Upper Canada during the War of 1812-1814 and in his assessment of the importance of the Niagara frontier, the choice of site was a mistake—it neither protected the town of Niagara nor did it command the entrance to the Niagara River. Officers who manned the fort said this clearly but no one paid any attention to them until the Americans took it in May, 1813, and held it until December 10th. When the

British got it back they rebuilt it but since it had been replaced by Fort Mississauga it was allowed quickly to fall into disrepair and finally in 1815, Sir Gordon Drummond gave orders that "the expense of keeping up the old and useless Fort George, already tumbling into ruins, be discontinued." Today, however, Fort George is restored with eleven of the original fourteen buildings in good order. It is a very good example, as contrasted to Fort Erie, of the evolution of a frontier fort of the time. While the visitor is in the area he might also take a look at the Naval Hall which is near Fort George but closer to the river. This is a collection of four clapboard buildings which was used by the Provincial Marines during the American Revolution but is famous mainly because the first parliament in Upper Canada was held there in 1792.

However Simcoe was also interested in defending Toronto which was, by the time of his regime, the largest settlement in Ontario. Accordingly he built Fort York. (Simcoe changed the name of the settlement from Toronto to York and then it reverted to Toronto at a later date.) Like the other forts, Fort York was almost completely rebuilt to meet the exigencies of the War of 1812-1814. The fort which can be visited today is not a reconstruction but a restoration of the actual buildings which were erected at that time. For this reason it is perhaps the most authentic of the old forts in Ontario. Easy to reach since it is located at the north and east of the Canadian National Exhibition gates off Lakeshore Blvd., it is a real treasure house of historical displays and museums which reproduce faithfully the living conditions under which officers and men fought, the armament they used, the kind of buildings they had to defend. It is open all year round and there are regular showings of films of early garrison life within the fort. There is also the colourful Fort York Guard, dressed in scarlet uniforms of the early nineteenth century, who drill on the parade ground.

Another major reconstruction of a fort which had its genesis in the War of 1812-1814 is at Kingston—Fort Henry known as "The Citadel of Upper Canada." Kingston had an earlier fort which the British had reserved for a battery as early as

1788 and in 1791 constructed a guardroom. This establishment was known as Fort Frederick and it too was expanded during the War of 1812-1814. Fort Henry, however, was the most important defence post and it eventually became the major British stronghold in Ontario, contributing largely to the reputation of the City of Kingston, as a "military town." Kingston, too, has the Royal Military College (built on the site of old Fort Frederick) which is the Sandhurst or West Point of Canada. Fort Henry itself was by far the most elaborate British fort ever erected west of Quebec and today it has been virtually restored intact as it was at the height of its functioning days between 1832 and 1836. This was the home of many famous British regiments on garrison duty here until Canada became a nation. Since 1870 native Canadian troops manned the fort until 1891 at which time the practical value of this kind of fortification was greatly diminished and Fort Henry gradually fell into ruins.

Restoration was begun in 1936 and since 1938 it has become one of the top attractions to visitors in the province. No pains have been spared to make it an authentic and fascinating showpiece. Every aspect of nineteenth-century military life can be seen here. Cannon of the period which actually still work have been remounted on the ramparts; the quarters of both officers and men have been authentically refurnished. In the shoemaker's and tailor's shops skilled craftsmen ply their ancient trades. There is a museum with displays of infantry, cavalry, artillery and naval arms and equipment unequalled anywhere else in Canada. To all this has been added real showmanship. The now world-famous Fort Henry Guard, a precision trained group of Canadian university students, display nineteenth-century infantry drill, fife and drum corps and artillery salutes as well as the routine of muzzle-loading cannons. Every Wednesday evening through July and August the guard performs a special retreat ceremony. This highly-trained group, authentically dressed in the uniform of the old Imperial Garrisons and carrying the equipment of the Royal Garrison's Artillery and British line regiments of 1867 (Canada's Confederation year), have appeared twice at the Royal tournament

in London, England. This is by far the best military display of
the past to be found in Ontario.

But what do the forts tell us? In the first place, their history
reveals that the concept of setting up heavily-armed outposts
as key defence positions was outmoded at least by 1890, something which the French had not learned fifty years later when
they built the Maginot Line. Of more immediate concern, perhaps the forts are the living reminders of the uneasiness which
began in the days of the American Revolution and which it
took a war and then some to dispel before the United States
and Canada could claim to have the longest undefended international boundary in the world.

The war itself, fought in 1812-1814, really was not much
of an exercise as wars go. To this day, both nations claim that
they won it. I remember once being highly incensed at Queenston Heights, scene of one of the more spectacular battles of the
war, trudging up the spiral staircase of Brock's Monument
behind an overweight American lady who was finding the
going rough. "I don't see," she complained to her husband,
"why we should go to all this trouble to climb a monument
these people put up to celebrate a war they think they won."
As a matter of fact, it is part of the legend of Ontario that we
did win it. If you read our version of the story we won it
against superior numbers, by superior courage, gallantry and
bravery and through expert generalship. In a country which is
remarkably lacking in military heroes we have had to draw
heavily upon the war of 1812 since it is the only formal war
we ever fought in this province.

General Isaac Brock (whose monument so exasperated the
American lady) is just about our only major military hero.
According to the way I learned it at school, he kept charging
up a hill until he got shot for his pains and this, since he was
on our side, has earned him a niche in provincial history from
which it will be hard to dislodge him.

Then in the same area and in the same war we have a
gallant lady called Laura Secord. Today her name is perpetu-
ated, as is the way with practical minded Ontarians, in a
chain of shops which sell excellent chocolates. The connection

between her reputed exploit in the war and the candy-making business is one which has always eluded me but her attractive face appears on every box of candy just the same. In 1813 the American General Dearborn succeeded in taking Fort George and from this base sallied out on various enterprises. One of these was a scheme to surprise a British advance post which was held by Lieutenant James FitzGibbon with the usual "handful" of soldiers and some two hundred Indian scouts. Somehow, in a way never quite satisfactorily explained, Laura Secord, the wife of a Niagara settler, overheard two Americans talking about the proposed surprise attack. At dawn the next day she wended her way through twenty miles of American-held territory to give the warning to FitzGibbon. How she did this is a bit confusing. One version is that she drove a cow in front of her so she could tell American sentries that it had been lost in the woods and she was taking it home. Another version is that she carried a milking-stool with her so she could tell the same vigilant sentries that she was looking for her cow, lost in the woods, so she could milk it. In any event, however she did it, she is said to have reached Fitz-Gibbon who, and this point seems to get very little attention in our histories, already knew about the attack through his own scouts and intelligence service. But after all, surely we have to have something and so today Brock has his monument and Laura Secord her candy box.

The plain fact of the matter is that most of the citizens of Ontario do not give very much thought to these battles of long ago. Today the province is growing so rapidly and its people so preoccupied with its development that they no longer need myths and legends of battles long ago to bolster their self-assurance.

THE REBELLION OF 1837

However, in the century between the cessation of the War of 1812-1814 and the beginning of World War I, the province did have a few alarums and excursions of a military nature.

The first of these occurred a little better than twenty years after the end of the war when Ontario came the closest it has ever come to civil war. This event is called the Rebellion of 1837. From a political point of view it had significant effects but from a military point of view it is negligible. There was a similar uprising of about the same proportions in the Province of Quebec.

In Ontario, the Rebellion of 1837 consisted of one battle—and it is even stretching it to call it by such a name. The rebellion was about responsible government. In Ontario its leader was a fiery little publisher of Scottish nationality whom we shall meet again; his name was William Lyon Mackenzie. For many years prior to 1837 Mackenzie had been waging a verbal war against a group of entrenched office-holders in the province who came to be known as the Family Compact. He charged they controlled elections, traded favours, were not interested in developing the province and its resources and exploited every facet of provincial life for their own advantage. Most of it was more or less true and, as the population of the province increased, more and more settlers came around to accepting his point of view and supporting him. Not a man of even temper and moderation in any event, he was further exasperated not only by the indifference of his enemies but by personal attacks against him. For example, at one juncture the young bloods of Toronto raided his newspaper office and dumped his press into Toronto Bay. Finally, in exasperation, the "Little Rebel"—as Mackenzie has now, almost affectionately, come to be known—decided it was time for action.

In secret he and his friends attempted to recruit men for armed combat. Over a hundred miles to the west in a new area which was just being opened up, called the Huron Tract, Mackenzie found the only fully-trained military officer who had any sympathy for his cause. He was a Dutch immigrant of considerable means, a veteran of the Napoleonic Wars, and a former colonel of the Dutch Army, named Anthony G. Van Egmond. Mackenzie promptly made him commander-in-chief and Van Egmond probably is unique in the military annals of the western world inasmuch as he is probably the only commander-in-chief who saw his army for only a matter of a couple of hours before they went into battle which the commander-in-chief said was ill-advised and refused to join himself.

Mackenzie's forces, such as they were, had been instructed to gather at what was then far up Yonge Street in Toronto at a place called Montgomery's Tavern, which incidentally cannot be visited because it was torn down many years ago. Here Van Egmond made a rendezvous with his "troops" which to his consternation were not the well-trained, well-armed group of men Mackenzie had led him to believe they were but rather a rag-tag and bob-tail assortment of disgruntled settlers, many with no weaponry whatsoever save a pikestaff. Mackenzie's plan to march boldly on Toronto and, by surprise, get control of the main blockhouse containing the city's powder supply was quickly vetoed by Van Egmond.

Ironically enough, there is a reasonble chance that it might have worked because the Lieutenant-Governor of Upper Canada at that time, Sir Francis Bond Head, was an extremely obtuse gentleman who refused to believe that anyone would have the temerity to take up arms against the British Crown. Once again that wily British regular army officer, James Fitz-Gibbon, comes into the picture. Again, his intelligence informed him of Mackenzie's plan, this time without the assistance of Laura Secord. It was only with the greatest of difficulty that he succeeded in getting permission to defend the blockhouse, but had the Mackenzie irregulars moved fast enough they would have attained at least their first objective. As it was, by the following morning FitzGibbon decided to send out an exploratory party which Mackenzie's scouts (far less reliable as a source of military intelligence) mistook for a major attack. Again, against Van Egmond's advice, Mackenzie ordered his men to go forth and engage the regulars which they did with the inevitable disastrous results. And that was the end of Ontario's "Civil War."

Mackenzie himself fled to the United States but Van Egmond, who had not even been in the battle, was intercepted on his way back to the Huron Tract and imprisoned in York County jail where, before he could be brought to trial, he died of pneumonia brought on by old age and overexposure.

In Queenston, near Brock's famous battlefield and in the beautiful Niagara Peninsula, can be found a house which is now a public museum. It is known as Mackenzie's Printing

House because it was here that his newspaper the *Colonial Advocate* was published in 1824. Later, he moved it to Toronto. In Toronto, on Bond Street, is what is known as Mackenzie House which is also preserved as a museum and is an excellent reproduction of a house of that period. The interesting thing about this particular house is that when it was safe for William Lyon Mackenzie to return to Toronto (where he had been its first mayor in 1834) his attempt at rebellion seemed almost to be condoned because a group of his admirers bought the Bond Street residence and furnished it for him so that he might live comfortably in his later years. He died in 1861. There are no other remains of the rebellion of 1837 in Ontario.

THE FENIAN RAIDS

Just before the outbreak of civil war in the United States a curious organization called the Fenian Brotherhood of America was organized. Its object was to snatch Ireland from the British Empire and make it a republic. The branch of the brotherhood in the United States was led by John O'Mahony who decided that the Fenians' contribution in North America would be to attack and take Canada. With the coming of civil war this enterprise had to be abandoned until the spring of 1866. At this time the Fenians, almost exclusively made up of expatriate Irishmen—a race well known for its capacity to imagine and pretend—were firmly convinced that the people of Canada were weary of Britain, that there were two hundred thousand Canadians at least who were ready to join them, that the United States government would not interfere with their plans, and that without either adequate training or arms they could beat the regular British army units stationed in Canada at that time. It is hardly necessary to say that Canadians, and this included particularly the people of Ontario, did not even take the group seriously.

In this they were wrong. General John O'Neill assembled almost a thousand men at Buffalo and a large amount of ammunition which, much to his surprise, was promptly seized by the United States government. However they thought they still had sufficient arms to make a successful attack and on

June 2, 1866, they boarded some canal boats at Black Rock and were towed across the river by tug landing at Fort Erie where they cut the telegraph wires, tore up the railway tracks and then, instead of proceeding to known military establishments, set up a camp. Now the military geniuses of Ontario were in a considerable state of surprise and disarray. Quite typically, having no plans, they called out battalion after battalion of both regular army units and militia and poured them down toward Fort Erie and, indeed, into almost every other direction in Ontario including many sections which the Fenians could not by any possible stretch of the imagination reach.

In the Fort Erie region the battle quickly assumed the colouring of real comic opera on both sides. The Welland Canal Field Battery (which had no field guns) and the Dunnville Naval Company engaged the enemy and, since they had virtually no arms and were not a land fighting force, were quickly driven off by the Fenians. At Ridgeway, the Queen's Own Regiment and the Thirteenth Battalion, both of which had been sent into the fray without blankets, greatcoats or proper field equipment, also took up battle with the Fenians where, as one Ontario historian modestly puts it "They did not prosper." The main reason they did not prosper was because they were under some strange illusion that the Fenians had crossed the river and were equipped for cavalry attack. There was not a horse in the Fenian camp. However, after these few successful skirmishes the Fenians were impressed by the huge hordes of men (they did not know were ill-equipped) who were pouring into the Niagara Peninsula. Their imaginations carried them the rest of the way and they proceeded to retreat across the river where a United States ship, the *Michigan*, captured them and held them in Buffalo as prisoners. Thus ended the Fenian Raids, the last direct attack made in Ontario.

But for a long time, the citizens of the province were uneasy. In my own part of Ontario I have heard old-timers recount many hilarious tales of restless young men who pretended to be Fenians and rode through the countryside at night beating drums, playing fifes and generally raising hell. On one occa-

sion they were so successful that an entire village was evacu-
ated for over twenty-four hours. To my knowledge not a single
Fenian ever entered my part of Ontario.

Ontario's lack of colourful military history is a source of
frustration for a certain element in our population. Those who
hold tenaciously to what we generally call "our noble British
heritage" find it a little embarrassing to live in a province with
so few examples of one of the major facets of the British tradition—the red coats, the thin red line, etc. Somehow, many
who live here are a bit schizophrenic about our military
position. When the Boer War came along a sprinkling of
Ontario young men volunteered for service. In both World
Wars I and II the province proved that it could indeed provide
excellent fighting men, in all branches of the armed services,
and in impressively large numbers. The record of Ontario
regiments constitutes a role of honour indeed and the satisfaction which the people of the province took in the exploits
of its fighting men is manfested in almost every town and city
in the province. There are very few centres which do not have
a cenotaph or similar war memorial, most of which were
erected after World War I. The majority of these monuments,
while they attest to a very proper respect for those who gave
their lives for their country, are not worth looking at. Anyone
who travels extensively through the towns and cities of Ontario
and keeps a vigilant eye out for the war memorials will come
to realize that he is seeing the same monument several times
although in different locations. The truth is that after World
War I a group of Scottish stone masons assembled half a dozen
standard designs depicting Canadian soldiers in various attitudes of gallantry, mass produced them and through expert
salesmanship virtually littered them all across the Ontario
countryside. This is not true, however, of Canada's war memorial and cenotaph in Ottawa.

THE ULTIMATE REMEMBRANCE

The National War Memorial is no mass-produced hunk of
granite. It took a long time to appear in concrete form, so
long that (like our flag) it cropped up periodically in political

campaigns. It was only unveiled (by his late Majesty King George VI) in 1939, a few months before we were embroiled in another war. It stands just to the southeast of Parliament Hill in what is known as Confederation Square. It is called "The Response." It is crowned by two figures, one bearing a laurel wreath and the other a torch, which are supported by a granite arch. Through this arch a group of fighting men and women, representative of all the branches of the Canadian Forces who fought in World War I, crowd eagerly and heroically. It is beautifully rendered, full of action and represents exactly what the late monarch of Canada said it did:

One sees at a glance the answer made by Canada when the world's peace was broken, and freedom threatened . . . it depicts the zeal with which this country entered the conflict . . . something deeper than chivalry is portrayed. It is the spontaneous response of the nation's conscience. The very soul of the nation is here revealed.

This is the side which Canadians generally, and Ontarians particularly, are loath to reveal even though deep down in their hearts they respond to the panoply and pageantry of war. In this nation and in this province we have generated very few distinctive symbols of that side of our character which is indeed warlike. Like the cenotaph itself (which was designed by two British artists) whenever we want to express this side of our nature we borrow from Great Britain. Perhaps this explains why such a large number of Ontario's best-known regiments are highland regiments. And certainly it must have something to do with the colourful and dramatic but quite incongruous display which the government of Canada arranges in front of the Parliament Buildings every day during the summer months. Here representatives of various Canadian regiments are carefully drilled in parade-ground routines such as changing the guard, etc., dressed in red coats, and with towering busbies and all the accoutrements which one associates with the guard at Buckingham Palace. It is difficult to understand that the government which supports this kind of anachronism, so essentially foreign to the Canadian scene, should at the same time be the pioneer amongst the western nations of the world in the unification of its armed services, the elimination of distinctions between army, navy and airforce, and the introduction of a common uniform designed to meet the demands of modern warfare and with no regard for the trappings of any heritage whatsoever. It is only one more aspect of the great Canadian riddle and nowhere is the enigma more apparent than in Ontario. Any visitor who comes to this province will enjoy his visit much more if he merely accepts all the delightful things to see and do, regardless of how contradictory they appear to be, and let it go at that. The citizens of the province have long since learned to live with their own confusion.

Also in Ottawa, which is on the Ontario side of the great Ottawa River, is the nation's ultimate tribute to its valiant men who have fought in both World Wars. This is the Peace Tower which stands in the middle of the centre block of the three buildings which comprise the Houses of Parliament on Parliament Hill. The original centre block, which had a somewhat stubbier tower, was ravaged by fire in 1916, supposedly by saboteurs, and only the Parliamentary Library remained standing. When it was being rebuilt after World War I it was decided that the present great tower would be erected not only to celebrate Canadians fallen in conflict but also to impress upon all viewers that Canada's basic motivation was for peace.

The main lobby of the tower is called Confederation Hall. A short flight of stone steps leads to the shrine, richly ornamented with carved stone and stained glass. In the centre is the altar of remembrance, carved with the arms of Canada and bearing on its surface in a gold-framed glass casket, with kneeling winged figures at each corner, a book of heavy opaque vellum. It is an illuminated book containing the names of all the men and women who died on active service in both World Wars. Except for a certain few days each year, one page is turned each day and every page is exposed to view once a year. Above this quiet room, visited almost every day by relatives of those whose names are inscribed in the great book, is Canada's famous carillon—fifty-three bells in all, the largest weighing twenty-two thousand, four hundred pounds and the smallest ten pounds. The carillon is played for concerts, participates in every national ceremony and presides over every formal gathering in the quadrangle before the centre block. The music of the bells is the signal for every unified call to attention both in sadness or rejoicing. Far above the bells is the clock with its four huge dials which can be seen from many parts of Ottawa. It is controlled by the Dominion Observatory and the hours are struck on the largest bell which is called the bourbon. The quarter hours are struck on the smaller bells in the familiar Westminster chimes.

Here, then, is the consummation of Canada's and Ontario's impulse to war. Its grandeur representing heroic deeds fought in other lands contradicts the historic facts of Ontario's own military past. Here is a province whose only major war was a massacre of an Indian tribe, which only once fought seriously an enemy on its own territory and which, although it made an attempt, has not experienced the ravages of civil war. Despite this, what does remain of this past is well worth looking at and that is the way Ontario would like it to be. This province would not be what it is today if it had had to suffer the setbacks of consistent bloody conflicts. We have restored our forts rather well; we go through the motions of a colourful tradition but deep in our hearts we are glad that we have been blessed by peace in our land.

CHAPTER FOUR

Man Bites Dog

It becomes quite clear to any traveller in Ontario as he visits the museums, the old forts and the Indian relics and missions that the real battle which was waged in this province was not man against man but man against nature, and that was some battle. Indeed, it looked for a while after the British had conquered this territory that the battle might never be fought. The British government seemed, on the whole, to take about the same attitude as the French before them.

This was rough and terrifying country, thickly covered with forest and filled with rushing, hard-to-navigate rivers and streams. One thing known for certain was that it was a seemingly inexhaustible source of rich furs. The temptation was great to leave the whole thing at that. Perhaps if the American Revolution had not come along this would have been the fate of Ontario for a much longer time. As long as the British held the prospering and now well-colonized areas down the Atlantic coast and ever extending westward, there was no real need to do anything about the wilderness to the north, but with the United States lost the picture was different. The Americans in their new-found energy and capacity to stand on their own feet might very well seek to wrest British North America from the motherland and make it part of the great republic. That, in turn, would mean not only the end of the profitable fur trade but it also would mean that over-populated Britain would have no place under the Crown in North America to send its thousands upon thousands of impoverished immigrants. In actual fact many of these people went to the United States anyway but if the then British Empire was to continue to be represented in North America, the wilderness would have to be opened up.

These facts were recognized readily enough but no one quite knew how to go about it. For a few years, while the Americans tried to take British North America, there was not much time to give to the problems of settlement. By the time Governor Simcoe arrived, he was still preoccupied with defence and with building more forts than farms. By the turn of the nineteenth century Ontario was still virtually a wilderness and, with the exception of the United Empire Loyalists and some other pioneer adventurers along Lake Ontario, the wilderness was still intact.

Governor Simcoe seems to have been primarily concerned, as far as settlement goes, with the establishment of his pet project—what has now become the City of Toronto. Originally it was a minor French fort. When the governor reached this particular spot he said, "Here a city will be built in the spring." From that point on a good deal of his energy was devoted to creating the city, to the detriment of the kind of expansion which was required to develop Ontario's great natural resources. For almost a hundred years or more, Torontonians lived under the happy delusion that they were, essentially, the entire province.

A typical Torontonian, and a great editor, John Ross Robertson of the Toronto *Evening Telegram*, wrote a series of articles in his paper between 1884 and 1914. They are most authentic reflections of the Toronto attitude. Writing about the founding of Toronto and its first forty-five years, Robertson summed it up this way: "By the end of that time Toronto had established a pattern of existence that still persists, had saved Upper Canada by her example and was clipping the wings of her aristocracy in order to make them market-conscious." Until very recently (and perhaps in some isolated areas of Toronto even today) most of those who lived in Ontario's capital firmly believed they had indeed "saved Upper Canada by her example."

And what was the nature of this inspiring example? It is well described by another early visitor named Dr. Bethune: "The society was excellent, having not less than twenty families of the highest respectability, persons of refinement and many of high intellectual culture. To these were added a small sprinkling of military. For the size of the place there was a large amount of hospitality exercised, and on a handsome and bountiful scale." From the point of view of those who really made Ontario, the sturdy pioneers who actually did the work of subduing the wilderness, the example of "hospitality exercised on a handsome and bountiful scale" was about as helpful as a bikini would be for an Eskimo lady.

The kind of people who dominated life in Toronto and who had satellites scattered in the United Empire Loyalist settlements both in Eastern Ontario and in the Niagara Peninsula were astonishingly unrealistic, indeed almost blind to the hard facts of life in the wilderness. A certain Major Littlehales who travelled west into the area between Chatham and Windsor pretty well exemplifies the approach of the gentry and the military to this new land. "After taking some refreshment of salt pork and venison, well cooked by Lt. Smith," the Major wrote, "we as usual sang God Save the King and went to rest." The keeping up of forms was far more important to these early adventurers into the unknown territory than any practical observations which might have helped the settlers after them as they took up the real struggles. Another visitor, in 1789, Lord Edward Fitzgerald, travelled into the same territory as Major Littlehales and in a letter home wrote an astonishing account of Indian women. "The Indians are delightful people, the ladies charming, and with manners that I like very much. They are so natural. Notwithstanding the life they live which would make most women rough and masculine, they are as soft, meek, and modest as the best brought

up girls in England." One explanation, of course, is that after
several weeks in the wilderness any female looked good to the
Irish peer but this romantic and sentimental approach appears
so often in early diaries and letters of visitors to Upper Canada
that it seems apparent that they were determined not to see
the brutal demands of eking out an existence in the forest
and regarded their visit as some kind of rubbing shoulders
with the exotic and the charming.

The military officers were no more down to earth than their
civil counterparts. Foppish in manner, preoccupied with good
form and determined to be elegant and stately on all occasions,
they contributed virtually nothing to the building of Ontario.
A good example is the story about Captain Cowan of the
navy and Staff Surgeon Fleming of the army who were extremely respected and popular in the colony because of their
reputation for being the politest men there. It is said that on
one occasion they met while crossing the old Chippewa
Bridge. As each proceeded to the middle of the bridge, he
paused every few minutes to bow to the other. When they met
they shook hands before they passed each other. Any honest-
to-goodness backwoodsman of Ontario would either have
laughed or been outraged at such nonsense. J. E. Middleton
who wrote a much-neglected but very rich history of Ontario
describes what the real makers of the province were like:

Jack was as good as his master—if Jack could fell a tree
as well, if he had the strength of arm and willingness to work.
It was a matter of course for the hired man to lose his heart
to the daughter of the house, brave in her deerskin petticoat
and her broad-brimmed sunbonnet, for she was a worker too.
It was a matter of course for the young couple, married by a
Justice of the Peace according to law (but not according to
the social custom in England) to take up land of their own,
build their own ingle, and found a family as good as the best.
Physical strength was a necessity to clear underbrush, chop
hardwood and pine, grub out stumps, reap the wheat with
sickles and thresh it with a flail. But physical strength alone
was not sufficient. The pioneers had need of patience, content-
ment and a whole galaxy of spiritual virtues which made them

notable in their generation. They may have been lacking in
the knowledge that comes from books, but in the solitudes they
learned to think as well as to strive. So also the women toiled
and endured; washing, cooking, spinning, weaving, patching,
quilting, making soap, making clothes, and serving the needs
of a succession of babies. We who regard with affection the
noble landscapes of this Ontario, the rolling fields, the clumps
of bush, the gentle streams, the orchards embowered in bloom,
think too seldom of the broad-shouldered men and the broad-
hipped women who commanded the wilderness to blossom,
who reaped a forest and made a garden in its place.*

This is the true picture of the men and women who really
created this province. They did not stop in the middle of the
bridge to bow and shake hands, they did not sing "God Save
the Queen" and go to rest after each meal, they were not families of the highest respectability and the most bounteous hospitality, they were men and women such as Middleton describes.

It would, however, be wrong to assume that many of those
who came from "gentler" families did not adapt to the endurance which was the lot of every successful pioneer regardless
of what class he came from in the old land. Anne Langton,
whose family settled a few miles north of Peterborough, considered themselves of the highest respectability and were extremely class conscious, has left a series of diaries which have
been brought together under the general title *A Gentlewoman
in Upper Canada*. From the diaries it is apparent that she was
very much preoccupied by certain niceties and conventions
which did not apply in the wilderness but it is equally obvious
that this woman, faced by the harsh realities of pioneering was
just as much of the stuff from which the successful subduing
of Upper Canada was made as any of her more sturdy compatriots. Here is a typical entry from the diary:

When I look back I sometimes wonder how we managed
for those months when we had no fire in the house, and every
culinary operation from baking bread to heating water was
performed on the dilapidated cooking stove, whilst eight or
nine meals were regularly served each day and ten or twelve

The Province of Ontario—A History, 1615-1927, by J. E. Middleton and
Fred Landon. (Toronto: Dominion Pub., 1927).

mouths fed bread. This stove stands about ten yards from the back door under a little shed . . . Here was many a nice dinner cooked with all proper varieties for a party of five or six (sometimes more), besides the eternal almost daily bread baking, and everlasting frying for breakfasts and suppers . . . In due time we shall have things complete and comfortable, and wonder how so many conveniences could be dispensed with, I daresay we must exercise our patience some time longer."*

Resourcefulness was the necessary ingredient for the pioneer regardless of what class of society he came from. And yet, individual initiative, hardihood and sheer physical strength were not enough in themselves. As in every other situation known to civilized man, there had to be leaders. In good measure, the success of the conquest of the Upper Canadian woodlands is due to the fact not that there was an efficient and sympathetic administration at York or Toronto but that in most of the key sections of the province remarkable men undertook the responsibilities of leadership in the colonization process. Not all of these men were either democratic or, sometimes, even honourable. But they were strong, and in every instance, colourful and highly individualistic.

THE TALBOT AND THE CANADA COMPANY SETTLEMENTS

In Southern Ontario, which is still the thickly populated section of the province though by far the smallest, the original settlement was based on agriculture. The pattern of settlement depended largely upon the kind of leadership and the kind of motivation behind the leadership which existed in any particular section. When the Canada Act was passed in 1791 creating Upper Canada, the area now known as Ontario, there were still large blocks of land which, by previous treaties, belonged to the Indians. After 1791 the British government systematically set about buying out these areas from the Indians and setting up reservations of a much smaller size in

*A Gentlewoman in Upper Canada. The Journals of Anne Langton. Edited by H. H. Langton. (Toronto: Clarke Irwin, 1950).

various parts of the province. By approximately 1830, most of the land had been purchased from the native Indian tribes and was held by the Crown. As areas were surveyed into townships, one-seventh of the area of each township was set aside as Crown land and one-seventh as Clergy Reserves; the remainder was available for purchase. As we have seen, the first substantial block of settlers were the United Empire Loyalists who were given land holdings by the Crown. After that, the disposal of land by the government proceeded at a very haphazard pace, mostly in the area east of Toronto and under no organized system whatsoever. Without the machinations of daring and imaginative leaders, settlement in the province would have been extremely slow and ineffective but, in varying degrees of magnitude, enterprising people appeared who bought large tracts of land and vigorously promoted the sale of farms within their domain to land-hungry settlers.

One of the earliest of these was an astonishing, tyrannical and vigorous gentleman called Colonel Thomas Talbot. One Canadian writer has described Talbot in these terms: "The 'Great Pasha of the Wilderness' was a man of violent opinions, most of which he inherited from his father, who had them from his father, who had them from George I, which explains why he was reputed to be a hard man to get along with." The colonel was indeed a difficult gentleman. Born in 1771 within the castle of Malahide, the family seat nine miles from Dublin, he chose a career in the army and was commissioned as an ensign at the age of twelve. He first came to Canada in 1790 and was invited to join John Graves Simcoe's staff in 1791 when Simcoe proceeded to his new post in Upper Canada. Talbot was recalled in 1794 and served in various European campaigns against Napoleon for the next six years.

During his time with Simcoe he had travelled a good deal through Western Ontario and was particularly taken by the fine lands which lay between the north shore of Lake Erie and the Thames River at London, Ontario. He returned to Canada in 1800 resolved to acquire a large section of this particular land, insisting that Simcoe had promised it to him—five thousand acres in all! Already he was displaying the stubbornness which characterized him for the rest of his life and finally he did make an arrangement with the Colonial Office whereby he received five thousand acres, mostly in the Township of Dunwich, on the basis that he would divide the tract into fifty-acre farms and for each settler he located on one of them he would receive as a reward two hundred acres from lands elsewhere in the same township. Under this plan he could have received a maximum of twenty thousand acres but, as things turned out, before he was through the colonel actually controlled sixty thousand acres of some of the finest land in Ontario.

By 1804 he was under way but it took him five years before any large number of settlers were attracted to his holdings. The first settlers to come were treated with great kindness and respect by Talbot but as things began to prosper his attitude changed.

Near Port Talbot on Lake Erie which was the first village erected within his territory, Talbot built a succession of dwellings for himself culminating in an elaborate structure which was generally known as a castle and, of course, called Malahide after his ancestral seat. The "castle" still remains near Port Talbot where it is privately owned, lived in and enjoyed. But before the colonel had died in 1846, his castle was a magnet which attracted numbers by the score in a mood of both fascination and fear. Talbot's reputation was widely known. He was irascible, quarrelsome (he quarrelled with almost every major official in Upper Canada before he was through), occasionally fought a duel and as he was "sizing up" a prospective settler seemed to take an almost masochistic pleasure in giving the poor fellow a hard time. Mrs. Jameson has left a description of a typical sight, any day of the week, around Talbot's Upper Canadian Malahide Castle: "On leaving my apartment in the morning I used to find groups of strange figures lounging around the door, ragged, black-bearded, gaunt, travel-worn and toil-worn immigrants, Irish, Scotch and American, come to offer themselves as settlers. These he [Talbot] called his land pirates, and curious and characteristic and dramatic beyond description were the scenes

which used to take place between this great pasha of the
wilderness and his hungry, unfortunate clients and petitioners."

As the colonel's health failed, and after several rough-and-
tumble fights which the colonel often lost, Talbot decided it
was better not to meet applicants face to face and instead
took refuge behind a sliding window. If an argument developed and the applicant looked dangerous, the colonel merely
slammed the window shut and retired to safety. The man
generally given the credit for having reduced the colonel to
this state is still, to this day, a hero among what Dr. Kenneth
Galbraith has called in his book of reminiscences *The
Scotch*. This man was one, Duncan Patterson who, having
been refused a location that he desired by Colonel Talbot,
threw him on the ground and held him there until Talbot
promised he would give him the lot he wanted. He kept his
word too.

Nevertheless, of all the settlers whom the colonel dealt with,
usually in a fractious and unpleasant way, the Scottish were
the ones he despised most and particularly those who were
of the temperance persuasion whom he described as "damned
cold water drinking societies." Although the nearby city of
St. Thomas is reputed to have been named after Talbot, he
was no churchman at the best of times and at the end of his
life supported no religious activities whatsoever. Ironically,
one of the most interesting historical landmarks in the city of
St. Thomas is St. Thomas' church which was built in 1824.
The entire area of the Talbot Settlement is delightful country,
the shore of Lake Erie abounds with pleasant fishing villages
and quiet resort areas and the prosperity of the countryside
generally proves beyond all question that, whatever his failings might have been, Colonel Talbot knew good land when
he saw it and pioneered—much more successfully than most
—in getting it quickly and well settled.

By far the most ambitious land settlement scheme ever to
occur in Ontario was developed about twenty-five years after
Talbot began his experiment by the Canada Company which,
through the activities of the Scottish novelist John Galt,
acquired a million acres in what is known as the Huron Tract.

Trooping the Colours, Ottawa

Skyline of Ottawa from the Macdonald-Cartier Bridge

Parliament Buildings, Toronto

The story of the opening of the Huron Tract has been told many times.* Besides Galt who was the founder of both the city of Guelph and the Lake Huron port of Goderich, the ill-starred Colonel Van Egmond of the 1837 Rebellion was a leading figure in the early days of the settlement and so was Dr. William "Tiger" Dunlop, one of the most fabulous men ever to come into the province of Ontario.

Of gigantic proportions, red-whiskered, jovial, hard-drinking and large-hearted, Dunlop ranged through the wilderness, bringing in settlers, encouraging them, helping them and, in short, taking exactly the opposite attitude to that of Colonel Talbot. Dunlop, too, came of a distinguished British family and established a Canadian version of his family estate at Gairbraid just north of the town of Goderich. Today nothing remains of Gairbraid, but the tomb of Dunlop and his brother Robert can be visited. There was nothing funereal about the "Tiger." He too battled most of the leading figures in the province at one time or another but it was always on behalf of the settlers who came into the Huron Tract. Dunlop not only had the characteristics of leadership but also the humanity of the truly great and, above all, a sense of humour which delighted his friends, almost everyone he met and is still manifested in his famous will which is considered to be one of the most distinctive—and hilarious—legal documents ever signed and sealed in Ontario.

The Canada Company carried on business in Ontario for over a hundred and twenty-five years and by that time had left behind what is generally regarded as the richest agricultural area in Canada. The Huron Tract area which extends west from Guelph in a triangle of which Lake Huron is the base does not contain much in the way of historical sites but it is just about the most beautiful pastoral countryside to be found anywhere in North America. The beaches along Lake Huron are the finest in Canada and there is an abundance of excellent accommodation in the quiet resort areas along the lake, at such places as Bayfield and Goderich and, for the swingers, groovy Grand Bend where a winter population of a few hundred expands, on summer holiday weekends,

*See the author's *Settlement of Huron County* (Toronto: Ryerson, 1966).

to over ten thousand. For the camper, besides the many
privately-operated facilities, there is the Pinery Provincial Park
just south of Grand Bend, an excellent place for enjoying the
delights of Lake Huron's great beaches and its famous sunsets.
And behind it all lies the leadership provided by the great
men of the early days of the Canada Company.

Not all areas of Ontario were fortunate enough to have
adventurous individuals or land companies take the leadership
in settlement but some did very well on a less ambitious basis.

THE "PENNSYLVANIA DUTCH"

Special mention should be made of a great number of Americans (not United Empire Loyalists) who came into Canada
after 1800 and in many areas provided leadership. These
people did not come because they expected or deserved
political favours but because they were pioneers in the true
sense of the word, seeking the adventure, the challenge and,
of course, new land which was shrinking rapidly in the eastern
section of the United States and was available at the worst
at a very low cost (and sometimes for nothing) in Upper
Canada. By far the most significant group of immigrants from
the United States were those who came from Pennsylvania—
the well-known "Pennsylvania Dutch." These people usually
came into Canada via Youngstown and Niagara-on-the-Lake
and fanned out to the east as far as such towns as Markham
just north of Toronto and to the west to the Kitchener area.
The city of Kitchener was originally called Berlin but, in the
sensitive years of World War I the name was changed to that
of the gallant but ill-fated British general.

Today, the most colourful reminders of the settlers from
Pennsylvania are the Mennonites. They settled in tightly knit
communities both in the Markham district and just to the
north of Kitchener around the town of Elmira. Elmira is a
quiet town and the best time to visit it is late in March when
they have their famous pancake and maple syrup festival,
although it is beautiful countryside at any time of the year.
Similarly, at any time of the year the traveller in Ontario can
see something which is probably not duplicated anywhere else

in North America—a whole community which is literally back
in the horse-and-buggy days. These are one group of Mennonites. Not all Mennonites have stuck stubbornly to the old
ways. They come in varying degrees: the advanced group
which, except on certain theological and doctrinal matters, is
indistinguishable from the rest of the Ontario community; the
in-between group which will use modern farm machinery,
drive an automobile as long as it is painted black and has no
chrome or other ornamentation, still wear sober black clothes
and resolutely refuse to wear a necktie (their attitude to turtle-
necks has not yet been determined); and the strictly orthodox
Mennonites of the old school who create a picturesque and
interesting sight on a Sunday afternoon when they are driving
to or from their very plain clapboard churches.

What can be seen on this occasion is as close a facsimile of
what it was like in Ontario one hundred years ago as it is
possible to find. Almost every type of horse-drawn vehicle,
except highly ornamented carriages, of a bygone era, is in use.
Large, sober-suited families—the women wearing skirts to the
ground and bonnets chastely surrounding their heads—can be
seen going to church in a surrey drawn by a team of very fine
horses at a sober gait. And, at the other extreme, a gay young
couple in a racy buggy with a high-spirited mare can be seen as
they take off for church in what must be the last century's
equivalent of squealing tires. These are a sober, change-resist-
ing people but a leisurely drive through the farm lands they
occupy will quickly dispel any notion that, although they may
disapprove of the use of the combine, they are not efficient
farmers. Here is some of the best cultivated, most envied and
most beautiful farm land to be found anywhere in the world.
It is well worth a visit.

The Mennonites, as seems to be the way the whole world
over, are split into various sects. So too were the Quakers who
also came from Pennsylvania, and in the Markham district
only a few miles north of Toronto is the last memorial of such
a deviationist group. This is the Sharon Temple, sometimes
known as the Temple built for music. This structure which
looks something like a wedding cake was built by the Children
of Peace, a group of Quakers who broke with the orthodox

members because they loved music and built their worship of the Lord around it. Every line of this beautiful structure has a symbolic meaning and its acoustics are superb. Here the Lord was praised indeed in the service of song and for many years the Sharon Temple was renowned throughout the area for the great and inspiring concerts which were held there. Today it is a well-preserved museum, in beautiful condition and a delight to the eye if no longer to the ear.

EARLY NEGRO SETTLEMENTS

Still another unique type of settler in Upper Canada was the fugitive negro slave who, prior to the United States Civil War, was smuggled into Canada via the underground railway whose most important terminal was at the border city of Windsor. More than one present-day civil rights activist may be surprised to know that slavery existed in Upper Canada until 1793 when, for the first time, a law was passed preventing the bringing of negro slaves into the province, limiting the term of contract for binding the slave already in Ontario to nine years and decreeing that the children of slaves should become free at the age of twenty-five. At that, this was really advanced legislation for the time. Indeed it is the first legislation against slavery in any British country. The first European country to take such action was Denmark, only one year earlier. Through this legislation, the coast was cleared for the U.S. abolitionists who became increasingly active about the middle of the nineteenth century. In 1858, the famous John Brown whose "soul goes marching on" and who was often in the district, held a convention in the First Baptist Church in Chatham which, although greatly altered from those days, still stands. It is said that the famous Harper's Ferry Raid in Virginia was planned at this convention.

Near the town of Dresden the interested traveller can visit the grave and the home of the Rev. Josiah Henson, the escaped slave whose life is supposed to have been the model for Harriet Beecher Stowe's famous novel, *Uncle Tom's Cabin.* The Henson house is now the nucleus for what is known as the Uncle Tom's Cabin Museum complex and is well worth visiting. From the point of view of settlement, the most significant operation is that which centred around the village of South Buxton. Here, in 1849, a group of American abolitionists purchased four thousand, three hundred acres of land which was made available to free fugitive negro slaves for settlement. Throughout the period of pioneer settlement in Western Ontario the negro settler was by no means uncommon throughout the area from Windsor to London and even slightly farther north.

Thus the savage battle which man waged against the forces of nature to create the beauty and the productivity of present-day Southern Ontario involved all kinds and conditions of men. Every group made its distinctive contribution from the snobbish would-be aristocrats, the half-pay army officers, the hard-skinned and tight-fisted immigrants from the British Isles and the Continent (especially Germany), the shrewd Yankees, the humble Quakers, the patient and hard-working Mennonites and the fugitive negroes—a motley company in very truth, but a source of the greatness of Ontario today.

Wherever one may go to catch a glimpse and intimations of that great and critical struggle one cannot help but find it difficult to realize fully what these great hearts of the past were up against. A rather romantic account of an early American traveller, written in 1832, gives us this picture:

The regular and elegant wall of trees on either hand whose spiral tops reach (seemingly) to the heavens, their beautiful evergreen hue, the deep impervious shade beneath their small and straight yet intertwining branches, all viewed together, appears at once pleasing, sublime and solemn. Some of the trees are very large and in no other place have I seen a forest so compact, such a vast quantity of timber on any particular space of ground.

The actual settlers found it less sublime and more terrifying because they had to cope with this compact timber which grew so thickly that light was almost eliminated and they worked in a twilight gloom as they struggled to chop down trees of immense girth, plagued by black flies by day and mosquitoes by night. It is possible, however, for the present-day explorer to get some approximation of what it was like for an immigrant settler to move off into the unknown wilderness on foot in search of the land-holding where he would seek to build for himself and his family a new and better life. To do this, is at the same time one of the easiest and most difficult things for modern man: he has to get out of his automobile. Then on foot he must take to the Bruce Trail.

THE BRUCE TRAIL

The fact that the Bruce Trail was conceived, built and is used very extensively is proof positive that man does want to see and experience nature from the same perspective as did his ancestors. The plan was conceived in 1959 by the Hamilton Naturalists' Club. A committee to study its feasibility was formed in 1960; and in 1963 the Bruce Trail Association was incorporated.

What they wanted to do—and what they did—was to provide a 450-mile walk extending from Queenston, through the Niagara fruitlands; up into the Caledon Hills and down into the valleys of the Pretty and Mad rivers; along the highlands of the Blue Mountains and into the Bruce Peninsula up to its tip at Tobermory.

The idea was to keep the route as untouched by the technological age as possible; to provide a walk in the woods at any point (few do the whole 450 miles all at once). It is great for a couple of hours of getting away from it all; for a day's excursion or for a total holiday. The proof of the need is the number of enthusiastic hikers who use the trail, to say nothing of the fact that most of the land it covers is privately owned and used because the owners themselves could easily recognize the get-back-to-nature urge.

A hike through the Bruce Trail or part of it serves, amongst many other things, to remind us once more—and very forcibly — that at the time of settlement Ontario was completely covered by woodland. And yet, in almost every settler's mind the accent was on land not wood. In these days when it costs a small fortune to build a few feet of shelving for books, one constantly asks himself "What ever did they do with all that wonderful wood from the original forests of Ontario?" For the greater part of Southern Ontario the answer is: They burned it. For the average settler the great felled trees were something to be got rid of as quickly as possible. Of course wood was used for heating purposes but a man who cleared fifty acres of timber had enough firewood, regardless of what heating system he used, to last him for several lifetimes. All he wanted to do was get it out of the way as quickly as possible.

When he had time he would burn the wood more carefully in order to get the pure ash required to turn it into potash for which he could get solid money. But literally thousands of Upper Canadian farmers sent potential fortunes in lumber up in smoke. They were not exactly stupid. A good many of them did know that elsewhere in the world, particularly in Europe, there was a market for the excellent standard of timber available in Ontario but the problem was to get it there. Lumber is a cumbersome product and transportation facilities were minimal. Even when the railway came the bulk and weight of timber made transport too costly and so the wood of most of Southern Ontario was burned again, this time to fire up the steam-engines of the railways.

THE LUMBER "KINGS"

There was, however, one answer to the problem—a large fast-flowing river leading directly to a major seaport and there was only one place of early settlement in Ontario where this condition could be found.

This area is where the capital of Canada now stands along the Ottawa River. In 1799 a shrewd Yankee, taking advantage of a British attempt to lure Americans to Canada, secured land directly across from where the capital, Ottawa, now stands on the site of the present day city of Hull. This was Philomen Wright. Wright was a man of means and he wanted to practise agriculture as he had done in his New England home at Woburn, Massachusetts. But for him it was sinful to waste all that good timber cut to clear the land. And the timber in this area on both the upper and lower Canadian sides of the Ottawa River was almost perfect lumber—tall, straight-growing, flawless white pine. Wright was convinced that the trees could be felled, trimmed, dumped into the Ottawa River and made into great rafts which would float down to Montreal ready for transport by ship to a Europe which needed lumber badly. The only catch was that the Ottawa River was hard to navigate and every time Wright talked about his lumber project the skeptics said he would never get his rafts past the turbulent rapids of the Ottawa and St. Lawrence rivers.

Instead of taking someone else's word for it, in typical Yankee style Wright decided to explore the route for himself. He found there was a way he could take timber out by using another river instead of the St. Lawrence which would bring his logs slightly downstream from Montreal. No one believed he could do it but he took the chance, and in 1806 sent a team of lumbermen to cut the white pine along the shores of the Ottawa. In the spring of 1807 he floated the timber to the village of Hull, made it into a raft, got it past the Long Sault Rapids of the Ottawa and finally, by-passing the other rapids in the St. Lawrence, got it to the port of Quebec.

Before he died Wright was one of the richest and most influential men in the area. His adventurous tackling of the problem of floating lumber to a major port proved to be an example, and a profitable one, for settlers who came to the Ontario side of the Ottawa River. The second settler in the Ontario district was Braddish Billings who quickly saw the possibilities of the Ottawa timber trade. Two years after Wright had begun his operation, Billings and a young friend and partner named William Marr went up the Rideau River, cut their first timber along its shores, took it out and sold it to Wright. This continued for three years when Billings went into business for himself and thus began lumbering in Ontario.

Although many fortunes were made, the Wrights continued to dominate the timber business in this area until the 1850's. In this decade two young men, one from Vermont and one from the eastern townships of the province of Quebec came to the Ottawa-Hull area. The Yankee was Ezra Eddy who started up in business in Ottawa making clothes pins, wash-boards, bowls and pails of wood. He also made matches. The second was John R. Booth who worked for the Wrights for a while and then set up a little shop to manufacture split shingles. Both Eddy and Booth were men of imagination, ambition and enterprise. Almost simultaneously, they saw the possibilities of not only utilizing the fine stands of pine as a source of timber supply for Europe but of combining it with manufacutring enterprises in their home territory. By this time Ontario was growing rapidly and wood was needed for construction purposes. Booth ranged as far west as the eastern shores of Georgian Bay to Parry Sound, acquiring vast tracts of timber rights all the way through. Twenty years after he had been working for the Wrights at $9.00 a week he owned a vast kingdom of timber rights larger than many European countries. He employed two thousand men in his mills and factories in Ottawa and had another four thousand working for him in the woods. With his own money he built a railway from Ottawa to Parry Sound through five hundred miles of wilderness. He developed Parry Sound into a port and built a fleet of ships to operate out of it. Before he died at the age of ninety-two they called him the king of Ottawa.

Ezra Eddy was of the same ilk. But most of his operation was on the Quebec side of the river. In Hull he too developed a great industrial enterprise primarily based on matches and the name Eddy still remains synonomous with matches throughout all of Canada today. From the windows of the Members' dining-room in Canada's House of Parliament one looks directly across the river and still sees huge rafts of logs, vast piles of pulp wood and a great sprawling industrial com-plex which is the E. B. Eddy Co. The Eddy Company today includes the empire of the king of Ottawa because the Booth and Eddy enterprises have long since been merged.

One thinks of Ottawa as primarily the centre of government for Canada and it is, but long before Queen Victoria placed her finger on a map at a little point called Bytown and said, allegedly, "Here will be my capital," Ottawa had another and very vital significance because it was the beginning of one of Ontario's greatest industries. From this point on, lumbering became the Ontario settler's second great area in which he attempted to subdue nature and turn it to his own advantage. Almost all of northern Ontario is still woodland despite the ravages of forest fires, and the ruthless, thoughtless cutting of trees for many decades without any attempt at reforestation. Fortunately, laws have now been passed preventing this and the province is still rich in woodland and, with careful harbouring of this magnificent natural resource, it can be a source of prosperity for many years to come. It is also one of the greatest hunting and fishing preserves in the world. The visitor to Ontario can still go into the northern woodlands dotted with a thousand lakes, and, in season, fish or hunt to his heart's content or, at least, to the legal limit. Another kind of journey is also worth taking up the Ottawa River north of the capital.

John R. Booth was not the only lumber king; he was just the biggest. In Ottawa several Booth mansions are still to be seen and one of them now houses one of the capital city's exclusive clubs. Proceeding northward up the river there are other towns to visit, all of them towns whose genesis was in the lumbering trade. My favourite spot is Lake Coulonge, now a quiet picturesque town where, without looking very far or very hard, the traveller can see the elegance of the mansions of the lesser lumber kings who flourished in the latter half of the nineteenth century. The best place to find it is on the Quebec side of the river in the town of Fort Coulonge.

A long time ago Ontario became aware that the richness of its woodland and the great abundance of natural wildlife therein could not be completely trusted to chaps like Booth, Billings and the other lumber kings. As far back as 1893 the government of Ontario decided to take an area of twenty-seven hundred square miles almost in the middle of Booth's empire which stretched from Ottawa to Parry Sound and set it aside as a national park, a forest and game preserve. This is the most famous of all Ontario's parks and is known throughout North America. It is, of course, Algonquin Park. Algonquin Park as a game and forest reserve is the best run, the best organized and the best example of how conservation can cease to be merely a word in a geography textbook and become meaningful in the lives of literally hundreds of thousands of vacationers.

Like the Bruce Trail, Algonquin Park is for those who have some kind of primordial instinct which drives them to experience an approximation to the life of early man, roaming freely in the wilds. Evolution undoubtedly is slow but today's man rarely wants any more than the approximation. Hence, an excellent highway—Queen's Highway 60—runs through the southern end of the park. It is easy to get into Algonquin from either the east or the west. Within the park, man has made convenient campsites. There is, as it seems there inevitably must be, a place where one can buy souvenirs. For every tourist with some kind of camera slung around his neck there is no need to get off the highway in order to find a wealth of photographic subjects. Deer abound; the bears roam freely in this section of the park. But that section of Algonquin which a large percentage of its visitors see is only a fraction of the whole. To the north lies most of the great acreage, still relatively unspoiled but, it must be confessed, not the greatest fishing area in Ontario.

The regulations governing activity in the park are strict. It is necessary to obtain an angling license if you want to fish. Firearms of any description are prohibited and cannot be taken into the park. Hunting, of course, is out; so is cutting timber for any purpose whatsoever. There are many public campsites, however, and sites for cottages can be leased. There are regular canoe-trip routes and the superintendent of the park and his rangers are a helpful lot.

THE CANADIAN SHIELD

At the beginning of the twentieth century very little was known of the area which comprises by far the largest part of Ontario and stretches from about the 80th to the 95th degree north latitude bounded on the north by the shores of James Bay and Hudson Bay. This is the section of Ontario which is part of the Precambrian or as we more patriotically call it the Canadian Shield. The lumber kings did not go this far north;

they were not interested in it. The supply was plentiful enough without getting into this wild territory. Nobody else had much interest in it either until in the first decade of the twentieth century it became apparent that the settled farmlands of Southern Ontario could not possibly accommodate all those farm lads who knew only agriculture, thought only agriculture and, like all their Ontario compatriots, were still convinced that Ontario's role was farming. This was the decade of the opening of the great plains area in the Prairie Provinces and thousands upon thousands of farm boys headed west. They did it happily and optimistically because the publicity, largely ground out by the two great transcontinental railways of the day—the C.P.R. and the Grank Trunk—painted the west as the promised land. And yet, there were many who resisted the idea of leaving their home province.

A group of adventurers decided to take a look at Ontario's north and settled at Haileybury and New Liskeard on the shores of Lake Timiskaming where they did well. No one paid much attention to the rock underneath the land but there seemed to be a layer of good soil and soon the people surrounding these two pioneer towns of the north were clamouring for access to the south via highway and railway. The pressure was great enough to force the Ontario government to send ten survey parties into the north in 1901. Included in each party were geologists and soil experts, and the reports came back to the south and generated wild enthusiasm. They said that between Lake Timiskaming and Lake Nipigon there was an area of about sixteen million acres of first-rate arable land. This came to be known as the Clay Belt but it has never realized its full potential as farming country because something else happened.

The report also said that this area contained "Almost unlimited quantity of the best spruce for the manufacture of pulp and paper." Here was another cash crop, not requiring homesteading and all the back-breaking slow-paced endeavour of homesteading. The Ontario Legislature authorized the construction of the Timiskaming and Northern Ontario Railway which is now known as the Ontario Northland and here a lucky accident produced something far more exciting than the north's potential for spruce. True enough since 1900 vast areas in Northern Ontario have become the source of pulp in quantities which are truly astronomical and which have made fortunes for large corporations such as Abitibi and Kimberly-Clark and brought many millions of dollars of revenue into the province.

GOLD! AND NEW ONTARIO

But the accident during the building of the railway was something else again. At a point 104 miles from North Bay the railway workers, with no more than their picks and shovels, uncovered a vein of rich silver ore and the boom was on.

My friend of later years, Big Bill Forrest, was in his teens in the year of the Cobalt strike, 1903. In his old age, with a jar of Canada's finest between us (and it was not maple syrup although on one occasion Big Bill filled a bottle with just that and made a hot and thirsty Premier of Ontario drink a full tumbler) the old timer would reminisce about the first of his many adventures. "Cobalt," he said, "was a poor man's camp and that's why I was there. The veins were so close to the surface and in many cases so rich you didn't need any fancy equipment, any heavy financial backing or much of anything else except a good strong back. Why the Lawson Mine ran twelve thousand ounces to the ton which is a hell of a lot richer than anything I ever saw taken out of any other mine anywhere! Me, I was too young to know which end was up. I thought all I wanted was a good job and that was easy enough to get and, like the fool I was, I took it. When I came to my senses all the good claims had been staked out so I just shoved off." But others, of a less impatient or less adventurous turn of mind, stayed and in half a century Cobalt produced more than a quarter of a billion dollars worth of silver.

Because it was his first venture into the prospecting territory in the north, Big Bill headed south again (he returned many times later) but more experienced prospectors, already infected by the prospectors' virus, started a systematic search for other Cobalts. They didn't find them but six years later they found something even more exciting—gold! Only about ninety miles north of Cobalt, southwest of what was called Porcupine Lake, three young fellows, Harry Preston, Benny Hollinger and Alex Gillies were prospecting. Preston slipped on a steep hillside and stripped the moss from the rock to disclose a ledge of quartz twenty feet wide leading to a dome-shaped structure that was literally studded with gold. The claims staked by these prospectors became the famous Dome Mine. Hollinger and Gillies staked a number of claims west of the lake and then tossed a coin to see how they would be divided. Hollinger won the toss and selected the six claims he considered best and thus began another great gold-mining venture in Ontario—the Hollinger Mine. At the same time and just east of where Hollinger and Gillies were working, Sandy McIntyre staked four claims which began the McIntyre-Porcupine Mine, one of the great producers of the country. The full story of Hollinger and McIntyre is one all too common in mining history. When these men started out they were broke; they had to be grubstaked just to get a chance to do some prospecting and when they hit it rich their backers took over. Benny Hollinger and Sandy McIntyre each ended with only a few thousand dollars reward for what virtually can be called the starting of one of Ontario's greatest industries—the mining of gold.

The kind of mineral wealth which lies in the Canadian Shield while vast is difficult to mine. It requires heavy capital investment to turn it into the most stable of all tangible products in the world of finance. The first money was generated right in Ontario's northland. One of the gentlemen of the north who made a fortune in the easy mining at Cobalt was Noah Timmins. Timmins picked up Benny Hollinger's claims and it was his determination as well as his money which turned Hollinger into the great enterprise it became.

From 1906 onwards, thousands of square miles to the east and west of the original discovery areas were the happy hunting grounds of hundreds of prospectors, everyone carrying the same dream—sudden and great wealth taken out of the earth. The next major area to be discovered and developed was at a campsite known as Kirkland Lake in 1912, and here some of the prospectors, learning from the unhappy fate of fellows like Hollinger and McIntyre, took another route, more difficult but by far more rewarding. The most famous of these are Harry Oakes and Bill Wright. Oakes was one of the original stakers of what became the famous Lakeshore Mine and he stubbornly stayed with it through all the phases of financing and production and ultimately became one of Canada's richest men. As is sometimes the way of self-made men, Harry Oakes was obsessed by dreams of recognition, prestige and social acceptance. For many Canadians of his era (maybe there are still a few around) the ultimate tangible evidence of the achievement of these goals is to acquire a title but Canada for a long time now has been unsympathetic to titles. Although he built a great mansion near Niagara Falls, and contributed handsomely to that city, Oakes eventually had to move to the Bahamas where he was soon created a baronet only to be murdered and burned in his bed one fine sultry tropical evening. The murder of Sir Harry was one of the big stories of the world in 1943 even though we were in the middle of World War II. It has never been solved.

Bill Wright was another sort of fellow. Retiring, a bachelor, and by many considered to be a miser, he was known, despite his great wealth, deliberately to wear old clothes so panhandlers would not bother him as he walked down the financial centre of Canada—Bay Street in Toronto. Wright, like Oakes, had survived because he became thoroughly familiar and adept at the machinations required on the Toronto Stock Exchange in order to finance the production of gold. Here he met one of the greatest "charmers" Ontario has ever produced, an eager, vital and handsome young stockbroker called George McCullagh.

McCullagh, born in London, Ontario, while not of a poor family certainly was not rich. He is reputed to have made a million dollars on his own before he was thirty years old, starting from scratch. This impressed Wright. McCullagh, like Oakes, was a seeker of fame and influence but he was of another generation. No title for him but rather a position where he could influence and perhaps dominate opinion-making in his native province. In the Toronto of that day (the 1930's) the two prestige morning papers were the Tory *Mail and Empire* and the Liberal *Globe* and both were floundering largely because of the activities of Joe Atkinson, founder of the *Toronto Star*, a Hearst-type newspaper once described as "the Star which keeps Toronto blinking." It was easy enough for McCullagh to put the two morning papers together with the help of Bill Wright's money and thus establish the *Globe and Mail* which, today, is certainly one of Canada's most authoritative newspapers as well as one of the most successful. McCullagh built what for that time was the most modern newspaper publishing plant in North America on the corner of King and York Streets and named the building after W. H. Wright.

Since the first decade of this century, billions of dollars in gold have been mined in Northern Ontario. The original site where Preston, Hollinger and McIntyre made their strike has produced well over a billion dollars itself. Towns, which began as makeshift enterprises, keeping in mind the transient nature of most gold rushes, have settled into a pattern of comparative prosperity. In the original region four good solid towns have grown up over the years—Timmins, Schumacher, Porcupine and South Porcupine. To the east lies Kirkland Lake, now a well-established community of some twenty-five thousand population. To the south is Cobalt, still going strong, Hailey-bury and New Liskeard.

This is great country to travel through and yet, curiously, it is not much given to looking backward even though it has been in thriving existence for half a century. About the only museum I know of in this area is in Porcupine where, not even housed, one can find an interesting collection of items relating to the early history of mining in the district including a "little giant" drill and steam locomotive. Most of the great mines, although much reduced, are still in production and these can be visited. For me, the real satisfaction lies in following the excellent highways which traverse this area, enjoying the beauty of the country (particularly in the fall of the year) and taking back, from the colourful characters of the early days, the incentive to contemplate the future with hope.

During the dread depression of the 1930's, Ontario and its people suffered deprivation as did everyone in North America but in Ontario depression was not quite so desperate as in most other parts of the continent. It was during this same decade that the gold mining industry of Northern Ontario was at its peak and it has always struck me as rather strange that few economic analysts have paid very much attention to what I am sure is more than coincidence. Producing the most stable commodity in the world in terms of many millions of dollars annually undoubtedly provided a good deal of the ballast which, comparatively, kept the Ontario financial ship a good deal steadier than most of the other provinces or states.

OTHER MINING IN THE NORTH

The gold mining area of Northern Ontario is only a relatively small portion of this vast territory. Besides the pulp industry which pervades all of Northern Ontario there are many other sources of wealth in the Canadian Shield.

The most impressive of these is in the Sudbury area where something like between 80% and 90% of the world's nickel is produced. As everyone knows (except me until I read about it in six different books) nickel is the bastard ingredient very often found in the mining of copper. Until they learned how to separate it from copper it was such a nuisance that it was nicknamed "Old Nick" and hence nickel.

One hundred years ago, during the building of the C.P.R., large copper-nickel deposits were known to exist in the Sudbury area. The first copper mine was established by William and Thomas Murray, two adventurers from Pembroke, but the first major mine was established by Samuel J. Ritchie who started the Canada Copper Company at just about the time when it was discovered that nickel was very useful in hardening armour plate. Dr. Ludwig Mond, a German-born scientist working in England, developed a process for separating nickel from copper which was put to use in the Sudbury area and

Dr. Mond himself came out and bought 2700 acres at Coniston nearby and opened the Mond Mine. Even Thomas Edison is reputed to have prospected in the Falconbridge area immediately adjacent to Sudbury. Today, of course, the giant which is International Nickel dominates the industry.

As is the usual fate of big business, Inco has long been the target for many slings and arrows. As one approaches Sudbury, at least one of the reasons is apparent. Almost the whole visible area has been defoliated. The terrible fumes, which used to belch from the smokestacks of the smelters separating the nickel from the copper, are alleged to have killed almost all the vegetation. Whatever it was, the visitor's first impression of Sudbury with its gigantic mounds of slag and lack of greenery is one of desolation and spoilage. But Sudbury is a very hefty town indeed. It is perhaps the most cosmopolitan city in Canada. Workers from almost every race under the sun are to be found in this city. For the careful observer, Sudbury is unique in Ontario—there is a little bit of almost everything here. On a payday night its streets are turbulent and in many ways it is one of the province's toughest towns. Yet the caressing touch of great wealth is here too. There is a gracious living in Sudbury and excellent tourist accommodation. Altogether it represents that interesting paradox which inevitably derives from men battling nature for gain and succeeding on a grand scale. No one has seen all of Ontario until he has seen Sudbury.

Straight west from Sudbury one enters the vast, sparsely populated segment of Ontario—huge, still relatively untouched and still, except for a few significant exceptions, relatively unknown. The potential for Ontario's future may well lie in this territory. If this seems an extravagant fantasy, think about Elliot Lake.

Elliot Lake is just at the edge of the big chunk which comprises Northern Ontario. If you go along Highway 17 for a little over sixty miles west of Sudbury and then turn up a short eighteen miles you will be there. And yet, at the end of World War II, what was in the Elliot Lake vicinity was unknown. What was there was that substance which the mushroom clouds of Hiroshima and Nagasaki had shown to be the most interesting, the most dangerous and one of the most valuable elements in the world—uranium. What went on after that is one of the most beautiful examples in North America of how man has perfected his techniques for subduing nature. No more the haphazard, slap-dash confusion of "gold rush days," once the initial prospecting had been accomplished. Now, modern technology is applied under the aegis of provincial and federal governments. After a very brief period when the settlement was a trailer-camp town, the town planners and developers stepped in and from their drawing-boards a model town emerged. Three splendid hotels (one of them with the largest beer room in Ontario) were erected, the streets and shopping plazas were quickly developed. Well-planned and well-placed homes, in an atmosphere very like suburbia any-where in Canada, quickly took shape along with schools and a community centre.

This wonder town is in the large old federal constituency of Algoma East, the home constituency of the former Prime Minister of Canada, the Right Honourable Lester B. Pearson. In the good days, I made many trips with "Mike" to Elliot Lake and never ceased to be flabbergasted by the buoyancy, prosperity and the quickly acquired elegance of life in the middle of Ontario's northland. More than once in those ex-pansive days, we sat down to a Sunday "brunch" preceded by champagne, followed by a smorgasbord the like of which could have been approximated in very few places in either North America or Europe—a bewildering array of hors-d'oeuvre, salmon freshly flown in from the west coast, several kinds of caviar and some of the best pastries and imported cheeses I have ever wrapped my tongue around. And all this was achieved in less than a decade.

Then, of course, came the decline. We were still making regular visits to the town when the bottom dropped out of the uranium market. Now the pressure was on. In its very short history Elliot Lake somehow managed to create citizens who behaved as if not only had they spent their own entire lifetimes there but their fathers and grandfathers before them. In short, although their average length of time in the town was under fifteen years, they had made an identification with it which one usually associates with several generations. They were not only anxious for their economic survival but they were pressing hard to ensure the survival of what they regarded as a beautiful and unique experiment. Today Elliot Lake is no longer a boom town but it certainly is not a ghost town.

One manifestation which emphatically asserts that the new town of Elliot Lake is with it along with the oldest towns in Ontario is the fact that—and here we go again—it too has aquired a museum, the Elliot Lake Mining and Nuclear Museum, and a very intersting one it is too, including pioneer uranium-mining equipment, models of uranium mine building and various items relating to the natural history of the area. Altogether this is a town worth visiting because in it is the most successful example of a planned community to be found in Ontario and perhaps in Canada. A few years from now when the saga of Elliot Lake is seen in a more objective perspective it may well be that this town will be regarded as a pioneer community, an early example of a new type of planning, utilizing the technological skills of the twentieth century to combine economic growth and social progress.

The next major city west of Elliot Lake is Sault Ste. Marie which has a special sort of pride in its existence inasmuch as at this border point the usual pattern is reversed. It is on the Canadian side—the Ontario side—that the action is to be found. Across the river there is another Sault Ste. Marie in the State of Michigan surprisingly much smaller than its Canadian counterpart.

The Canadian Soo goes back to the days of the Northwest Company and the Ermatinger House (privately owned) still stands—over one hundred and fifty years old. It was built in 1814 by a fur trader. The great Algoma Steel Mills are in Sault Ste. Marie and constitute the major industry. This enterprise has been an important factor in the development of the huge area farther west where man still struggles to subdue nature and bring iron from the Precambrian Shield.

At this point it is worthwhile to take another look at the map of Ontario. Fixing ourselves at Sault Ste. Marie one can look to the east and the west and it will come as a surprise to most of us to discover that by far the greater proportion of

Ontario is to the west and virtually untouched. Here one can find the great pits of the Steep Rock iron mine; the great grain elevators and the Lakehead cities of Port Arthur and Fort William; and the beautiful Lake of the Woods country with Fort Frances, Kenora and Dryden as its principal towns. This great territory was basically the realm of the Northwest Company and its remains can still be found. Fort William was the site of a French post, Fort Kaministikwia, and later a main post of the Northwest Company; another trading post was at Fort Frances and is marked by a plaque. Similarly the Hudson Bay Company was active in this region and after many a bloody battle it ultimately gained control and in 1821 merged with the Northwest Company.

Here the battle to subdue nature has hardly been joined. This "wilderness way of the voyageurs" is still largely un-tamed. While its cities and towns are fine and comfortable the thousands of square miles of lake, rock and woods primarily represent sporting country for the visitor and that is another story.

CHAPTER FIVE

Paddle Your Own — Relax! Enjoy!

Over 70% of the boundary lines enclosing Ontario are waterways—the great bays, Hudson and James, the Great Lakes, the mighty Ottawa River and the chain of lakes and rivers stretching from Lake Superior toward the neighbouring province of Manitoba. Within the boundaries is a myriad of lakes, still uncounted and probably many which have never yet been seen by a white man. It can be said, then, that, among other things, Ontario is full of water.

In the first stages of settlement, where there is water there must be some kind of craft which the explorer or pioneer can use to turn the waterways into highways. In Ontario this craft was the canoe. And it was a special kind of canoe because the country immediately north of the great lakes was rich in birch, trees with bark ideal for building light, waterproof vessels. The word canoe comes from a Spanish word "Kanawa" and it was first used by Christopher Columbus. The name stuck and the usage became common throughout North America. So did the canoe itself. Jacques Cartier found it in the Maritimes; Champlain found it in Quebec and as he moved west into Ontario he found it there too. Both the missionaries and the traders as well as the explorers quickly adopted it, realizing that no vessel built on European lines was nearly as adaptable to the country and its particular demands as the canoe. When the British came they too used the canoe and that elegant lady, Mrs. John Graves Simcoe, thought highly of it as she recorded in her diary at Toronto on September 14, 1793:

We walked to the spot intended for the site of the town [York—later Toronto]. Mr. Aikens' canoe was there—we went into it, and himself and his men paddled. We went at the rate of four miles per hour. I liked it very much: being without the noise of oars is a great satisfaction—to see a birch canoe managed with that inexpressible care and composure which is the characteristic of an Indian, is the prettiest sight imaginable.

Although locks and canals soon made the use of other more elaborate and faster craft feasible in all the settled parts of Ontario, somehow the canoe has won its way into the heart of the white man as an ideal method of conveyance for the fisherman, the hunter and the vacationist. It is firmly rooted and besides that it is still the best way to get maximum enjoyment for travelling in the great inland waterways, the little lakes and streams which abound in Ontario. Of course, the birchbark canoe is almost extinct.

A few years ago I went to an Indian fair on a reservation which perhaps better be nameless. Amongst the exhibits was a birchbark canoe which even to my eyes looked a little clumsy. In the course of the day I talked to the chief, admiring many of the exhibits and particularly singling out the canoe. He looked a bit uncomfortable when I asked him if it was for sale. "Quite a few of the men spent most of their spare time during last winter on that," he said evasively. "You mean they would want a very high price for it?" I asked. "Well it's not exactly that," the chief said, "the fact is I don't think it will float."

However, it is easy to find good commercial canoes which will float and which handle beautifully. I still think the wooden cedar-strip canoe is the best but this too is hard to find. Canvas canoes are good and, today, you can even get—God save the mark—aluminum canoes. These you can have.

Whatever type of canoe seems appropriate, a group of out-doors-minded people can have a wonderful time almost any-where outside the highly urbanized area of Southern Ontario for a day, a week or for a carefully-planned long canoe trip. Despite the fact, which I have recounted earlier, that except in the far north it is very difficult to get away from civilization completely, canoeing is still a wonderfully exhilarating experi-ence but don't try it in the heavy traffic of our popular inland waterways. The canoe is still a touchy lady and she needs to be handled with care and respect. She is light and graceful and if you give her her due she will perform beautifully, but true to her heritage she prefers the grandeur and solitude of the wilderness and she does not take kindly to the other craft which have usurped her place in the more popular and popu-lous vacationlands of Ontario.

BOATING ON THE GREAT LAKES

In the past decade there has been a tremendous upsurge of in-terest in boating in this province. Throughout the summer every busy highway manifests a large number of automobiles drawing trailers on which are mounted all kinds and descrip-tions of power craft. Both the natives of Ontario and the many thousands who come to vacation here every summer have dis-covered the carefree delight which is to be found in the modern version of paddling your own canoe. Today there are several categories, each with its own mystique, in its particular usage and its own particular snobbery.

At the top of the roost is the cabin cruiser. In Ontario the suitable places to enjoy this mode of carefree enjoyment are the ports of the Great Lakes and the two great canal systems— the Trent and the Rideau. All along the lakes and all through the canal systems the popularity of this type of vacationing now insures that the Saturday sailor and his fun-loving crew can find all the essentials and the amenities which make for a happy holiday. Marinas abound, good dockage is readily avail-able; so too is fresh water and plug-in power. But best of all, good fellowship and a kind of loose camaraderie of the sea will be met with anywhere a skipper wants to take his pleasure craft.

And where will he take it? The Great Lakes are still large and can be sometimes formidable bodies of water. They are to be treated with respect and sailed cautiously. Regardless of the size, and the power and seaworthiness of your craft, it is prudent to keep within range of the shoreline as much as possible. Lake Huron is perhaps the finest lake for sailing but it is also the most temperamental and given to sudden squalls which can easily founder the boat. In any event, if you are going to sail the lakes it is not only wise but a lot of fun to get your charts, plan your route, set your schedule and relax and enjoy being what you probably are—a fresh-water sailor of the vacation-time ilk. There is nothing wrong with this at all and, as in most situations, in the long run it is better to be whatever you are. Of course a little bit of showing off is allowed. Anyone interested in the human comedy cannot help but get a large kick out of a group of Saturday sailors congregated around the dock of a marina watching still another of their kind trying to manoeuvre his forty-footer into the last available space. In most cases, not one of them—including the proprietor of the marina—is of the breed that goes down to the sea in ships. They know a little bit about the internal-combustion engine; they can read a chart and know the port is passed to the left. They are also wise in the cost of boats and somewhere along the line they have picked up some odds and ends of what they think is sea-going talk. Sometimes they wear yachting caps but they are all having fun.

Indeed, fun is the objective of all those who sail the vacationland waterways. Let us not for an instant confuse this kind of challenge (such as it is) with the real struggles of man against nature. True enough, it is possible to get caught in a bit of weather but let us face it—most of the victims of marine tragedies in small boats brought it on themselves either through carelessness or an ill-placed bravado. If the waterways are treated with the respect they deserve, and the impulse to extend oneself beyond his capacity is resisted, they are completely safe. Everything for helping craft in distress is present but no one has yet found a way of providing common sense which, really, is all that is needed for safe enjoyment.

With this in mind, there are two acceptable ways to enjoy the Great Lakes whose Canadian coastline is entirely in Ontario. Those who own smaller craft are well advised to establish a home port and work out from there on expeditions of suitable length. There is no dearth of suitable "home ports." Starting along the St. Lawrence and proceeding westward I would recommend, for those who want to sail in the river rather than get in the Great Lakes, the stretch between Kingston and Brockville. To go much farther downstream is to get into the locks of the St. Lawrence Seaway.

While undoubtedly the Seaway has already been a great boon to commerce on the Great Lakes and the St. Lawrence and has an even greater potential still to be reached, it has not improved conditions for pleasure-boating. During Canada's centennial year I made this trip down to Montreal along with many hundreds and perhaps thousands of similar pleasure craft. It must be stated that once we got into the Seaway complex we entered another enviroment. While a good deal of care was taken, the immensity of the huge locks has destroyed most of the scenic value. More important from a practical point of view, it must be remembered that these locks were primarily built to accommodate large ocean-going vessels. Quite properly, pleasure craft have to take second place, with the result that inordinate delays are sometimes encountered with no diversion and amenities for those who are merely sailing for pleasure. But from Kingston to Brockville it is another story. This is the country of the Thousand Islands and perhaps the resort town of Gananoque can be considered its centre and capital. Along this stretch the vacation atmosphere predominates and the scenery is excellent. This is a good place to keep the boat and it is also a good place to keep in mind if one is planning an itinerary of sailing.

On Lake Ontario almost any of the small ports will serve very well. It is merely a matter of convenience. If I were going to keep a boat on the Lake Ontario coastline I would gravitate to the Bay of Quinte area which it seems to me is one of the most neglected vacation spots in the province although this should not be taken to mean that many people have not already discovered its delights. The scenery here is excellent, particularly in Prince Edward County, that irregularly-shaped peninsula which is almost an island jutting out into Lake Ontario, connected by bridge to Belleville and by a narrow neck of land to Trenton. The reason this area is particularly attractive is that it offers three types of sailing. You can sail the bay, you can go out into the lake or you can proceed up through the Trent Canal system which begins at the town of Trenton. But you can pick almost any place as a base. Cobourg is good, so is Port Hope or Newcastle or if you get past Toronto into the Burlington Bay area Oakville is excellent and the sailing conditions are first rate.

The same broad choice applies to Lake Erie which has even more small ports to choose from. These include Port Dover, Turkey Point, Port Rowan, Port Burwell, Port Bruce, Port Stanley, Port Talbot and on down to Erie Beach, Erieau, Point Pelee or Kingsville.

Prejudiced though I am, I would prefer to sail Lake Huron, particularly if I had a craft of larger size. Here one can start at Sarnia or Point Edward and choose maybe Grand Bend or Bayfield or Goderich or Kincardine, Port Elgin or Southampton on the lake proper. If one is more interested in sailing into Georgian Bay you can start at Tobermory and then move around the shoreline of the bay perhaps picking Lion's Head, Owen Sound, Meaford, Collingwood, Penetanguishene or Midland at the south end or if one prefers more rugged country Parry Sound or Pointe-au-Baril on the east shore of Georgian Bay, or, on the north shore, Killarney which is a beautiful part of the world and a nice run over to one of the finest boating areas in the province—Manitoulin Island. The main port here is Little Current but there are many other places which one might choose.

Lake Superior is a little different, more sombre, less light-hearted and not likely to be reached unless you are based on its shore.

But before you decide to operate a pleasure craft out of anywhere it might be well to remember that the Department of Transport requires the licensing of *all* boats using the Trent,

Rideau and Quebec Canals. For foreign pleasure-craft a permit is necessary which can be obtained free of charge at the customs port of entry.

The simplest kind of cruise in any of the lakes is simply to hop from port to port but this is probably the least interesting way to spend a vacation on the water. It is much better to pick specific points which one might like to visit and then see if they can be reached by water. This will involve using the inland waterways as well as the lakes.

THE TRENT-SEVERN ROUTE

The busiest of these is the Trent Canal-Severn River route. By using it one can travel from Lake Ontario through the heart of the province into Georgian Bay. It is little wonder that this is the most popular and has the heaviest traffic of any of the water routes. It is probably also the most fun. On this route you can forget all about cabin cruisers as the only suitable means of transport. Here you can use almost anything and this is precisely what people do. Approach any lock at the height of the season and one will see a miraculous cross-section of everything that floats in the way of pleasure-craft—elegant fifty-footers, and their smaller and more modest counterparts, inboards of all descriptions including some huge ones with the most elegant of fittings, any kind of boat that you can fasten an outboard on, and houseboats. These latter I must confess I have a prejudice against. I put them in much the same category as I would put a western saddle on a good standard-bred jumper. I guess they are comfortable and judging from the frilly curtains (and sometimes even flower boxes!) one often sees at their windows it may be that people buy them at the insistence of some hausfrau who has got to be fussing with the housekeeping even on a vacation. But let us face it, they are a nuisance on a congested waterway, especially at busy locks, for they are slow and cumbersome. However every man to his taste.

The Trent Canal system should really be considered when mapping out a trip. One need not merely follow the system itself but use it as a connecting point from Lake Ontario or

Georgian Bay. If you start on Lake Ontario you begin at Trenton; if you start from Georgian Bay you begin at Port Severn. Either way, lies prime vacation land.

One of the reasons for the wide variety of craft to be found on the Trent-Severn System is that with the exception of a couple of large lakes, weather is no hazard at all. It was not always thus. This system was first used by Champlain in 1615. Then it was a matter of long portages between the network of small lakes and rivers which stretched through from Georgian Bay to Lake Ontario. Since that time, over the years, canals have been created joining the navigable waters of the rivers and lakes to form a placid system of water highway. Although the sailing is easy, the scenery is far from bland. One of the reasons that this is one of the most heavily-travelled pleasure waterways in North America is the fact that it traverses such splendidly scenic territory. Heavy traffic also implies excellent service. There is so much boating of all kinds going on in the Trent-Severn System that there is an abundance of all kinds of marine services available within easy reach of any point along the route. Marinas, dockage, overnight accommodation, stores for provisions, etc., are most plentiful and of first quality.

Starting from Lake Ontario and moving northward the first section of the route is up the Trent River for a distance of fifty-one miles and eight locks. This is pleasant pastoral country. The largest town on the route is Campbellford and the second largest settlement is Hastings which is at the end of this section just before the river emerges from Rice Lake.

Rice Lake is twenty miles long and three miles wide and for diversion instead of making a direct crossing the sailor can take a side trip around the lake. It is lovely and well worth exploring. It is said that by some migratory freak a band of Hopewell Indians worked their way up from the Gulf of Mexico to this lake thousands of years ago establishing a strange civilization whose nature is far from being fully understood and documented. However, for the curious some relics of this culture have been found in huge burial grounds at Roach Point, a government park with wharves, campsites, fireplaces, etc. The two points which I find most entertaining and pleasant in the Rice Lake section are Bewdley and Gore's Landing.

The third section is the Otonobee River which is between Rice Lake and the City of Peterborough. This too is a beautiful run but there is a decided shift in sea level here with the result that there are many locks to be negotiated before arriving at the granddaddy of them all—the famous liftlock of Peterborough. This is the largest liftlock in the world—sixty-five feet. For the traveller negotiating the Peterborough Liftlock for the first time there is a real thrill and a magnificent view, and yet no discomfort whatsoever.

From Peterborough north to the picturesque town of Lakefield is a short run but full of locks, by no means the most pleasant section of the route but very necessary if one is to enjoy the best which comes after Lakefield. Now we are in the Kawartha Lakes section which for many, including myself, represents just about the acme of pleasure cruising. The first lake is Katchiwano, a weedy lake in some places but with a good well-marked channel running through it leading into the next which is Clear Lake. From this point on one can take his time investigating the various lakes which are all joined together and make for easy cruising. These include Stony, Lovesick, Deer, Buckhorn, Chemong, Pigeon, Sturgeon, Cameron and Balsam. They are all delightful little gems of lakes and, of course, all well serviced.

Everyone who sails this area has his own particular favourite place. For many it is Bobcaygeon. Here, at Gordon's Boat Works, is the home port of *Yo-Ho II,* skippered by Fred Peel, and as rollicking a vessel as has ever sailed the system. *Yo-Ho* is the epitome of good times and happy landings. Wherever she sails, wherever she docks, her presence is felt immediately. Her hospitality is legendary and her capacity for good fun is unlimited. We have danced on the dock in the moonlight; we have entertained the casts of a score of Straw Hat Little Theatres scattered along the route; many a small boat in distress has been towed to the nearest dock while its passengers have enjoyed open-handed hospitality on *Yo-Ho.* The inhibitions of the staid and stuffy work-a-day world are left behind. On one occasion the effervescent skipper, emerging from a small general store with a strawberry custard pie in his hand, suddenly pushed it into the face of one of his guests standing at the side of the boat. "That," he said with considerable satisfaction, "is something I have wanted to do all my life ever since I first saw it in the movies years ago." For me, *Yo-Ho* and scores of similar familiar craft of the Trent-Severn System are the embodiment of the fine careless and happy atmosphere which sailing this route can engender. Sober clerics tear off their Roman collars, dynamic business men say "To hell with the telephone," dignified dowagers squeeze themselves into slacks and forget to blue their hair. Sailing on the Trent is a fun thing and that is the way to make most of it.

From the Kawarthas to Lake Simcoe is a twenty-two mile run which is a narrow channel and some people call it dull. I couldn't disagree more. For me it is like sailing through the canals of France. As we move peacefully along this stretch I expect to see vineyards and a Norman chateau on the horizon. It is a magnificently pastoral, rich and satisfying countryside.

Then comes Lake Simcoe, the biggest lake on the route, some thirty-five miles long and thirty-two miles at its widest point. This is the one spot on the route where the sailor needs to exercise care. It is a lake of sudden squalls and since it is small can be extremely choppy, making for an uncomfortable voyage unless one has mastered the art of running small craft through churned-up waters. The lake is not always this way but it happens often enough to justify caution in the sailor. I like to make two stops on this run. One at Jackson's Point where one can spend a pleasant evening at the Red Barn Theatre and the other at Orillia, the sunshine town made famous by Canada's greatest humourist, Stephen Leacock.

One proceeds from Lake Simcoe and Lake Couchiching into the Severn River and sails down into Georgian Bay. This is fine true sailing through countryside which becomes increasingly rugged as one approaches the bay. There are only two locks and, now, one remaining marine railway. This is a unique experience. At one time there were two but one has been replaced by a lock. However, as long as it lasts one should try to negotiate the marine railway. Here one's boat is run onto rails which are under water, fastened securely and hauled over a hill and down into water on the other side. And when you take this expedition keep an eye out for Big Bill, long-time veteran of this tricky manoeuvre and if you want to be his friend for life set a glass of hospitality within easy reach. Many of the old characters of the waterway have disappeared but Big Bill still carries on. Keep an eye out for him. And then having negotiated the marine railway carry on right through until you come to Port Severn and reach the sparkling blue and open waters of Georgian Bay where another sailing adventure awaits you.

THE RIDEAU CANAL ROUTE

The Rideau Canal System goes much farther into the past than the Trent. To understand its lovely but, in today's terms, illogical route one has to go back to the end of the war 1812-1814. Once more we are reminded of the great uneasiness felt in the minds of Great Britain's statesmen because of the Americans looking for rapid colonization plus, as always, a misunderstanding of the country.

To proceed west either for the purposes of defence or colonization the jumping-off point was Montreal. Keeping in mind that all the routes at this point were waterways, there were three possible ways to go. First there was the obvious: up the St. Lawrence directly to where it emerges from Lake Ontario, that is at the point where Kingston now stands. This is the route which ultimately came into use, carried the great burden of all traffic toward the west and still does as far as waterways are concerned. However, the British were very much aware that the greater part of the south shore of the river was in the United States and they did not consider that the development of this route was a good military risk. Secondly, they could have taken the route generally used by the Indians and commonly called the route of the Grand Portage, this is up the Ottawa to Lake Nipissing and across to Georgian Bay and thence into Lake Huron. Had this route been developed it just possibly might have opened up the northern section of Ontario faster but the British wanted to get west via Lake Ontario.

The answer was to make a loop by going up the Ottawa River to the Chaudière Basin which is where the capital of Canada stands today, hence, down the Rideau River, the Rideau Lakes, the Cataraqui River which empties into Lake Ontario at Kingston. This was the route chosen by the British and it is interesting to note that when they decided to do it it was considered as a military project, put under the control of a professional soldier, Lieutenant-Colonel John By of the Royal Engineers who was living on half-pay in England when he received his orders to proceed to Canada to take command of the building of the Rideau Canal. His clerk-of-the-works was John MacTaggart who has left a terse description of the way in which the system was to be built:

The Rideau Canal, when constructed, will be perfectly different than any other in the known world, since it is not ditched or cut by the hand of man. Natural rivers and lakes are made use of for this canal and all that science or art has to do in the matter is in the lockage of the rapids or waterfalls, which exist between extensive sheets of still water or expansive lakes. To surmount this difficulty dams are proposed and in many instances already raised, at the bottom of rapids or sometimes at their head, or even, as the case may be, in their middle, by which means the rapids or waterfalls are converted into still water.

In essence this is what was done. Colonel By made his headquarters in Ottawa and, as we have seen, since it coincided with the development of lumbering, the military project combined with the industrial interest to lay the foundations for what has become the capital of Canada. About four miles of the Rideau System now lie within the boundaries of the capital and provides an interesting short excursion for many thousands of tourists who visit Ottawa each year. But the real travel, of course, lies outside the city.

The canal system as it finally emerged some forty years after it was first begun in 1826 is very much like John McTaggert's description. The falls and rapids for which lockage had to be constructed are today known by the names of the early pioneers who followed the construction of the route and settled where locks were being constructed. Thus, as we proceed from Ottawa down to Kingston we pass Burritt's Rapids, Nicholson's Rapids, Merrick's Falls, Maitland's Rapids, Edmund's Rapids, Smith's Falls, then Oliver's Ferry and on to Chaffey's Rapids where, since a mill was built, the settlement became known as Chaffey's Mills. From this point one proceeds to Davis' Rapids and Jones Falls and thence into a stretch of marshland known as Cranberry Marsh which leads into the Cataraqui River which flows directly into Lake Ontario at Kingston.

The many lakes which are utilized in the system and lie between the Rideau River and the Cataraqui River are known as the Rideau Lakes and this, like the Kawartha Lakes, is some of the finest vacationland in North America and certainly in Ontario.

The difference between utilizing the Rideau System and the Trent System is that, up to this point at least, the Rideau is much quieter and more placid. As was true of a good number of "military projects" in the first half of the nineteenth century in Upper Canada, this one never had any military use or importance whatsoever. It did serve, as one can see from the names of the locks, to bring in a batch of pioneers to begin the process of settlement. But this part of the country is not very good land and while British officials might not take this into account potential settlers certainly did. The result is that this part of Ontario is still not heavily populated. By the same token, this expensive waterway—it cost over a million pounds to build—has had virtually no commercial use.

It is a curious thing that vacationers by and large seek to go where other vacationers go. Hence the Trent, flowing through well-settled and thriving sections of Ontario, seems to attract thousands upon thousands of boatmen while the Rideau where there is not really very much action attracts, comparatively speaking, very few. As a result there are no resort towns (with the possible exception of Chaffey's Mills where there is a quite active resort area now) and the amenities of travel are much more spotty and fewer in number than in the Trent. For the traveller by boat, one cannot get past the fact that there are forty-seven locks between Ottawa and Kingston, a stretch of one hundred and twenty-six miles of canal. These locks are worth seeing. They were built before the days of reinforced concrete and each one is a masterpiece of the stonemason's art. If one is seeking a vacation utilizing Ontario's waterways, the Rideau should not be ignored. It provides a pleasant contrast to the bustling Trent and the scenery is indeed gorgeous.

From the vacationer's point of view, the attraction of both the Trent and the Rideau routes lies not so much in the fact that a canal system has made them navigable but rather that the systems utilize a number of picturesque lakes and rivers. The same is true of still a third area in Ontario, this time up far into the north in the Lake of the Woods district.

LAKE OF THE WOODS

Until comparatively recently most inland cruising was confined to the two great canal systems but far in the vastness of Northwestern Ontario a new area for pleasure boating has opened up and it is a busy and delightful spot. Although this whole section of Ontario is filled with lakes it is in the large Lake of the Woods where pleasure boating is now in full swing. Although the lake is only sixty-five miles long and about the same distance wide it has, because of its extremely indented shoreline, a shoreline longer than that of Lake Superior and it contains some twelve thousand islands, more than on any of the Great Lakes except Lake Huron. It has a fresh charm of its own. First, because of its long shoreline and many islands it has many clear channels for sailing; again, because it is far away from the heavily urban and industrialized area the fishing is still superb and finally, as one might expect, the water is remarkably clear and sparkling. Because of its isolated position and the fact that there is no really clear sailing into it except via the Rainy River this is a lake where one has either to bring his boat in by trailer or base it permanently on the lake. The result is that most of the boating on Lake of the Woods is by smaller craft, inboard or outboard motor-powered boats.

Access to Lake of the Woods is via Trans-Canada highway and the place to go is the city of Kenora, a busy town with a population of some twelve thousand with all the services and amenities which the pleasure sailor requires. From Kenora one proceeds through one of two channels: the Devil's Gap Channel or the Keewatin. Both are picturesque routes and both lead into an area where the lake expands into a large pool from which three more main channels radiate.

The southerly channel leads into the Rainy River and thence to the town of Rainy River some ninety miles away. This is the old through route which was first traversed by Jacques de Noyon who discovered Lake of the Woods in 1687. Most travellers will merely remain in this channel and stay in Lake of the Woods.

The second channel which proceeds westerly leads to Clearwater Bay. Although one is at all times in a lake only sixty-five miles broad and long he has the impression that he is travelling through a series of lakes and rivers and the variety of scenery never flags. The same can be said for the third channel which leads southwesterly to White Fish Rapids and to what is locally known as the Upper Lakes.

Within the confines of this remarkable lake one can perhaps find more variety and travel fewer miles than anywhere else in Ontario. This is one of the reasons why a small craft is completely adequate and satisfactory for sailing Lake of the Woods.

Besides Kenora there are two or three other major settlements which the sailor will encounter sooner or later. For example, there is the Devil's Gap Bungalow Camp, a luxury resort developed for those who find no pleasure even in roughing it slightly. Then there is the little town of Keewatin which has all the necessary service requirements. Sioux Narrows is another little town with a particularly happy atmosphere, handy both to the highway and to the lake where, for some reason or other, visitors always seem to have a good time.

It is estimated that in the short time that Lake of the Woods has become popular with tourists some fifteen thousand small craft will ply its waters during the summer season. What has happened here undoubtedly will happen in other places as the great northwest is developed but at the moment Lake of the Woods is quite satisfying and draws people from all of the midwest of the United States, from the neighbouring western province of Manitoba and from all sections of Ontario. It is a different experience in many ways from sailing in the softer south but especially for those who enjoy a bit more of the rugged outdoors it has an attraction which they prefer to that of any of the other inland waterways.

SAIL OVER STEAM

Ontario, then, has no dearth of opportunity for those who would seek to find relaxation and enjoyment on the water. And yet, we have not even mentioned sailing at its finest— honest-to-goodness sailing using canvas instead of a motor, inboard or outboard.

Any one who has tacked his way across a river down to the harbour mouth and into the lake, no matter how decrepit he may become or how much he will yield to the convenience of motor-powered craft, will never accept that kind of boating as a real substitute for sailing. Certainly, any boy brought up within range of the Great Lakes has an opportunity for some exciting sailing, the kind which will test his skill and give him a genuine respect for wind, water and sail.

I learned my lesson when I was a boy. In those days the best we could manage was a small sailing dinghy, with a centre board and a rudder fastened with nothing more than a large cotter pin, and a single mast with a small mainsail and a bit of a jib. At my home port, Bayfield, on Lake Huron, we had a small flotilla of such craft, each captained by a proud owner whose little skill never matched his sense for adventure. What we learned of the art of sailing we learned the hard way and we learned it from the best of all teachers, the freshwater fishermen of the Great Lakes. And at Bayfield we had some of the finest—the Castles, the Thoms and the Mac-Leods—and of them all perhaps Louis MacLeod was the greatest. On a clear day, with not a cloud in the sky and only a soft, moderate wind Louis could stand on his dock, sniffing the air and tell us "There'll be a squall out there in about half an hour." We never listened to him; we went out anyway. And no matter how many times he told us, and no matter how many times he was right, we still went out. And sure enough the squall would hit and, sure enough, at least one of us would go over before we got back to port. Louis was always standing on the pier watching our amateurish efforts, the motor in his fishing tug idling, ready to go out, haul us in and, after we had our usual lecture, charge us $5.00 for the trip. Out of that group many of us ultimately were picked for competition crews from the Royal Canadian Yacht Club of Toronto and other similar clubs. The time to learn sailing is when one is very young, and Ontario's lakes provide just about the best training ground to be found anywhere inland in North America.

For those who would bring their sailing craft into Ontario I would recommend that they stick to the lakes. Sailing, for example, is at its very best in the tricky waters and winds of Georgian Bay but anywhere along the Great Lakes will do. And the places to look for are those where there are fishermen located. These men are almost always bred on the lakes and they understand and sympathize with the lore of the fresh-water sailor. Go into any fishing port on the lakes with a sailing craft and you will find companionship, understanding and help, if you need it, from those who know how to help properly.

Of course, there are small craft sailing on many of the small inland lakes but this is largely for those who have cottages on the lakes themselves. It is not possible to sail through the canal systems.

Ontario is virtually a paradise for anyone who wants to do serious sailing or boating. If the trip is carefully charted and planned one can get to almost any point of interest in Ontario or within easy striking distance of it and to get there by boat adds an extra dimension to a vacation.

On the other hand, for the more sedentary, a summer cottage or a resort hotel can be an experience of complete fulfilment and what Ontario has to offer here is almost unlimited.

FAMOUS MUSKOKA

Perhaps the most famous of all the resort areas is Muskoka. Originally this magnificent vacationland was the discovery of very rich Americans, the railway barons and the steel millionaires of another era. (The Melon family, for example, still has a vacation retreat in the Muskoka area.) These were followed by the not-quite-so-rich millionaires of Toronto. Today Muskoka is for everybody.

"Muskoka" is an Indian word meaning "Blue Skies" but the Indians have long since gone. Indeed the two hundred and fifty thousand-acre tract, which comprises this area which extends from the island-studded Lake Joseph to the pine-clad shores of Lake-of-Bays, was ceded to the Crown for four thousand pounds by the Indians in 1815. But the blue skies are still blue.

This area is about a thousand feet above sea level which makes for an unusually clear atmosphere and low humidity. One of the first attractions as Muskoka was developing as resort land was that it was a haven for sufferers from hay fever. Similarly the many lakes are refreshing and clear.

As it has developed over the years Muskoka is now the most thickly populated area as far as motels, hotels and available cottages are concerned. It is the major vacationland of Ontario. Nevertheless, the basic rugged grandeur of this area of rock, pine and lake still remains· but in addition all of the requirements for the contemporary swinging vacationist are available. In Muskoka, it is still possible to find many spots where one can enjoy peace, quiet and solitude and feel very close to nature. On the other hand, the more sophisticated delights of our era are also available. There are excellent golf courses, and there is an airport just out of Bracebridge and many first rate hotels and motels. Just one word of caution: even though four-laned Highway 400 leads out of Toronto and carries on a good way up to the Muskoka area the weekend traffic is very close to the saturation point. The vacationist with a bit of time on his hands would be well advised to avoid the weekend rush. Once there he can relax and enjoy it.

THE HALIBURTON AREA

Muskoka is not by any means the only resort area in the province; it is just the most famous and the most highly developed. Another district in the Laurentian Shield is to the east—Haliburton. This is more rugged terrain and not as sophisticated as Muskoka. Generally speaking the people who are lured to the Haliburton area do not demand, or indeed want, very much in the way of vacationland razz-ma-tazz. Nevertheless this is a well-developed resort area with the small town of Haliburton more or less in its centre. The lakes are profuse as in Muskoka and, if anything, the air is cleaner and more invigorating.

Generally speaking, this area is known as the Haliburton Highlands. The main artery into it by land is Highway 35, north from Highway 7 and a network of roads branching off it to the east as one gets into the Haliburton area proper. One of my favourite towns here is Minden which is the county seat of Haliburton, a lumbering town in the days of the lumber kings of Ottawa whose empire stretched right through this territory and where today there is one of the finest views to be seen in Ontario from a splendid park site called Panorama Park, a rock bluff overlooking the Gull River. Here too is Bethel Church an almost unbelievably charming little church which is generally known as "The little old church in the wildwood."

Still going east between Haliburton and the Kawartha Lake area, which is immediately below it, and the Rideau Lake area there lies a splendid tourist area comparatively untouched by man. This comprises the northern halves of the Counties of Hastings, Lennox and Addington, and Frontenac. It takes a bit of research and a bit of exploring but for someone who wants a vacation in an area just as charming and scenic but even more rugged than Haliburton here is an excellent place to search.

The principal attraction of this large area is that it is much easier to reach from the populated centres of Ontario than the far north and yet it has much of the basic grandeur of the Precambrian Shield. Originally it was lumbering country, again part of the lumber kings' empires, and later the scene of sporadic mining ventures developed at various centres throughout the district. The Precambrian Shield is rich in minerals and at various times iron, copper and even silver have been extracted in this area and most recently, immediately after World War II, uranium which was mined extensively for a few years in the Bancroft district. The development was never of the proportions reached at Elliot Lake but the uranium mines near Bancroft caused more than a flutter and made more than a few dollars on Bay Street in Toronto. Somehow industrial development has not occurred here to any great extent. The original settlers who drifted into the area and attempted to farm soon found that the shallow land on top of the great shield was not productive. Apparently, it can fulfil a greater function by providing a haven for those who seek the delights and rewards of an outdoor life at vacation time. In this area there have been some ambitious attempts but so far this cannot be called well developed resort territory.

I think particularly of Bon Echo, north on Highway 41 off Highway 7 at Kaladar, where the father of my old friend and the distinguished Canadian writer, Merrill Denison, decided he would create a luxurious retreat for wealthy Americans. Today one can see some of the remains of the ambitious cottages which were erected by a man long before his time. Amongst other things Mrs. Denison sought to make this wilderness paradise a centre for writers and artists and the great slab-faced rock which gives the place its name has an inscription from Walt Whitman on it. Pleasantly, if ironically, the most important contribution to the literary world to emerge from Bon Echo was Mrs. Denison's own son, now almost the dean of Canadian writers, who first made his mark in Canada, went the usual route to the richer fields of New York and now is back in this country.

In trying to get oriented to Ontario's vacation land, Highway 7 is an important boundary line. Broadly speaking, the land north of Highway 7 is the vacationland which falls into the category of the more rugged, pine-clad, rock-bound northern terrain. South of Highway 7 there is also excellent holiday country but in the softer and the more civilized mode. For example, we should retrace our steps through that museum-laden area of Eastern Ontario if only to be reminded that we can enjoy a lot of good vacation country. This means the shores of Lake Ontario.

GREAT LAKES RESORTS

There are ninety-one well-developed Provincial Parks in Ontario, another even one hundred Conservation Parks in the province and sixteen St. Lawrence Parks Commission parks in Ontario. To unravel them, an almost indispensable guide is a map issued by the Department of Highways which both lists and shows the location of all these parks as well as a good number of other interesting things such as the two hundred-odd picnic areas, campsites, historic sites, ski areas, etc. This simple little map, very well organized, is almost basic equipment for anyone who seeks to travel throughout this province and enjoy the great outdoors which is his for the taking.

However, there are areas which are not designated on this map and these are the ones I would like to mention to fill in the picture. We have already done it for the north country; now let us return to the shores of Lake Ontario.

A much neglected strip is between Bowmanville and Brighton. This area includes the old ports of Newcastle, Port Hope and Cobourg. The Port Hope-Cobourg area was one of the first to be discovered by Americans, before the turn of the century and in the early decades of this century, as fine, indeed prime, vacationland. It is impressive to drive along old Highway 2 and still see the great summer estates which were built at that period. They were not built for nothing. Here is fine beach country, excellent swimming and the charm of old towns. They should not be neglected in considering a holiday in Ontario.

By the same token, one can unhappily eliminate the western tip of the lake circling around from Toronto to Hamilton and beyond at least as far as Grimsby. This is such heavily industrialized territory now that the charm of the lake is virtually obliterated.

The north shore of Lake Erie is also good beach country.

And speaking of beaches, the Coney Island of Canada—Crystal Beach—is at the eastern tip of the lake almost directly across from Buffalo. This is hardly the place for idyllic relaxation but it has the most wildly extravagant carnival air (if you like that kind of thing, and many people do) to be found anywhere in the province. The rest of the lake has not been too badly tampered with but unfortunately Lake Erie is a shallow lake, very vulnerable to pollution and erosion, and between the two has suffered more than any of the other Great Lakes.

The eastern shore of Lake Huron perhaps represents the acme of fresh-water beaches. Once I made a tour all around the lake and it was a revelation to discover that the American coast of the lake was entirely different. Here the beaches were meagre, the sand poor if available at all, and the water badly polluted. On the Canadian side the beaches are magnificent and for a cottage holiday it is hard to beat them. Curiously enough, with few exceptions, extreme overcrowding has not yet occurred along the extensive shoreline of Lake Huron. This means that there are many fine places to roam quietly and peacefully.

One of the exceptions is Grand Bend, a really go-go resort town, but only a few miles south is the quiet Kettle Point where archeologists say a tribe of Indians known as the Neutrals developed one of the first manufacturing industries in North America. At the Kettle Point-Port Franks area is one of the most important chert beds on the continent. This is the source of flint, and flint was the key to Indian technology and survival. The Neutrals who were a much-advanced tribe actually developed a monopoly over these beds and learned to process on a mass production basis the nodules of flint which were here in great abundance. They skilfully took advantage of the fact that their two great neighbours—the great Huron tribe to the north and the even greater Iroquois tribe to the south—had different preferences in the way of flint.

The flint nodule is rather like a fossilized onion. It has a hard core covered by several layers of flint which will peel off if the nodule is subjected to the right kind of pressure in the right spot. The Hurons preferred the outer flint and the Iroquois liked the harder kernels of the core. In the vicinity of Kettle Point post moulds have been discovered which indicate a real flint workshop where many men could be engaged in simultaneously cracking the nodules of flint and separating the two types. These were then traded to the appropriate tribes and ensured the neutrality of the small tribe for many, many years. Flint from the Kettle Point area has been identified as far west as the Rocky Mountains.

From this point right on up to the tip of Bruce Peninsula one can stop almost anywhere at any of the towns and villages and find some of the best beaches anywhere in North America and, some travellers say, in the world. Motels, cabins and cottages are readily available.

The Bruce Peninsula is a long finger separating the main body of Lake Huron from the large clear waters of Georgian Bay. At its very tip is Tobermory a small town of much character which, in the summer months, is entirely dedicated to vacationers. One of the main reasons is that Tobermory is the mainland port for one of the most picturesque ferry services to be found in the province. The ship which plies between Tobermory and Manitoulin Island provides more than a service, it provides a short and extremely pleasant (most of the time) fresh-water voyage. The traveller can have his car as well as himself carried across to the picturesque island. If he chooses, he can make the voyage through the night and can, for a modest sum, rent a stateroom and have a good sleep. I would not recommend this. The bracing air and the sparkling waters are too good to miss. The voyage is just long enough to provide a pleasant and unusual interlude to highway travel. It is possible to reach Manitoulin Island entirely by land if one follows Highway 69 along the eastern shore of Georgian Bay, and then Highway 17 to Espanola, taking Highway 68 over a causeway to the island. This is an interesting trip but it is much longer and I would certainly prefer to take the ferry which pulls into South Baymouth, a gateway to one of the most delightful vacation islands to be found anywhere. With a coastline of many inlets and several inland lakes Manitoulin is still relatively unspoiled and almost unbeatable for a relaxing, almost folksy, holiday.

Manitoulin Island was part of former Prime Minister Lester B. Pearson's riding of Algoma East. Once on a fishing trip up to the island I left a pair of pyjamas at a motel. On my return to Ottawa I wrote to the proprietor whom I had remembered with warmth and asked her if she would mind sending my pyjamas to the National Liberal Federation Headquarters in the capital city. This she did and along with the package was a long letter of happy reminiscences from the gentle hostess of the motel who told me in detail what a considerate and kind-hearted man the Prime Minister was, pointing out that I had slept in the same bed that he had used on many occasions and finishing by telling me that not once had he forgotten his pyjamas.

On Manitoulin, Prime Minister or no, every visitor is treated with unfailing warmth and consideration. I can think of no part of Ontario where hospitality has achieved such a beautifully unobtrusive peak of excellence.

SUNNY HURONIA

The southern curve of Georgian Bay takes us down through Cape Croker and Wiarton to Owen Sound and from here, around to Penetanguishene and Midland, we are on the coastline of Huronia, the best-organized and best-promoted vacation area of Ontario.

Collingwood is a good place for a visit in Huronia. Here is the largest youth hostel in Canada and within a radius of a few miles are many things to do and see. For example, six miles from Collingwood are the scenic caves up the side of the Blue Mountains. This is a series of caves, deep and cool where sometimes one can find last winter's snow still there in midsummer. This is the area of Ontario's famous Blue Mountain pottery. Here too one can visit Craigleith Provincial Park where, if you are lucky, you might even find a fragment of an ancient vertebrate that probably lived in Huronia three hundred and seventy-five million years ago. There is also Devil's

Glen Provincial Park, situated on one of the most imposing gorges in the province.

Wasaga Beach is farther along the south shore of Georgian Bay. This is a boisterous spot, thickly populated in summer, from time to time the rendezvous of leather-jacketed motorcycle gangs from Metropolitan Toronto and, on the other hand, the site of the Ontario Zoological Park. A visit to the park is like a safari. Here lions roam and roar through the forest, hippos swim in the pools, coyotes, tigers and an Indian elephant are all found as well as the wolf, the jaguar and even water buffaloes. There is a small primate house for monkeys, mainly from Africa, and a bird conservatory housing many varieties of the most colourful bird of Africa, Asia and Europe. And there is a genuine beaver pond. The beaver is the symbol chosen by Canadians because he is a hard-working fellow with great skill and tenacity. A visit to the beaver pond in the Zoological Park can tell every Canadian a good deal about the attitudes of his pioneering forebears.

Penetanguishene is the second oldest settlement in Ontario. It was the gateway to Huronia for the French. Later Governor Simcoe (in 1793) chose it as the naval headquarters for the province he envisaged. In 1828 Sir John Franklin, explorer of the Arctic regions, assembled his expedition at Penetang. While in this area the Officers Quarters Museum, beautifully reconstructed and other restorations of the ambitious naval establishment which was once here, are worth a visit. Nearby are the hulls of two vessels raised from the harbour. One is the American vessel the *Tigress* which was drawn from the water in 1927; near it is the British craft the *Tecumseh*, raised from the harbour in 1953. This is a country thick with the lore of the past and everything which has been found has been skilfully restored or reconstructed to give meaning and sense to the traveller.

Midland is the final important point on the south shore of the bay.

As already indicated, the reconstructed Huron village and the reconstructed Ste-Marie among the Hurons are two of the best and most interesting reconstructions to be found anywhere in Canada.

All this is sunny country, happy country, country whose charm has been accepted for what it is, one of the most attractive places for a visitor and a vacationer. All the legitimate artifices of the twentieth century have been employed to heighten the attraction of the Huronia countryside and coastline but they rarely distort and never spoil the delight which comes from the nature of the country itself and its colourful past.

THE THIRTY THOUSAND ISLANDS

The St. Lawrence River has its Thousand Islands; Georgian Bay has its Thirty Thousand Islands. The most interesting and best developed complex of the Georgian Bay islands are those which fan out from Honey Harbour at the southern end of the eastern shore of the bay. The centre and largest of these islands is Beausoleil which, along with thirty-eight others, or portions of them, make up Georgian Bay Islands National Park. Beausoleil Island has eighteen campgrounds. There are two nature trails and three circular hiking routes along the forty miles of this island which is heavily wooded particularly at the south. There is a good beach, tennis and badminton courts. There is also good dockage for craft cruising through Georgian Bay.

A hundred miles northwest of Beausoleil Island but still within the complex which makes up the national park is the famous Flowerpot Island, composed of flat lying limestone and sandy, dolomitic limestone. The "flowerpots" which give the island its name are vertical pillars of rock which have been eroded away by the action of the waves. The tops of the pillars have been preserved because they are composed of more durable rock and because wave erosion is more effective below the surface of the lake. These make a picturesque and much-photographed site and are well worth seeing. The best way to get to Flowerpot Island is by boat from Tobermory.

Flowerpot Island marks the western extreme of Georgian Bay Island National Park. Most of the islands are to the east fanning out from Honey Harbour. For the sailor, cruising among the Georgian Bay islands is pure delight even though some of the channels are tricky. They are all well marked and a little care is all that is required. This is also great fishing country and if one is not cruising through the islands he can still reach good fishing grounds from the eastern shore of the bay.

Honey Harbour itself is a standard resort area with first-rate accommodation. Moving north one comes to the town of Parry Sound which has an excellent harbour and attracts many boatmen. However, Parry Sound is not primarily a resort town. It has a busy and bustling life of its own and a strong sense of identity. Some years ago a talented Canadian actor, Don Harron, created a character he called "The man from Parry Sound." I doubt if the citizens of the town particularly appreciated Harron's definition of their character. "The man from Parry Sound" appeared in several versions of *Spring Thaw*, a mildly satirical review which has become a Canadian theatrical tradition. In Don Harron's version, the man from Parry Sound was supposed to represent a typical Ontario citizen with narrowly provincial attitudes. Such people do exist in the province of Ontario and probably even in Parry Sound but they represent something which is much more typical of a past era than the present.

Let us take a look at Don Harron's man from Parry Sound. First he wore work clothes and in the old Ontario definition this meant the clothes of a working farmer. Well, once Ontario was primarily rural and in a harder age it is certainly true that working from dawn to dusk, day in and day out throughout the hot summers and frigid winters, represented the epitome of virtue for many people. When one has to do something rather unpleasant in order to survive it makes the going much easier if he can persuade himself that such activity is highly pleasing in the sight of God and will undoubtedly earn for him one of the better mansions in Heaven. Today, however, very few citizens of this province have to work like this for survival and, while vestiges of the old attitude hang on, Ontarians have long since emancipated themselves from the curious idea that hard work (which God thought so little of He made it a form of punishment according to the Old Testament version) has any particular virtue.

Yet as a people we have come to this position slowly. Even with magnificent opportunities for relaxation and enjoyment as our natural heritage, we still have had to inch our way very slowly to a position where we could enjoy all the good things the province of Ontario has to offer. And we had another hang-up too.

The fictitious man from Parry Sound was "provincial" in the narrow-minded sense of the word. He was both jealous of and suspicious of strangers and the fact of the matter is that this too at one time did indeed represent an Ontario attitude. This mood was further aggravated by the proximity of our successful and wealthy neighbour to the south. At one point in our history we were easily convinced (and it must be said that our American cousins have no inhibitions about trying to convince us) that our way of life in Ontario was more drab, less affluent and less glittering than could be found, say, in the State of Michigan. It was all a painful misconception, perhaps a symptom of growing pains and, saddest of all, derived from nothing more substantial than the sight of American citizens who drove more expensive automobiles than one could find in Ontario. We had our values so little sorted out that we actually resented this without realizing that in the surroundings of our everyday life we had just about the best country to live in in terms of natural enjoyment that a man could find anywhere on the surface of this earth.

Times change. With the era of instant communication, coupled with Ontario's astonishing affluence, our old provincial values have righted themselves. Today Ontario has developed and takes care of its "tourist attractions" as well as any state or province in North America and a great deal better than almost all of them. The interesting thing is that we primarily do it for ourselves. We are certainly happy to share the opportunities for relaxation and enjoyment with anybody for we are still a gregarious and hospitable people. We truly like to be good neighbours and good hosts. It is a part of our character that we rarely talk about and which still makes many of us both clumsy and defensive. At least one can say that our hearts are in the right place, we do like to have fun and we like to share it with anybody who comes to visit us.

Up to now at any rate, we have not developed any objectionable pride in these characteristics. We have one of the best highway systems in the world and yet most of us are not sure whether we actually believe this or not. We have this great and wonderful vacationland and most of us don't like to talk about it very much. And we still have one bad hang-up: we think it is only good in the summertime and we still apologize for our winters.

WINTER FUN

It is a fact that no part of Ontario, including what we somewhat ironically call "The Banana Belt" (the Niagara Peninsula), has what could in any way be described as a salubrious winter climate. We get cold weather and plenty of snow and there is no way of getting around it. In Southern Ontario the actual winter period is relatively—and for some disappointingly—short. Usually, up until around the Christmas season we do not have either many heavy snowfalls (and if they come they inevitably go away quickly) or very low temperatures. For Southern Ontario, January and February are the only true winter months which we can count on and even then we are subject to periods of thaw when most of the snow is likely to go away for a few days at least. But it always comes back during these months. March can be its traditional blustery best and then we are into April and spring. But north of the line which Highway 7 makes across the province winter comes earlier, is more consistent, and stays longer. In short, while winter sports can be enjoyed in all parts of Ontario they can be counted on only north of Highway 7.

In Ontario you quickly learn that wintertime, too, is fun time. The great sports are skating and hockey, curling and skiing.

Every settlement, town and city has its skating rink. In the south they are now almost all equipped to make artificial ice which is usually laid down sometime in October and carried through until the next spring. Here tens upon thousands of hockey teams for youngsters anywhere from the age of five and up are organized and every lad who takes to the ice is a potential N.H.L. star. Similarly, there are literally hundreds of figure-skating clubs organized throughout the province where the scintillating legend of Barbara Ann Scott still persists. And above and beyond that an Ontarian of any age is often impelled to take down his skates and go to the nearest rink simply for the sharp exhilaration which comes from skating for fun.

The royal sport of curling probably came to Ontario with its first Scottish settler. Certainly wherever a group of Scotsmen pioneered, they promptly began curling activities. Immigrants travelled light and a set of curling "stanes" was heavy and unnecessary baggage. The primitive curlers of Ontario fashioned their own stones from ice-borne granite fragments which were readily available in many parts. In those where granite was not obtainable the settlers showed a ready ingenuity in making circular curling blocks out of wood of beech and maple and banding these heavily with iron which furnished the needed weight. Some of those early curlers found these wood stones so effective that they preferred to use them even after Ailsas and other famous Scottish stones came into general use in the province. The first organized curling club in Ontario was in Kingston in 1820 and the next was in Fergus in 1834, Flamboro in 1835, Toronto and Milton in 1837 and Guelph, Galt and Scarboro in 1838.

The same pattern was true as the great Ontario northland was opened up. The town of Haileybury was the first to produce curling in the north when they organized a club in 1907, to be followed shortly after by New Liskeard. Since that time some of the finest curling teams in Canada have come out of Northern Ontario.

Today, curling has become even more popular than ever. The whole of the province is dotted with curling clubs, some with their own ice and some which use the ice of the local arena, sharing it with the hockey and skating enthusiasts. Like the skaters, the curlers of Ontario are deeply involved in this great game and they bring a zest to it which is as refreshing as a clear sparkling winter day in the province itself.

Skiing is a relatively new winter sport for this "land of

snow." In the pioneer days the settlers quickly adapted from the Indians the snowshoe, an oval-shaped frame made of bent wood and interlaced by the soft gut of one of the many animals that roamed the forest. Except in the lightest snow, the snowshoe keeps the traveller on the surface and, as it was with the Indians, so it was for the first settlers primarily a utilitarian device. There is a fine art to snowshoeing and, with feet encased in soft moccasins, the traveller can move rapidly along forest trails or open spaces.

As roads were developed and horses and sleighs came into general use the snowshoe was no longer required for travel. By the last decade of the nineteenth century and through the Edwardian years of the twentieth and indeed up until the nineteen-thirties snowshoeing was, much like bicycling, a sport and recreation rather than adapted to utility, except in the far north. As a boy, I can remember the care which each lad took of his snowshoes, making sure that the gut was soft and resilient, and the pride he enjoyed when he acquired a new set of moccasins which, for a reason I do not know, we called "shoepacks." These were beautiful to wear, the equivalent of bare feet in the summer time but in a hot room they had an unholy smell which rose from the rank oil we used to keep them soft and pliable. Perhaps it was this far from delectable aroma which hurried the demise of the snowshoe but I am more inclined to think that the passing of snowshoeing as a recreation is another significant manifestation of an age which has to go faster and faster. Snowshoeing through an Ontario winter is a leisurely sport and cannot be compared to the excitement which comes from gliding down a good ski run through the exhilarating crisp winter air, a sensation almost of disembodiment, a feeling of flying through space.

In a short twenty years Ontario has caught up with the majority of other countries of Northern latitudes where snow is fairly plentiful in winter. The province is not blest by any ranges of real mountains—no Rockies or Alps. Even the famous Laurentians of the neighbouring province of Quebec provide ski slopes which just cannot be found in Ontario. Typically, however, the people of this province put to use the ingenuity of a technological age when they want something badly enough and this is how we got most of our good ski slopes today.

Altogether there are well over one hundred ski areas in the province ranging from the mediocre to the very good. Naturally enough, most of the better ones are in the northern sector. There is excellent skiing in the Haliburton area around Bancroft, in the Tay Valley west of the town of Perth, and around Atikokan. The renowned summer resort of Muskoka is almost as active in the wintertime now with a wide range of slopes to choose from around Bracebridge and Huntsville. Here the ski lodges are deluxe and are often associated with motel developments which operate equally actively in the summer time.

In Southern Ontario there is a strip which extends from Lake Huron just south of the shores of Georgian Bay across to about mid-point in the province around Barrie. This is known locally as the "Snow Belt." Here the strong northwest winds, coming over long expanses of the Great Lakes, dump heavy accumulations of snow. Here too are the closest to mountains which can be found in Southern Ontario—the Blue Mountains area. Some of the earliest and best-developed ski areas are to be found here especially around Collingwood. But anywhere except in the southernmost tip around Windsor some form of skiing is available. Oftentimes artificial snow has to be created and the season is a bit chancy but Ontario's winter-loving people will not be denied. There is skiing at the swinging summer resort of Grand Bend; there are many ski slopes within the boundaries of Metropolitan Toronto itself; there is skiing just outside the city of London and the city of Kitchener; there is skiing on the Niagara Peninsula around Fonthill; there is skiing handy to the capital, Ottawa. In the real north, of course, skiing facilities are available adjacent to almost any major town—at Sudbury, at Coppercliff, at Espanola, at Elliot Lake, at Haileybury, at Sault Ste. Marie, at Port Arthur and Fort William and, in addition to these, some other excellent slopes farther into the northern woods if one is seeking a more quiet atmosphere. Most of them are accessible by highways which are kept clear the winter round.

One of the earliest forms of recreation in the days when Ontario was largely rural in character was the hayride in summer and the sleighride in winter. No matter how you look at it, there are obvious advantages for those of a romantic turn of mind in the commodious sleigh which cannot be found in the back seat of an automobile. There is little doubt that sleigh rides would still be popular and quite often groups of young people try to organize them. Unhappily, this is almost impossible to do in the Ontario of today. For one thing the roads are plowed, saturated with salt and kept bare to the pavement all through southern Ontario and even if one could find a team of horses to draw the sleigh he would be hard put to find a road on which it could glide. A suitable substitute has not yet been found and probably never will be but a newcomer, a Canadian invention, has appeared on the scene and met instant success. This is the snowmobile.

In the twenties and thirties, when only the main roads were thoroughly cleared, there was a primitive version of the snowmobile which consisted of a light car (usually a Ford) equipped with heavy tires and massive chains on the rear wheels and with runners replacing the front wheels. They were usually owned by country doctors and many an errand of mercy was performed because the old snowmobile allowed the physician to reach the scene of emergency and distress quickly through the rigours of what was then a typical Ontario winter.

The snowmobiles of today are another kind of bird entirely. The name of one of the first snowmobiles to be marketed on a mass basis is "Skidoo," a trade name which, like Frigidaire, is now almost generic. Skidoo is highly descriptive of what this streamlined snowmobile can do. It is strictly for fun. It is fast and highly manoeuvrable and people of all ages and in increasing numbers are giving it a try. Its charm is that it induces a sensation which is carefree and abandoned. It can be used anywhere where you can find an open field, either day or night. Almost all major towns and cities now have snowmobile clubs for groups of people with their own vehicles. They go out to rented farmland and have a ball. The vogue of course is extending south into the United States but for a fun time with a snowmobile Ontario tops the list.

There are other minor winter sports carried on in the province, among them ice-boating on the St. Clair and Ottawa Rivers, and fishing through the ice in any of the small lakes which freeze over entirely. On Lake Simcoe, for example, hundreds of fishermen's huts dot the lake throughout the wintertime.

Ontario is not a province whose citizens hibernate in the cold weather. As leisure time increases and highway travel becomes easier and more certain every year there is almost as much action in the wintertime as in the summer. It is enjoyment with a new dimension, more active, more invigorating, with the added attraction of a roaring fire and a cosy snug cabin at the end of a day's healthy exertion.

It is a legacy from older and more rugged times that the people of Ontario have derived a completely erroneous reputation for being smug, slow-moving and self satisfied. The atmosphere of the province gives the lie to this every day, summer or winter. Travel any highway in the province in the summer and perhaps every sixth car will be carrying a trailer or a boat behind it and, in winter, about the same percentage of automobiles will have a ski-rack on top. The streams which were used to power gristmills and sawmills are now used for fishing. The lakes which were considered helpful for water travel are now used for pleasure craft. The hills have been turned into ski slopes and the beaches into summer resorts. The great areas of woodland have had to be protected from lumbering and turned into provincial or national parks where the hundreds of thousands come to enjoy camping out. While the province thrusts ever forward in its agricultural and industrial development it has superimposed upon the entire map a network of places where people go to relax and enjoy themselves.

No matter where you are in Ontario you can have fun, and on any given day of the year thousands of Ontarians can be found making full use of the recreational facilities of the season.

Little wonder that Ontario is a happy province.

CHAPTER SIX

Pomp and Circumstances

In the earliest years of the settlement of Ontario the closest we came to an organized social structure largely revolved around what might be called "officialdom." For the most part, only those who were involved in government, the military or other similar official duties had either the time or money to devote to the frivolities of society. As a result, most of Ontario's early social calendar derived from such events as the birthday of a monarch, the changing of the command of a regiment, the marking of such patriotic days as St. George's Day, the date of some famous battle, or the opening or closing of a Legislature.

For example, the first full-scale social event in my own part of the country—Huron County—occurred when the news reached the town (the primitive settlement of Goderich) several weeks after the event, that King William had died and a young girl called Victoria had acceded to the throne. Couriers went out into the bush to round up the scattered settlers and as soon as they could be assembled (many of them walked up to twenty miles) a full day of festivities was arranged. A monstrous dinner consisting mostly of what could be harvested or shot in the woods, was held at noon followed by a round of toasts to the new Queen. There were no glasses, but a pail of whisky with a dipper in it was passed from one patriotic citizen to another followed by a pail of water for those "weaker spirits" who couldn't take their whisky neat. The afternoon was given over to impromptu games of skill such as tug-of-war and lacrosse. In the evening the provision sheds were were cleared and a great ball was held which lasted all through the night. This is official society in Ontario in its most primitive form.

In the capital city of Toronto and garrison cities such as Kingston and London the social rituals were much more elaborate. In the early years most social events were held in the largest hotels of the cities (in Toronto the Steamboat Hotel was a favourite for balls and routs) or in the officers' quarters of the forts. In the major towns, as they developed, at least one hotel would try to include a ballroom in its facilities. Later as population increased major centres would develop their own halls which could accommodate large social events of all kinds.

In 1849 in Toronto the most beautiful of these was erected —St. Lawrence Hall. It was designed by one of the leading architects of the time, Mr. W. Thomas, and was described as "from the example of Jupiter Stator, of Corinthian order, the centre being a portico of three-quarter columns, its carved work of a rich and varied character crowned by a cupola forming a circular open temple within which was a bell of over two thousand pounds in weight." For many years St. Lawrence Hall was one of the most famous concert halls in Canada and the centre of a glittering social life which developed in the province's capital. Lectures and travelogues were very fashionable and were held regularly. Many of the anti-slavery speakers from the United States came to seek Canadian support from the platform of the St. Lawrence Hall. Magicians, ventriloquists, phrenologists and midgets were featured. Local musical organizations, orchestras and choirs performed here. Under John Carter, the organist of St. James' Cathedral, the first performance of "The Messiah" was offered in 1851. By the late fifties and sixties St. Lawrence Hall was on the circuit for great foreign artists making a North American tour. Adelina Patti came in 1860, and Jenny Lind sang there. In this century St. Lawrence Hall had little usage. It was grey and dirty and rundown but as part of its centennial program the city of Toronto restored the great hall to its former glory and today it stands on King Street a beautiful reconstruction whose elegance and perfection of line is a delight to the eye amid the city's towering skyscrapers.

Social life around the Ontario Legislative Assembly encountered many difficulties in the early days largely because the various buildings available were never really suitable. The original legislative building, which was the second brick building in what was then known as York, was destroyed by fire in 1814 and the Legislature had to meet in Jordon's Hotel. New buildings were built in 1818 and were used until 1824 when they too were enveloped in flames. The next year the Legislature met in the Toronto General Hospital Building and the year after that in the Court House. Finally, in 1832 a group of public buildings on Front Street between John and Peter Streets were occupied by the Legislature. At various times some of these buildings were used as a university, an insane asylum or a military barracks. However, most of the official life of Ontario was conducted on Front Street until 1892 when the new Legislative Assembly Buildings were erected in Queen's Park. We shall take a look at them later.

The ultimate seal of social approval and acceptance was invested in the lists of those who were invited to the openings of the Legislature and the various social events which occupied the city while the government was in session. For example, around 1837 a Scottish housekeeper called Louisa McColl married one of the brothers who were her employers. This man was Captain Robert Dunlop who had very recently been elected the first Member of the Legislative Assembly for Huron. At the time the ceremony was performed there was no clergyman available. Since both the brothers were of Scottish descent they resorted to an ancient Scottish custom often invoked in the Highlands when speed was important in establishing a marriage bond. Because of various factors including long lonely nights, beautiful highland lasses and a shortage of ministers the Church of Scotland recognized a marriage if the ceremony in the Scottish Book of Common Order was read over the two consenting parties by a layman.

In the case of the nuptials between Captain Dunlop and Louisa McColl (and here the unrestrained sense of humour of the Captain's brother who was the famous "Tiger" Dunlop is largely in evidence) the marriage service was read by the only coloured man in Huron County, who happened to be the Dunlops' butler. Shortly after the ceremony was performed the Captain left his bride and proceeded to attend the Legislative Assembly sessions in Toronto. In the long and undoubtedly lonely nights which followed, the new bride began to do a little thinking and perhaps have some misgivings. With that fine determination which marked the pioneer lady she caused a horse and cutter to be harnessed and set out by herself along the perilous winter trail which led to the capital. It would be romantic to think that the lonely new bride was pining for her husband and was ready to risk the perils of her hazardous journey simply to be in his company but all the records indicate that Louisa McColl was an extremely hard-headed lassie indeed. What she actually had in mind was recognition of the marriage and the seal of social approval which only could be conveyed by the acceptance of Toronto social groups. This she achieved.

To pursue the story to its end, it must be admitted that perhaps the Captain did have some lingering hope that his many happy years of bachelorhood could by some intricate device be restored. After Louisa McColl appeared in the capital, was introduced to the dowagers as his new bride and participated in the round of social events, the Captain completely capitulated. Back at the family home in Huron, "Gairbraid," a proper wedding ceremony, this time with a clergyman, was performed as soon as one was available.

THE GREAT HOUSES OF TORONTO

The other centres of social activity in early Ontario were the great houses. Curiously enough, these in no way resembled the stately homes of England where castles, sometimes even minor palaces, huge mansions and vast country houses set in great tracts of land and forest, have always been a social focal point. There was no shortage of land in Upper Canada or

Ontario but for some reason or other none of its original leading citizens or men of wealth seemed to be inclined to develop great country estates. Many of them owned large holdings of land but communications were of the most primitive and perhaps this is the reason why Ontario has never had the equivalent of Britain's "county gentry." The same pattern was largely true in the United States and perhaps already the American influence was dominating Ontario's social customs. In any event the social leaders of the province concentrated on building elaborate mansions in the cities. Again, because Toronto was the largest city, and the capital, most of the first great houses were built there.

The first house to achieve social recognition in Toronto was that of Captain Aeneas Shaw who, at the turn of the nineteenth century, built a commodious log dwelling for his family on what is now Queen Street West near the site of Old Trinity College. When Prince Edward, Duke of Kent and father of Queen Victoria, visited York in 1802 he was the guest of Captain Shaw and entertained there.

The first really imposing private dwelling was on Front Street just across the corner from where the Royal York Hotel now stands and was built by Dr. John Strachan, later Bishop of Toronto. It was a two-storey building of brick in the neo-classic style of architecture. It stood out so grandly in the primitive years of Toronto that when the doctor's brother James paid him a visit his first reaction on seeing the new mansion surrounded by its large and handsome grounds was, "I hope its a' come by honestly, John!" Apparently brother James knew his tricky brother very well because the machinations of the immigrant Scottish-Presbyterian-schoolmaster-turned-Anglican cleric are now a legend in Ontario.

Back in Scotland, James Strachan was impressed by what he had seen in the capital of Upper Canada and wrote "The society, both as in respects to ladies and gentlemen, is very superior, and such as few towns of England can furnish."

Shortly after, other great houses were constructed in Toronto and each made an important contribution to the evolution of society in the city. Among these were the Howard residence in what is now Toronto's High Park and which still stands and can be visited. There is a good restaurant in it where excellent food can be enjoyed although one will no longer meet the cream of Toronto society there.

Another great house which still stands is now the nucleus of the Toronto Art Gallery and locally known as the "Grange." "The Grange" was built by Mr. D'Arcy Boulton, a gentleman who had a reputation for polished manners. He was one of the first men to be called to the Bar of Upper Canada. The Grange is probably the finest specimen of the beginning of the great era in Toronto. From the time of its erection it became a social centre in the city and as the original portion of Toronto's Art Gallery has continued this function. In between it was occupied by one of Toronto's most intelligent citizens, Dr. Goldwin Smith.

Other important houses of those days included Beverley House where D'Arcy Boulton lived before moving to The Grange and which was enlarged by the first Chief Justice of Ontario, John Beverley Robinson; Cawthra House which stood on the corner of King and Bay Streets until about a decade ago when it was finally demolished to make way for the skyscraper which is the headquarters of the Bank of Nova Scotia; Rosedale House, the old home of Stephen Jarvis who was the Registrar of the province; and just beyond what was then known as Blue Hill Ravine (part of the deep winding ravines of Rosedale) stood a lonely unfinished frame house which was known as Roland Burr's Folly.

Perhaps the greatest folly in terms of great Toronto houses is Canada's only honest-to-goodness "storybook" castle—Casa Loma. This is the dreamchild of an adventuresome Ontario financier in the early decades of the twentieth century—Sir Henry Pellat. Sir Henry made a lot of money and acquired some very powerful ideas of grandeur which included the outfitting of a regiment and Casa Loma. Ninety-eight rooms in a spectacular façade of imported granite, complete with towers, turrets and balconies, secret stairways, gold-plated bathroom fittings and the first air-conditioner unit ever installed in Canada, Casa Loma was to be the solid physical manifestation of florid, flourishing Sir Henry. But—alas!—Sir Henry ceased to flourish. The great entrance—wide enough to

admit a carriage-and-four into the great hall led into a piti-
fully uncompleted dream. Ownership reverted to the City of
Toronto. What to do with Casa Loma, located on prime land
in the centre of the city but purposeless and profitless? It was
almost torn down. But Ontarians, with their real but well-
concealed romanticism, their deep attachment to the glory
associated with the British baronial castle of old, resisted. The
usual compromise formula was found. Today, Casa Loma is
operated by the Kiwanis Club of Toronto as a profitable showplace, is used for banquets and dances and can be toured for
a modest fee. It is one of the showplaces of the city even
though it never has and never will achieve the baroque perfection Sir Henry planned for it.

Eventually, as the city rapidly increased in population
select neighbourhoods evolved. By far the most concentrated
and the most imposing was on Jarvis St., now a street with a
somewhat dubious reputation but in the beginning an avenue
whose both sides represented block after block of monumental
Victorian houses, huge, ornate in architecture and the very
core of high society. Today one can still see occasional houses
which have more or less remained intact but most of them
have long since given way to the encroaching commercialism
of downtown Toronto. Even the bordellos which gave Jarvis
St. a new kind of notoriety in this century are being replaced
by high-rise apartments.

The next concentration of society in Toronto was Rosedale
which was the successor to Jarvis St. Today Rosedale is a
curious conglomeration. Many of the great houses still remain
but some of them have been turned into boarding houses.
Others are stubbornly occupied by descendants of the original
builders. Still others have been bought and Rosedale is still
a good social address in Toronto. Later still, as the city moved
northward, the area known as Forest Hill became synonymous
with the best in Toronto social life. Forest Hill, perhaps even
more so than Rosedale, is still an accepted address but the city
keeps moving ever northward and at the present time perhaps
the Bayview area represents the latest of this ever-fluctuating
social core of a great city.

In fact, in the cosmopolitan expansive mood of today's

Toronto, the rigidities of the old social structure have virtually broken down completely. But while it lasted, Toronto represented the acme of social achievement for the whole province. The leaders of Toronto society in any decade were known by name in the small cities, towns and hamlets and regarded as creatures considerably larger than life.

ONTARIO "OFFICIAL" SOCIAL LIFE

Along with its impulse to progress, tradition still rides hard beside. The people of Ontario stick stubbornly to many of the values of another era and nowhere is this better expressed, and nowhere is it more logical to find it, than in Queen's Park —the site of the Ontario Legislature.

The Ontario Legislature has got to be seen to be believed. In 1880 an architect from the city of Buffalo, New York, was commissioned to design a new building. What he produced was something so preposterous that it must be preserved forever because its like will never be seen again. To quote from an official description of the Parliament Buildings of Ontario the original building "combined elements from related Byzantine and Romanesque styles and added ornamental elements from Celtic and Scandinavian modes of the ninth to twelfth centuries." All this is rendered in red sandstone hewn from a quarry near Orangeville, Ontario.

What for many people was a horror has now come to be regarded with affection and even pride by most of the citizens of the province. Among other things, it is a solid symbol of the period when the province was a conglomeration of backwoods settlements but was prepared to take its stand as a full-fledged political entity in the waking years of the Victorian era. It still represents a feeling which persists in the hearts of most of the people of the province. We look at it and we experience a reverberation of what our grandparents must have felt. No more did they have to make do with flimsy public buildings which might be destroyed by fire (although the west wing of the present edifice was gutted in 1909 the wall remained intact); instead the new Parliament Buildings were the concrete evidence that the people of Ontario had indeed con-

quered the arch-enemy, the wilderness, and now were ready
to stand and grow.

The business which is carried on in this Legislative
Assembly still reflects something of the ambivalence of the
Ontario nature. One of the best spectacles to be seen in the
province is the opening of a legislative session. I looked at one
not long ago and it was typical. To open the proceedings the
representative of the Queen of Canada, the Lieutenant-
Governor, arrives. Although it was a dull November day,
damp and cold, he drove to the front door of the Legislature
in an open landau with outsized plumed hat tousled by the
breeze, the gold braid of his Windsor uniform glittering. His
entourage was followed by a company of mounted horsemen
wearing the uniform of some long-since-defunct regiment of
Hussars, steel-spiked helmets and all. A guard of honour made
up of two of the regiments of Ontario (this time Scottish
regiments because the Lieutenant-Governor at the moment
is of Scottish descent) were drawn up for his inspection outside the buildings.

The Queen's Representative was met on the steps of the
Legislature by the Prime Minister of the Province wearing
striped trousers and a director's coat. (Until recently the heads
of provincial governments were called premiers but it is a fact
that Canadian provinces seem to be getting more pretentious
all the time and now several of these government heads call
themselves prime ministers.) The Lieutenant-Governor and
the Prime Minister proceed through the heavily carved wood-
panelled halls of the building up to the Legislative Assembly
itself which is located on the second floor.

The Chamber is crowded. All the members of the provincial
parliament are there wearing their dark business suits and so
are their wives, dressed in high fashion; so too is the Judiciary
of Ontario, and a representative selection of some of the
province's most influential citizens. As in almost every other
Legislative Assembly in Canada, the Speaker is wearing his
tricorn hat and robes. Even the page boys dressed like students
of Eton College, helped to lend an old-world atmosphere.

This attachment to the ceremonials and symbols which
derive from the British monarchical system has puzzled our

'kiing near Huntsville

kiers silhouetted against sky

Skidoo-ing near Huntsville

Devil's Tooth Rock, Elora Gorge, Elora

A Sugaring-off Party at Bolton

At the Queen's Plate, Toronto   *Courtesy Ontario Jockey Club*

Harbour, Tobermory

Bob-Lo Island, near Amherstburg

Beach, Port Elgin

City Hall, Woodstock

cousins in the United States for generations. Wherever I encounter them, the subject of our relationship to the Queen comes up. "She owns you and the land you stand on," is a way in which this is often expressed. Strictly speaking, and much to the surprise of most Canadians, there is some truth in this. Without going into the legal technicalities it is true that all the territory which encompasses Canada is vested in the Crown. What Americans and for that matter people from other non-Commonwealth countries cannot understand is that through our long history of moving on "from precedent to precedent" the Queen would be absolutely powerless to do anything about a single square inch of Canadian territory even if she felt so inclined, which she doesn't.

This is just as well because no self-respecting Ontarian today would for a moment tolerate a situation in which the heroic struggles of the pioneers and the ambitious plans which we have for future developments could be interfered with by anyone outside ourselves. Perhaps our attachment (confused as it comes out in actual practice) to pomp and circumstance lies in a feeling that these symbols represent not what we actually are now but what we have emancipated ourselves from.

It was not always thus. Up until World War I Canada regarded itself as a colony of Great Britain, although in 1867 it achieved a parliament for itself and a considerable amount of self-determination. Nevertheless in the minds of the people we had a colonial attitude. We derived our legal system, our governmental system, our social values, much of our architecture, our educational values (the President of the provincial university — the University of Toronto — was always a Britisher rather than a native Canadian) and, above all, we relied upon Great Britain to defend us in the unlikely event that somebody might attack us.

After World War I a new spirit was in the air. Through the twenties, nationhood which had long been abuilding gradually became concrete and truly honourable. All this was a prelude to the first swinger in Ontario politics, The Honourable Mitchell Frederick Hepburn who arrived at Queen's Park in 1934 and for eight tumultuous years turned the

province upside down leaving it gasping but setting the tone
for a new era which continues to this day.

Mitch Hepburn, in his thirties, round of face with a deep
dimple in the middle of his chin, short, cocky and irreverent,
caught the imaginations of the Ontario voters in a way which
they had never experienced before. Long before political
scientists were using the word "charisma" Mitch Hepburn had
it. Ontario had never seen his like. Once he got rolling, people
in every corner of the vast province turned out by the hundreds
and by the thousands to hear him challenge the Establishment, paint a picture of promise and development, and convince his hearers that we could do things in Ontario which we
had not had the temerity even to dream about before his
advent.

Hepburn was a mountebank and a visionary. In the rambunctious confusion which he created there was an underlying
order which perhaps even he himself did not fully apprehend.
Without saying so, he sensed that the Ontario people were
ready to stand on their own feet and cease being good British
colonists. He closed Chorley Park, the official residence of the
Lieutenant-Governor. In his first campaign he promised that
he would sell by public auction all the Packard, Pierce Arrow
and Cadillac limousines which were the perquisites of cabinet
ministers up to that time. He did exactly that after he came
to power. He hired the most colourful auctioneer he could
find and the cars were sold off in Queen's Park right in front
of the Parliament Buildings. Of course, they were replaced by
newer models but there was no publicity given to this.

At a more serious level Hepburn took steps to assert
Ontario's claim for first place amongst the provinces of
Canada. Although he was certainly not the first provincial
premier to challenge the federal government he was the only
one to lay his own political future on the block in defence for
what he considered to be provincial rights. As it turned out
he lost the battle but he set the tone for a new and more
dominant role for the provinces in so doing. During his regime
the first four-lane highway to be built in the province was
constructed and opened—The Queen Elizabeth Way, which
runs from Toronto through the Niagara Peninsula to the

American border and still is one of the most important highways in Ontario. He was devoted to the development of provincial resources and allied himself with those who were
willing to risk capital to develop them.

The Hepburn years for many were an affront. "That young
feller is going to go too far," was the way a rural elector
of the old school summed it up. Perhaps Mitch Hepburn did,
but he gave the province the most diverting and entertaining
Legislature it has ever seen and his innumerable and fabulous
escapades are written into our folklore.

But above all, Mitch Hepburn gave this province an almost
unbounded confidence in itself. His extravagant exploits and
his own personal unpredictability perhaps were not the stuff
to develop the new spirit which pervaded this province after
his arrival but no one can take away the fact that it was
during the Hepburn years that Ontario took the turn away
from smugness, safety and introspection and headed toward
the exciting vista of expansion and development. The little
onion grower from Elgin County first set the province back
on its heels and then poised it ready for its exciting sprint into
the future.

SOCIAL LIFE IN THE CAPITAL OF CANADA

The Ottawa which Mitch Hepburn challenged also is in the
Province of Ontario. Although it is the capital city and
although over the years many plans have been put forward for
setting it up as a federal district which would be something
like the District of Columbia in the United States, this has yet
to be realized. Meanwhile Ottawa is part of the Ontario scene.
Many of the citizens of Ottawa would renounce this view.
They would say that the capital city has a character of its
own, an amalgam of the characteristics of all parts of Canada.
There is possibly some truth in this and if one seeks to pinpoint the difference between the Ottawa atmosphere and that
of the rest of Ontario you would have to say that Ottawa is
more self-conscious, stuffier and duller.

The business of government, of course, dominates the
Ottawa scene. The lumber kings have long since departed. In

their stead are the earnest men of the civil service, the well-meaning members of parliament, the frustrated members of the senate and the dashing delegations of the diplomatic corps.

All of these, of course, derive their being from what goes on on Parliament Hill. Taking it from scratch, what goes on here is almost identical to what goes on in Queen's Park in Toronto except, perhaps, more so. When Parliament opens, another landau transports another figure, also wearing a Windsor uniform and plumed hat, to the portals of the Parliament Buildings and substantially the same ritual is performed. Like those in Toronto, their Ottawa counterparts seem to find this both satisfying and exciting. Really the only difference is that, as stand-ins go, the Governor General of Canada would appear to be one notch closer to the ruling monarch than the Lieutenant-Governor of Ontario. In substance, neither one has any more power than the other.

It was not always thus. In the early days of Canadian nationhood our governors general did attempt to interfere and, quite often, successfully. They had two things going for them. One was that they were invariably members of the British aristocracy and usually related (by marriage at least) to the royal family. In those days this did indeed give them some power. Their boss at home (Queen Victoria) also interfered in governmental affairs with indifferent success but nevertheless with some. However, in Canada in those early days the British government itself was constantly meddling, constantly telling the Canadian parliament what it could and what it could not do and therefore the Canadian people and those they had chosen to represent them in government were quite used to being pushed around a bit. As the years went by Canadians grew stronger and the British influence waned but, as has been seen, it was not until the 1920's that economic nationhood really began to mean something.

It was during this decade that the royal representative then in Ottawa made the mistake of attempting to assert an authority which had long since passed out of his hands except (and this is still a most controversial constitutional issue) in the most strictly legalistic sense. This unhappy fellow was a gallant general of World War I, Viscount Byng.

In 1925 and 1926 two sworn political adversaries—the Right Honourable Arthur Meighen and The Right Honourable William Lyon Mackenzie King—were pitting their not inconsiderable wits against each other in an attempt to hold on to the office of prime minister. Lord Byng got himself caught in between. Had he lived even a decade later he probably would have known enough not to have become embroiled in the controversy at all. As it was he made a decision (the constitutionality of his act will probably still be debated by political scientists for many years) and promptly was caught in the wringer of Canadian politics. Right or wrong, his departure was unhappy, the last time a governor general ever had the temerity even to think of becoming involved in the cutthroat business of party politics in Canada. The last governor general in Canada to have a direct connection with the Royal Family (he married Princess Alice the aunt of the then reigning monarch, George VI) was the Earl of Athlone; the last governor general to be drawn from the British aristocracy was another famous general (this time of World War II) the extremely popular Viscount Alexander. Since that time Canada has had three Canadian-born governors general — Vincent Massey, Georges Vanier, and the present incumbent, Roland Michener.

Regardless of their political adventures and influence, socially speaking the inhabitants of the official residence of the governor general, Rideau Hall, have dominated the Ottawa social scene. Until very recently, an invitation to a Rideau Hall garden party would generally be rated higher than a pair for the Grey Cup, the Stanley Cup playoffs or the World Series.

Even the rite of going to church used to be able to excite the citizens of Ottawa no end. Of course it was expected that the royal representative would be an Anglican and it caused considerable confusion when one of Canada's most popular governors general, Lord Tweedsmuir, turned out to be a Presbyterian, thus giving St. Andrew's Presbyterian Church in

Ottawa a temporary edge over the Anglican Cathedral. But
these old prejudices have long since lost their impact and by
the time General Vanier took over the post not even an eye-
brow was raised when he regularly attended Mass.

The closest thing to the social pomp and panoply of Government House is to be found in the many embassies which are
now located in Ottawa, most of them in Ottawa's exclusive
residential area which is known as Rockcliffe Park. It is still
considered something of a coup to get on the embassies' entertaining lists. Today fewer and fewer of the really influential
people have time for this ceaseless round of elaborate gaiety
and more and more diplomatic guest lists contain a heavy
percentage of so-called influential newspapermen who are
primarily interested in the free drinks.

As a spectator sport, the goings-on of Government House
and the embassies do not have much to offer except for the
colourful guards at Rideau Hall, the synthetic changing of the
guard ceremony which is performed at noon through the
summer months in front of the Parliament Buildings, and the
occasional royal or semi-royal visitor who comes to the capital
and stays with the Governor General. Perhaps much more can
be learned by taking a quick glance at the grim gray and for-
bidding exterior of the Russian Embassy at the junction of
Laurier and Charlotte or at the stuffy Victorian exterior of
Laurier House the residence of two of Canada's Liberal prime
ministers — Sir Wilfrid Laurier himself and his successor
William Lyon Mackenzie King. The only significant difference
is that it is not easy to get into the Russian Embassy but, due
to Mackenzie King's highly developed sense of history, any
visitor can wander through Laurier House.

Unlike Washington, the residence of the Prime Minister
does not have the exciting symbolism of the White House. In
fact it was only during the regime of The Right Honourable
Louis St. Laurent in the 1950's that this country provided an
official residence for its prime ministers. It is at 24 Sussex
Street, a firm-looking grey stone building of considerable size
and indifferent architecture with modest grounds for the
function it fulfils and a good deal of shrubbery. Working in

this shrubbery one is almost sure to encounter a plainclothes-man of the Royal Canadian Mounted Police. During the tenure of John George Diefenbaker a mounted policeman in the red-coated famous dress uniform of the force was always in evidence. Before he became Prime Minister, Mr. Pearson used to say that one of the first things he would do when he achieved office was to get rid of the Mounties around the Prime Minister's house. However, by that time his good friend John Kennedy had been assassinated and the Mounties continued to patrol the grounds of Sussex Street during the Pearson regime.

For visitors to the capital the red-coated Mounties are still the Number One tourist attraction and the best place to find them is in front of the Parliament Buildings.

The Parliament Buildings themselves more by definition than by architectural grandeur attract most visitors to the capital. The point of interest which receives the most attention is the Peace Tower which has already been described. Visitors can take a look at the library, the only portion of the original main block which was not destroyed by fire. Immediately after the fire, in order to protect the contents of the library an R.C.M.P. constable was stationed at the entrance. He stayed there for over twenty years or at least a constable turned up for duty every day. It was not until a curious and unknown member of Parliament one day asked why a mounted police-man was always at the door of the library that it was discovered that no one had ever thought to countermand the order and so, for almost a quarter of a century, the library was guarded by a representative of Canada's finest. Actually the library is a very interesting place both to look at and to work in. There is not a really great library anywhere in Canada but the National Library is one of the best sources for reference work on Canada to be found anywhere. Architecturally it is fascinating with its unbelievably intricate carving reaching up into the vast pointed dome which, from the outside, is a landmark in the capital city.

A visitor can also take a look at the Government of Canada in action by applying for a pass which will allow him into one of the visitor's galleries of the House of Commons. Unless somebody is building up a storm that day, it is best not to tarry too long as a spectator of our legislatures in action. The question period can be lively; more often it is just plain exasperating and if one happens to be a Canadian citizen and listens to the inevitable spate of inane questioning which goes on in the Chamber most every day he is likely to come away from the experience thoroughly convinced that our members of parliament are more interested in making wisecracks and political hay than in governing the country. This is not necessarily so but it must be confessed that all too often the performance in the House of Commons is not reassuring to a sober-minded citizen.

If one is going to spend some time on Parliament Hill he should certainly look at the Peace Tower, go up past the great carillon, and visit the library. If the House is sitting it is interesting to watch the parade which includes the Usher of the Black Rod, the Sergeant-at-Arms and the Speaker as they make their way to the Chamber to open the day's proceedings. On the whole, it is best to leave it at that.

Lesser approximations of the official and political social life which occurs in Ottawa and Toronto can be found in a very watered-down version in most municipalities. Of late, the mayors of many of Ontario cities and towns have taken to wearing chains of office artfully designed by goldsmiths, which they hang about their necks on most official occasions or at least whenever they think of it. To date the most elaborate of these rigs is that which was concocted for a redoubtable Tory mayor of Ottawa and one of the first women ever to hold such office in the province, the fiery Charlotte Whitton. Miss Whitton, a short pugnacious lady much given to council-room brawling, apparently felt the need for some outward show of dignity to the office of the mayor of Canada's capital. In view of the fact that she was given to such japes as threatening council members with a water pistol it is understandable that she felt the need for some kind of impressive habiliments of office. What she came up with was a red robe trimmed with fur, worn with a lace jabot and topped with a tricorn hat. To my knowledge, no mayor of Ottawa or any other place has turned up in an outfit like this since Miss Whitton retired from municipal politics. But, during her tenure, she certainly was one of the sights in the capital.

SOME FINE PUBLIC BUILDINGS AND HOUSES

One legacy which Ontario has received from its early awe of things official are some extremely fine public buildings. These include an excellent group scattered throughout various parts of the province reflecting a neo-classic influence which pervaded Britain in the eighteenth century but, happily, carried on into Ontario in the nineteenth century before Victorian bric-a-brac became dominant. Such a building is the City Hall of Guelph which is rendered in fine stone work, and perhaps even better is the County Court House located in Peterborough. The County Court House in Picton is a little gem and the City Hall of Kingston is of the same genre but more elaborately rendered. Equally imposing is the County Court House in Brockville. The best example of colonial architecture which remains in the province in the form of a public building is the old Town Hall in Woodstock. The County Court House in London represents another architectural variation and is rendered in the form of a Norman castle. And at L'Orignal which was for many years the judicial and administrative centre of the old Ottawa district the original Court House which still stands is a distinct example of a French influence which can be found in many parts of the Province of Quebec but is rare in Ontario.

Besides the stately homes of Toronto and Ottawa the Province of Ontario is almost literally littered with fine and commodious houses. If a traveller keeps his eye open he can see excellent examples of all types of architecture which have evolved throughout the hundred-and-seventy-five-year history of the province. Slowly many of these are being earmarked for preservation under the aegis of the Ontario Historic Buildings Project which is associated with the faculty of Architecture of the University of Toronto and seeks to get a comprehensive inventory of all types of buildings of architectural value and interest. It is a mammoth project in which the traveller on

Ontario's highways and byways can participate. Actually if one is interested in this type of thing it is great sport to cruise through the Ontario countryside looking for interesting old homes. Because there are so many it has far more immediate results than, say, birdwatching. But let the traveller who is interested in this sort of diversion beware.

Only last summer two delightful young ladies turned up at my house one day asking innocently if there were any interesting old homes in my native district. With rash enthusiasm I bundled them into my car and within a five-mile radius of the town had showed them at least two dozen houses which provoked excited oo's and ah's from the two good-looking students. For me their visit was merely two or three very pleasant hours diversion until I found on my back doorstep a few days later a complicated set of documents which involved taking pictures of houses, recording their measurements and all sorts of other intimate details. This was followed by a letter from an old friend of mine who was involved in the project, a professor of architecture at the University of Toronto, who informed me that I was in charge of the project for this district. Since I am already involved in at least twenty more projects than I can do conscientiously this one I had to bypass, but it is still fun to travel Ontario looking for interesting houses.

And if you would like to become involved in the project I can assure you it is not difficult.

For a lot of travellers the houses which evoke the greatest interest are those of the "George Washington slept here" variety. In other words, houses where some of our great ones were born, lived or worked. A few of them are unfailing tourist attractions. Included among these is "Chiefswood," the birthplace of one of Canada's best-known poets, Pauline Johnson, whose father was a Mohawk chief married to an English bride. This house is located near the village of Onondaga. In the same area in the city of Brantford is Tutela Heights which is the homestead of the Bell family whose offspring, Alexander Graham Bell, is well known throughout North America. Bell himself is recorded as having said "The conception of the telephone took place during the summer visit to my father's residence in Brantford in 1874." Both the homes of Pauline Johnson and Alexander Graham Bell are open to the public. So too is "Woodside" in the city of Kitchener, the house which was the boyhood home of former Prime Minister William Lyon Mackenzie King. Another historic site (reconstructed and operated as a museum) is at Burlington and is the Georgian-type frame residence which was built by Chief Joseph Brant who received an extensive grant of land in this area because of the aid which he gave to the British. In Peterborough there is a cosy-looking stone house which is a symbol of the generosity of the citizens of that town. They banded together and built it as a gift and token of appreciation to an early physician of the district Dr. John Hutchison. In the County of Glengarry one can find the only remaining frame manor house which was built in 1790 by Sir John Johnson, a leader of the United Empire Loyalists.

SOCIAL LIFE IN THE CHURCHES

Official life and great and rich families by no means account for all the fun and games which can be enjoyed in Ontario. Social life at many other levels has evolved throughout the province's history. In any community, from the rudest pioneer settlement to the most advanced and sophisticated, the church has always been, apart from its devotional function, a social centre. In the early days, going to church was perhaps the only diversion which the hard-working pioneers could enjoy. Here they traded news, discussed crops, investigated scandals and did a little politicking on the side. As times progressed, the many auxiliary organizations of the church were deeply incorporated into the life of any community. The famous institution of rural Ontario, the "Fowl Supper," is a much-appreciated social institution which still persists. Anybody taking a vacation in Ontario would do well to pay attention to the local bulletin board which is usually found in front of the Post Office of small towns or, alternately, the Town Hall; in suburbia, on the larger supermarket billboards; and, wherever there is a weekly newspaper, in its columns. Here will be listed various church socials and for abundant and excellent Ontario cooking these are almost always sure-fire bets. Through the many years I have travelled this province, wherever I might happen to find myself staying overnight, one of the first things I would do would be to check out whether there was some church supper being held in the district. Generally speaking, the fare provided there is better than can be found in most hotels and restaurants and usually it's cheaper too.

The churches of Ontario have always been and, in some measure still are, intertwined with the social structure of the province. As a spillover from the days which we have been talking about when officialdom and the military set the social pace, the Church of England has tended to be associated with high social rank inasmuch as most of the early officials and officers of the British regiments tended to be Anglicans. In some communities this is still carefully nurtured although in practice it has little foundation in fact. More often in the smaller communities the church with the highest social standing could be any denomination which happened to have a large number of locally influential people amongst its membership. In a Scottish community this would tend to be the Presbyterian Church; in other communities the Methodist Church or the Baptist Church. Curiously, this social connotation seems to have been much more prevalent amongst Protestants than Roman Catholics.

In Toronto, which quickly became by far the largest city in Ontario, each of the predominant sects would have at least one church which was the "society church." To this day a bit of this hangs on. In Toronto today it is socially acceptable to attend the Cathedral but perhaps it is even better if you are a member of Grace Church-on-the-Hill; it is also socially acceptable for Anglicans, if they are of the high church persuasion, to attend either St. Thomas or St. Simon's Churches and, in a very special way (largely because of Ontario's great church musician, Dr. Healey Willan), St. Mary Magdalene. For the Methodists (in 1925 this became the United Church of Canada when it amalgamated with the Congregational Church and part of the Presbyterian Church) Sherbourne Street Church was very socially acceptable inasmuch as it was close to the mansions of Jarvis Street in the earlier days; today, like society itself, the best churches to attend in Toronto if you belong to the United Church are Timothy Eaton Memorial, an imposing Gothic structure on St. Clair Avenue West, or St. George's located in the same district a little farther north; Rosedale United is also right in there. The Baptists had an impressive and socially acceptable house of worship in Jarvis Street Baptist Church until it fell into the hands of a hell-raising evangelist known as Dr. Shields; after that the more prim and proper Baptists of the upper classes preferred either Walmer Road Baptist Church or Yorkminster. In the early days the Presbyterians belonged to two major groups—those who belonged to the Church of Scotland and those whose adherence was to the Free Church (commonly known as the Wee Frees) of Scotland. In early Toronto St. Andrew's Church was and is "The Cathedral of Presbyterianism" and Knox Church on Spadina Avenue is the most pretentious representative of the Free Church; Rosedale Presbyterian and Glenview in North Toronto are also considered very good, socially speaking.

In these churches social protocol was closely observed and vestiges of this attitude remain to this day. In many of them ushers and sidesmen still wear morning coats and striped trousers and outside of each an impressive line of chauffeured limousines can be observed each Sabbath morning.

Throughout the rest of southern Ontario there are some very fine examples of church architecture which are worth looking at. To list them all would be burdensome but there are a few which should be written into the record. At Niagara-on-the-Lake, where some of the best examples of early colonial architecture of all forms can be found, one should take a look at St. Andrew's Presbyterian Church whose congregation was formed in 1792 and whose present building was erected in 1831. It is generally considered to be one of the best examples of colonial-church architecture to be found anywhere in Canada.

In Guelph there is a magnificent twin-spired Roman Catholic church which stands on a rise of ground which dominates the entire city. Architecturally the church is a miniature copy of Notre Dame Cathedral in Paris. One of the pioneer Roman Catholic missionaries in Ontario was Father Macdonell who later became the first Bishop of the province. Macdonell was a Scotsman and a friend of John Galt who formed the Canada Company with Guelph as its principal city. Seeking first-hand information about the million acres of land which the company had acquired, Galt consulted his old friend Macdonell who was of great service to him and in return Galt offered the Bishop his choice of any site in Guelph for the purpose of building a church. Bishop Macdonell turned out to know the district well and he picked the best location in Guelph where the beautiful Church of Our Lady still stands.

In the city of Woodstock a lovely old church, St. Paul's, can be visited. It was built in 1834 and three years later was used to house and to shelter unhappy local supporters of William Lyon Mackenzie's ill-starred rebellion. In Toronto, apart from the "society" churches just mentioned, there is little Trinity Church which is the oldest original church building still remaining in the city, located on King Street East. It is a handsome brick structure built in the Gothic tradition. A little gem of an Anglican church is Old Christ Church in Lakefield just north of Peterborough which was built in 1853. Of quite different character is one of the few remaining log churches which can be found about four miles north of Huntsville just off Highway 11, well preserved and typical of the houses of worship which the pioneers constructed all through the province. It is called the Madill Church and was erected by Wesleyan Methodists. Later the pioneers built frame churches and one of the oldest remaining examples is Wicklow Church situated beside Highway 2, west of Port Hope. It was built in 1824 and is the oldest Baptist church in Ontario.

It would be quite erroneous to assume that church life in the Province of Ontario is largely a matter of either social events or of an outmoded past. The physical manifestation of the future of the churches of the province is to be found in the new churches which are being built everywhere. By far the most exciting modern architecture to be found in the province is in its new churches.

One of the first of these was Knox Presbyterian in Goderich. When it was first erected it attracted visitors from all over because it was so different from the kind of building which one usually associates with churches. But it suited the mood of Ontario and soon it was being copied and then surpassed in many parts of the province. One has only to go into any suburban area of any growing city to see some magnificent examples of contemporary church architecture, most of them designed by local architects. These are reverent but exciting buildings and the fact that there are so many of them in this province is an indication of how our people have tenaciously clung to the faith of their fathers but give it new expression in a dynamic, forceful kind of architecture which might have horrified their great grandfathers but, in its own sincere way exemplifies their own convictions. The swing to modern church architecture which permeates the entire province is not restricted to any religion or denomination. Some of the best forms of modern ecclesiastical architecture in Ontario are synagogues in north Toronto. And for my money by far the most exhilarating and dramatic example of modern church architecture I have seen anywhere is to be found in the city of Guelph in St. John's Church which is Roman Catholic.

FAIRS AND EXHIBITIONS

There were other early forms of diversion in Upper Canada besides those which were generated by the churches. Every early community, once it got itself established, would quickly form an agricultural society whose chief function was to hold spring and fall fairs. Originally these were highly competitive in nature and the local farmers could compete for awards for the best livestock and the best produce. Of equal or perhaps even of greater importance was the fact that these were great social events which were usually marked by parades of bands and school children and, at the end of the day, by a great community dance in whatever hall was available.

The fairs became increasingly elaborate and extended beyond one day into two or three, and in some of the major cities for a much longer period. They are still an active ingredient of the Ontario social scene and provide delightful entertainment for city-bound people who need an excuse to get out into the country. The spring fair is almost nonexistent. It was largely a series of competitions for the best livestock and especially horses. Since a large number of Ontario's farms have no horses and little livestock the spring fair is no longer practicable. But the fall fair certainly is and in the months of September and October there are literally hundreds of them held in the province. They are delightfully unsophisticated and beautifully entertaining and some of them have established impressive reputations including the fair at Rockton—which is billed as "the biggest little fair in the world"—and the fall fair at Kirkton.

One of the earliest fall fairs naturally was held at Toronto. As the city quickly became the centre of industry in the province it soon was not only an agricultural but an industrial fair which attracted people from all over Ontario. It had many sites but in 1879 an Exhibition Park, on lakefront property extending from Dufferin Street east to Bathurst Street, was formed and it remains today the site of what is no longer a fair but the great Canadian National Exhibition which presently runs for three weeks from mid-August until after Labour Day.

The C.N.E., as it is generally known, still concentrates on industrial and agricultural exhibits and while these have considerable interest this is not the reason why hundreds of thousands of people go to the "fair" annually. For at least half a century now the Ex has been the scene for some of the greatest extravaganzas the ingenious minds of promoters and showmen could devise. In the roaring twenties the world-famous marathon swims were held at the Ex attracting the greatest swimmers of the world vying for what was generally considered to be the top honour in professional swimming. Each year the midway for a few weeks collects one of the best assortments of sideshows, exciting rides and all the other appurtenances of a great carnival to be found anywhere on earth. Until North American automobile makers changed the date for introducing their new models the motor show at the Ex was again one of the best in the world and the elaborate Automative Building indicates the importance it once had.

Perhaps most publicized of all is the famous grandstand show which usually employs a cast of thousands for all kinds of amazing spectacles—tightrope walkers, trapeze artists, massed bands, the famous Royal Canadian Mounted Police musical ride, mighty historical pageants, and, one year even Canada's great little swimmer Marilyn Bell swimming in a tank! Major figures in the entertainment world, like Bob Hope, George Gobel and Danny Kaye, have performed at the grandstand show. For the individual performer in the world of show biz the grandstand show at the Canadian National Exhibition is considered to be one of the most challenging and toughest assignments an entertainer can take on. The saying goes "If you can make it at the Ex you can make it anywhere."

Exhibition Park consists of three hundred and fifty acres, and an army of gardeners works all summer to create elaborate floral displays in intricately arranged flowerbeds, beautiful stretches of green sward, gaily decorated walks and quiet islands of peace. Then the great show opens. From early morning until midnight thousands of Torontonians and thousands more of visitors descend upon the park in a mood of holiday abandon. They go through the buildings and look at the exhibits which range anywhere from the latest mousetrap to a capsule designed to explore outer space. Some of them even go to see the exhibits out of which the whole great show developed—the horticultural, the agricultural and the industrial competitions. Usually there are up to half a dozen bands playing in various stands strategically located throughout the grounds. There is one great bandshell with open-air accommodation for thousands and each year the Ex features a great concert band drawn from all corners of the world. Sousa once played Toronto Exhibition and so have the Coldstream and the Grenadier Guards.

In 1967, Canada's centennial year, the Canadian National
Exhibition which for a long time was the largest annual exhibition in the world faced the greatest challenge of its history.
1967 was a year for an official world's fair. Because it was
its one-hundredth-birthday year Canada had made application
to the international authorities and became the country designated. Several of the nation's major cities sought the honour
of having an official world's fair—and Canada's first—located
within their limits. The two chief antagonists seeking this
honour were the age-old rivals—Montreal and Toronto—and
Montreal, as the world now knows, won out and, on two
man-made islands, produced Expo 67. Expo 67 is generally
considered to have been one of the best if not the best world's
fair ever to be held.

As it got under way and the parameters of its achievement
speedily became known there were those who said it was a
mortal blow to the old and somewhat fusty Canadian National
Exhibition. The forecasts were gloomy. The doomsters predicted that attendance at the C.N.E. in 1967 would be so
low the fair would come close to bankruptcy and, looking
farther into the future, they were saying that it represented
another era and was no longer in the mood of the really hip
twentieth century. To the surprise of almost everybody, probably including some of the directors of the C.N.E., 1967 was
a bumper year. Even many tourists who had spent days, a
week, or even more at Expo came back to see their old
favourite on the lakeshore of Toronto. Probably better than
the founders and their successors will ever know, the Canadian
National Exhibition has a built-in appeal, in its own way has
kept up with modern Ontario and has created a distinctive
atmosphere which continues to pack in great crowds every day
it is in operation. Nevertheless those who are responsible for
the Exhibition have greatly accelerated their plans, opened
their minds and dedicated themselves to making sure that this
great entertainment tradition, still the greatest annual carnival
of them all, will continue to be one of the features which
makes Ontario famous.

A close cousin of the C.N.E. is the Royal Winter Fair.

Held in November, this too had its roots in Ontario's agricultural past. It was and still is the acme for competition in agricultural products and livestock. A blue-ribbon winner in any class in the Royal Winter Fair brings international recognition. On occasion, some famous food chains have even advertised that all their beef is from prize winners of the Toronto Royal Winter Fair. For most people, however, the Royal Winter Fair means the horse show. It was not so surprising as many people seem to think when Canada won its only gold medal in the 1968 Summer Olympics in the equestrian classes. The Province of Ontario is world renowned for its show horses and for the people who breed them, raise them, train them and show them. There are still several hunt clubs in Ontario including the Toronto Hunt Club and the London Hunt Club. Riding to the hounds is a reality in this province. Many of the same people who belong to the hunt clubs are involved in the horse show at the Winter Fair and they have made it one of the major events in Ontario's social calendar. Any evening one can see what passes for the aristocracy of Ontario, the women beautifully gowned and the men in top hat and tails, crowding their boxes in a glittering and gallant assembly. This in no way detracts from the real business of the meet which is some of the toughest international competition known in the equestrian world.

Ontario has two other major annual fairs, not as large or as impressive as the Canadian National Exhibition but still very worthwhile. These are the Western Fair which is held in London just after the Canadian National Exhibition, and the Central Canada Exhibition which is held in Ottawa just prior to the C.N.E. The Ottawa fair is in Lansdowne Park which is even more famous as the home of one of Canada's great football teams, the Ottawa Roughriders. Both the London and Ottawa fairs have extensive permanent grounds and buildings and between them they serve eastern and western Ontario well.

Similar in mood but more evanescent are the hundreds of carnivals which, mostly in the summertime, are held in almost every town and major village in Ontario. They are usually sponsored by service clubs or similar organizations which are seeking to raise money for worthy community projects. The fact that they are successful is an indication that the average Ontario citizen is highly responsive to any form of fun and that he will respond with enthusiasm to every opportunity to take part in a local carnival. As a long-time traveller of this province another one of my guide lines, in order to get the most out of what Ontario has to offer, is always to check in any part of the province where I might find myself to discover if there is a local carnival being held in the area. If there is, I can be sure of an evening's healthy enjoyment, losing a little money trying to win a turkey or a basket of groceries but losing it for a worthy cause. Too many people neglect the carnivals of Ontario which are one of the best ways to spend a pleasant summer evening anywhere. Now we are moving into winter carnivals as well with parades, ice sculptures, perhaps a hockey game, an impromptu snowball fight and lots of good clean action. These too are worth looking out for if you happen to be on the loose in Ontario in the wintertime.

PROFESSIONAL SPORTS EVENTS

In terms of spectator sport Ontario has plenty to offer. Canada's national game is represented in this province by the Toronto Maple Leafs whose home is the famous Maple Leaf Gardens on Carlton Street in Toronto. So popular is the Toronto team and so exciting the encounters which take place on the ice of the Gardens that there just isn't room to accommodate all those who want to see a hockey game. Saturday night until very recently was a traditional night for a local game in Toronto and tickets have always been scarce and hard to come by. This should not deter the enthusiasm. A little perseverance at the box office before the game will usually yield results even if it is "standing room only."

Ontario is the home province for three Canadian football clubs—the Argonauts of Toronto, the Tigercats of Hamilton and the Roughriders of Ottawa. These are great teams which draw enthusiastic support from all over Ontario and along with the Montreal Alouettes comprise the eastern section of the Canadian Football League. The western section is made up of teams from Winnipeg, Regina, Edmonton, Calgary and Vancouver. Although they play an interlocking schedule, the top eastern team meets the top western team in a sudden-death single game which is one of the sporting classics of the nation—The Grey Cup Game. The winner of the Grey Cup is the football champion of Canada. At least half of all Grey Cup games are held in Ontario, usually in Toronto, and the Grey Cup weekend is a legend.

In earlier and quieter times this contest was thought of primarily as an exciting sporting event and while this is still true it is now much more than that. Generally the credit for enlarging the Grey Cup Game into the most boisterous week-end which is experienced anywhere in Canada annually goes to the City of Calgary which in 1949 sent its representatives and boosters down along with the Stampeders (their local team) to participate in a Grey Cup Game. When they arrived in Toronto they had chuckwagons, cowboys, Indians, horses and a spirit of wide-open *joie de vivre* to which the Torontonians responded with fervour.

Ever since, the Grey Cup festival (wherever it is held) is the wildest celebration which can be seen in Ontario. It begins the Friday night prior to the Game when the downtown streets are clogged with thousands of happy sporting enthusiasts, sightseers and the hundreds of people who don't care anything about football but like a wide-open good time. The major hotels clear all but the most essential furniture from their lobbies. It is impossible to get a reservation and it is perhaps the closest that any staid Ontario city ever comes to a real *mardi gras.* On the Saturday of the game the famous Grey Cup breakfast is held with sports celebrities, old and young, in impressive attendance. Then comes the Grey Cup Parade, which undoubtedly is the most magnificent assembly of bands, beautiful girls, cheer leaders and floats in Canada. Then the game itself—usually on the last Saturday in November—and the inevitable riotous celebrations afterwards. I have been to Grey Cup weekends in Vancouver and Ottawa and Toronto, and the Ontario ones, in my opinion, have yet to be equalled. One might say that you have not truly lived if you haven't survived at least one Ontario Grey Cup weekend in your life.

This is the big time. Although we are often accused of being dominated by American influences, the fact is we have never really had professional baseball of the calibre of our football and hockey. At the present time there is not a professional baseball team in Ontario or, indeed, in Canada except Montreal which just got one. Toronto had a team in the International League for many years but support was so light that the franchise was finally moved back to the United States. But baseball and softball are played throughout the province in the summer months in all the towns and cities in a myriad of leagues. The same is true of football and even more so of hockey.

For excellent and exciting hockey any city and most of the major towns can provide great entertainment. The Junior A and Junior B teams in Ontario are almost as good to watch—and some people even prefer them to the professional teams. Generally speaking it is safe to say that almost any time one is in the mood to see good hockey he can see it in some easily available city throughout the entire province. For me there is one other area of hockey which is fascinating. You can observe this any Saturday morning in any place which has a skating rink. This is kids' morning and wherever you may find yourself it is worthwhile to go out to the local arena and watch the young toddlers—the hockey greats of tomorrow—as they learn the great game and, more important, imbibe the true spirit of good sportsmanship. Saturday morning is hockey morning in Ontario.

One of the most popular spectator sports in Ontario is racing in all its forms with horse-racing (running and harness) by far the most popular. Every year more regular race meets are held in this province and they are ever increasing in popularity.

The granddaddy of all the racing tracks in Ontario is the Woodbine which was originally in what is now almost the central part of Toronto. Some years ago when it was felt that a new track, with newer and better facilities, should be erected it was decided to move the Woodbine beyond the city limits to a site nearer Malton, northwest of Toronto but easily accessible to the city. The new Woodbine erected by the Jockey Club of Ontario is one of the truly great tracks of North America with the finest facilities for the horses, the horsemen and the spectators. Despite the fact that the new Woodbine achieved such a high degree of excellence Torontonians stubbornly stuck to the original Woodbine and the Jockey Club was responsive. The old Woodbine has been refurbished and continues to operate under the name, Greenwood. Both tracks have been—and the new Woodbine still is—the scene for the top social event of Canadian racing—the running of the Queen's Plate held in the month of June. This is the closest we come to the Derby or the Ascot.

On the day of the running of the Queen's Plate the cream of society appears resplendent in morning coats and grey toppers and with their beautiful women companions in splendid gowns and furs. Usually the weather is fine and, for any racing enthusiast, the running of the Queen's Plate is an experience which must be satisfied. Both King George VI and the present Queen of Canada, Elizabeth II, have appeared to present the royal guineas to the winner.

The program at new Woodbine is studded with important stake races all through the season. Another famous Ontario thoroughbred racing track is at Fort Erie.

Harness racing, once far more generally popular than thoroughbred racing, went into a decline for a while but now has emerged triumphant again. There are many great harness-racing tracks in the province, including the Garden City Raceway at St. Catharines, the Western Fair Raceway in London, the Windsor Raceway, the Mohawk Raceway at Campbellville and a great number of smaller centres including Goderich, Hanover, and Campbellford which now have regular weekly meets.

LAWS TO WATCH

Ontario's enthusiasm for the sport of kings is virtually unlimited and our enthusiasm reflects a good deal about our character, one facet which we don't talk about very much. At heart the true Ontarian is a gambler. He has proved it time and time again as he took long chances in almost every field of activity. For recreation he still likes to gamble and this is one of the reasons why we have so many excellent race tracks. And yet we continue with the pretence that it really is not very important to us; we have some of the most stringent gambling laws to be found anywhere in the western world.

For example, we cannot hold public lotteries. There is some fine print in the Act which allows us to hold little lotteries for charitable purposes but it is illegal for us to buy a ticket on the Irish Sweepstakes. Curiously enough, Ontario citizens appear every year among the winners. The fact of the matter is that despite our stringent laws thousands upon thousands of us buy sweepstake tickets, knowing very well that we are breaking the law. Betting until very recently was heavily restricted in Ontario with bookmaking completely forbidden. Now off-track betting shops are operating within very tight controls and surreptitious illegal betting still continues. Betting of course is allowed at all our race tracks. Here again we have an example of the strange Ontario ambivalence. One sometimes wonders if perhaps we aren't the kind of people who don't get a little added fillip to our enjoyment when we know that we are mildly doing wrong. The same thing seems to apply to our drinking laws.

Like every other part of North America Ontario had its prohibition period. It was ended in the 1920's but it was not until the middle thirties that public houses began to operate freely, and then only beer could be purchased. Bars selling spirits were not legal in Ontario until after World War II. And despite this slow but sure progression away from the unpractical restraints of the prohibition era there are still dry sectors within this province which continue to baffle travellers from other parts of the continent. The explanation for this is that we have a curious device called local option. Any municipality has to approve the opening of any public outlets for the sale of any type of alcoholic beverages, and there are a few places in the province which do not allow any form of alcoholic beverage for public sale, so let the thirsty traveller beware.

Another regulation which baffles many of the visitors from the United States and exasperates some Ontarians is the method whereby we dispense bottled alcoholic beverages to the public. If you want to buy a case of beer you have to go to a store which sells nothing but beer, known as a Brewers' Retail outlet. If you want to buy a bottle of whisky you have to go to another kind of store which is known as a Liquor Control Board store. Here you can also buy imported beer (you cannot buy imported beer at the Ontario beer stores). At the Liquor Control Board stores you can also buy all kinds of wines, domestic or imported. On the other hand, if you happen to be in a city where a specific winery has been allowed to have an outlet you can go to a wine store and buy the products of the winery which operates it. There are not many of these in Ontario. And finally, to compound the confusion, if you prefer a specific brand of beer you can go to a legal outlet at the brewery. Wherever a brewery operates it is allowed to have one store to dispense its own products. It is little wonder that a good number of the people who visit Ontario for the first time are somewhat perplexed and yet, on the whole, most of the people of Ontario have relatively few complaints about this system except one great nuisance. Whatever outlet you go to and whatever product you buy, except beer, and wine, you have to fill in an official purchase order which asks you for the assurance that you are over twenty-one years of age. Beer, wine and spirits cannot be bought in stores not run by government or approved agency not even, as is common in most parts of North America, in grocery stores.

If one wants to drink in public he has a new set of rules to master. For example, we have three kinds of restaurants: restaurants which are not allowed to serve any form of alcoholic beverage (these are in the majority); restaurants which are allowed to serve beer and wine only; and restaurants which are allowed to serve beer, wine or spirits. But if you drop into a restaurant and merely want a refreshing glass of beer, or a sherry, or a tot of whisky it is required that you eat food. If you don't want to eat food don't go to a restaurant: in that case you must search for what we rather euphemistically call a cocktail lounge. These are what are in more common parlance known as bars and here you can get any kind of drink. On the other hand, if you have your heart set on whisky be careful that you do not get into another kind of public dispensary called a beer parlour. These are found only in hotels and are permitted to serve beer only. And there is a further complication—some of these places are for men only; others are for ladies, or ladies and escorts. If you are a lonely male you are not allowed to have a pint of beer except in the company of other lonely males. These regulations do not apply to bars or cocktail lounges.

There are a few other things one has to be careful of. For example, singing or any other display of happiness is not encouraged. It is expected in Ontario that when you sit down to enjoy a drink you should be fully aware of all the serious possible moral, social and physical consequences which may accrue from this action. You may be having the time of your life but it is almost worth your life to show it.

There are a few other fine points which the imbibing visitor to Ontario should know about. For example, you are not allowed to be thirsty before noon if you propose to satisfy that thirst in a public place. On the other hand, if you want to satisfy your thirst in private, in your home or your hotel room, you are allowed to be thirsty at ten o'clock in the morning; that is you can go to the various outlets dispensing alcoholic beverages and make a purchase at that hour. You can then take it back to your hotel room and drink it but you cannot phone room service and ask them to deliver you a drink until twelve o'clock.

Indeed, until only a few years ago, this too was heavily frowned upon. The way the serving of alcoholic beverages to hotel rooms in Ontario became allowed perhaps indicates the pathway to a much simpler and saner set of regulations. During one of his fairly frequent trips to this country, Prince Phillip was staying at the Royal York Hotel in Toronto and had arrived late. He was thirsty. He phoned down for a drink and was politely told that it was illegal to be served a drink in the Province of Ontario in his hotel room and that his only alternative was to go down to one of the public bars if they were still open. The Prince's retort was something like "That is a lot of damn fool nonsense." Although Ontarians and countless other visitors to the province had expressed exactly the same sentiment it had no impact whatsoever upon the Government of Ontario and the Boards which it sets up to regulate the sale and use of the demon rum but, when it came from a royal personage, naturally Ontario officialdom reacted and reacted with considerable dispatch. There are those who say we are no longer a colony but sometimes the old complex will out. In any event the benefit of this particular episode has been greatly appreciated by natives and visitors alike.

Just another word of caution. When you buy a bottle of anything with an alcoholic content in Ontario you must take it straight home. Regardless of how inconvenient it may be to you, you cannot leave a case of beer or a bottle of anything alcoholic sitting around in your car. Buy it and take it home or else. This is probably one of the most frequently broken laws in Christendom which, of course, is the fate of all illogical regulation. The enforcement of the straight-home law is not usually too rigid but one which *is* taken very seriously is the transport in your automobile of an opened bottle of anything spirituous. This is out completely. For a vacationer, who has no home to go straight back to and who maybe only wants a small drink of whisky before dinner and is many many miles from the nearest public outlet there is no recourse if he wants to stay strictly within the law but to buy a thirteen-ounce bottle of spirits (this is the smallest size it comes in), pour himself his ounce and a half and enjoy it, and then pour the rest out on the roadside. The same applies to beer. It is not possible to buy beer in quantities of less than six; it is equally not legal to transport an opened carton of beer in your car.

Illogical and perverse as a good deal of other drinking regulations appear, they are a decided improvement over what we started with back in 1934. The gradual and cautious opening of cocktail lounges and bars and the gradual increase in the number of restaurants licensed to serve drinks has done

much to enliven the Ontario public social scene. Twenty-five
years ago there was very little for the average Ontario citizen
to do in order to while away an hour or two in pleasant idle-
ness. He could go to the movies or go for a walk and that was
about it. He could not see light entertainment such as a
cabaret show, hear good jazz (except in concerts which were
very rare) go dancing (except in Toronto which at its best
had only three places where public dancing was held every
evening) or just sit quietly with a few friends in a comfortable
place with some pleasant music as background and enjoy
relaxed sociability.

PUBLIC DINING AND ENTERTAINMENT

The changes in liquor regulations have greatly helped redress
some of the unfortunate disabilities and the result is that
Ontario is a much gayer and happier place for many of its
citizens. In most cities of any size, in the resort areas, and
very often in towns through which the tourist traffic is heavy,
one can now easily find good public entertainment at reasonably moderate prices. The entertainment available falls into
three rough categories: there is the pleasant bar with the background of organ or piano music and usually some highly
decorative serving girls; there is the bar or dining lounge with
more elaborate entertainment which can range from the noisy
and vulgar to international entertainment stars; there are the
bars or lounges which go in for more exotic forms of entertainment such as topless go-go girls, various types of "oriental"
shows, and very loud rock and roll combos. In addition there
are some places with specialties which are well worth looking
for. One of them is true jazz all the way from Dixieland to
progressive. Toronto, for example, is now considered to be
one of the best jazz cities in North America and for the
aficionado it can produce excellent performers any day of the
week.

The pleasant art of gourmet dining was virtually unknown
in Ontario until the relaxation of the liquor laws after World
War II. Of course, there were places here and there across
the province which had developed extensive reputations for

excellent food but these were the exception rather than the rule. Many of the hotels in small towns took pride in what their kitchens could produce but usually it was in hotels in big cities where the best dining was to be found. Almost invariably the reputation was based on good standard fare, and people in Ontario, natives or visitors, had at least to cross into Quebec or Montreal if they were looking for anything unusual or exotic with the possible exception of good Chinese food which has been available in the province for half a century.

Today all that is changed. Toronto has a range of cuisine at least as good as any metropolis of comparable size in the world. The range is wide—Chinese food is excellent and there are Japanese restaurants, Polynesian restaurants, Hungarian restaurants, Indian restaurants, German restaurants, French restaurants in profusion and, even, Canadian restaurants. With the advent of air transport, Toronto, like other inland cities, now can offer genuinely good seafood and there are many restaurants which specialize in these delectable items. Similarly the hotel dining-rooms have greatly improved and one can find not only a choice of fare but of decor. There are places of great elegance (usually fairly expensive), places not so expensively decorated but intriguing examples of the interior decorator's ingenuity, and places which more or less follow the standard pattern. The best way to eat well in Ontario if you are in a summer resort or in a small community is to talk to a few people and find out where the best places are. It it no exaggeration nowadays to say that anywhere in the province, if you find out where the good eating-place is, you will not be disappointed. In the cities it is a bit more complicated but a glance through the entertainment sections of the daily paper or in the handy guides which are supplied in most hotel and motel rooms will give you a good start. Good eating is no longer a problem in Ontario. It is the custom. Like anywhere else in the world, you have to work a bit to find the right places but they are there.

There are a few places which have rather unique qualities. One of the best known, perhaps, are the two towers at Niagara Falls each topped by a restaurant, one of which revolves so that the diner can see this great beauty of nature from all angles. It is literally true to say you can't miss these. If one has a penchant for dining at the top, the new Toronto-Dominion Bank Building in downtown Toronto, presently (I think) the highest building in Canada (but likely to be surpassed any day now since bank rivalry for tall buildings seems to be virtually limitless) has excellent dining facilties on the top floor. For sheer size and dominance since 1929 one cannot omit the Royal York Hotel which was, and is now again the largest hotel in the British Commonwealth. For a brief interlude it was surpassed by the Queen Elizabeth Hotel in Montreal. When it was built it seemed to dominate the Toronto skyline. Now as the clean-line skyscrapers sprout up all around it, it looks a little squat and dumpy but almost impregnable and perhaps it is. As hotels in Ontario go, the Royal York is in a class by itself. Although it has not been surpassed in size, there are now many rivals in terms of excellence of accommodation, and all the amenities which one expects from a great hotel. Nevertheless, the weight of the past and the building of a tradition still gives this old lovable monster a character of its own. Several generations now can look back to the main dining-room of the hotel where the genial Horace Lapp used to play for the supper-dance every night and where Moxie Whitney holds forth. The supper-dance at the Royal York is one of the few continuing public social events in Ontario. In almost forty years it has not changed very much and, indeed, the hotel doesn't change the band very often and hence provides a continuity the like of which is very rare in Ontario.

When I was at the University of Toronto, the supper-dance was one of the few places we could go for dancing during the week and most of us were fairly regular customers when we could afford it. A warm relationship built up in those days between the leader of the band and his clientele. Indeed, when he heard I was getting married Horace Lapp (who is a most accomplished organist) did not volunteer but told me that he would be playing at my wedding which he did. Almost twenty-five years later, when he heard my daughter was being married he made the same offer. There is still a touch of small-town coziness about even our most formidable social institutions and although we now have a reputation for being fairly tough swingers, most of us, deep down, are glad that Ontario is still this way.

We have changed tremendously in almost every respect since the earliest days of settlement in Ontario as far as our social existence goes, and yet much that is valuable remains. We like to think, and I believe we are justified in believing, that the passage of the years winnows out a good deal of the outmoded and the undesirable but leaves a residue of something of value. I think this is true of social life here in the province.

In rural Ontario we still have our fall fairs and they are as enjoyable as ever; our great exhibitions have improved and kept up with the times; both fulfil a function in the province still. Our natural recreational resources have been vastly improved but, considering the extensive use to which they are put and the hundreds of thousands of people who avail themselves of them, they are less touched by the deteriorating hand of commercialization than in most parts of the world. We still have lots of quiet stretches of beach, cool retreats in summer and wide open spaces for skiing, skating and snowmobiling in the winter. Our native games have become more organized and the facilities greatly improved but the overall effect is primarily that it provides an opportunity for more people to enjoy them. In southern Ontario our streams are not so good as they used to be for either fishing or canoeing but with the thousands of virtually untouched square miles of woodland to the north, and easy access to them, we are far better off than most people. Our public entertainment reflects the spirit of our times but it should be remembered that a large percentage of our people still prefer the quiet and restrained friendliness of the church social and similar modest entertainment and that any visitor is always welcome to participate in these quiet delights.

Over a century and a half ago the people of Ontario established a tradition for enjoyment which pervades the whole province and yet does not take it over. Like any other people, we can be driven to excesses but our average is very good indeed. Fun, relaxation and enjoyment are deeply imbedded in the life of Ontario and the fact that, no matter what kind of diversion you seek, you can find it in Ontario is the evidence that no opportunity has been lost to develop our potential for good and enjoyable living.

Sometimes when I think that we have all gone mad, that we are compulsively driven to earn nothing but more and more money and that the future bodes ill for all of us (and most of us as we grow older do get these thoughts), I take a minute to consult the local paper to see "what's on tonight." If I am in a small town I check out the local weekly and find even there a wide range of diversions. If I am in a city I look at the daily paper and find the same thing. We may be an aggressive dynamic people but we are not so far gone that we have forgotten how important it is to relax.

Timmins Mine
Beaver Valley, near Kimberley

Old City Hall, Toronto   *Courtesy Toronto Fire Department*

Nathan Phillips Square and New City Hall, Toronto   *Courtesy Toronto Fire Department*

Arts Library, University of Waterloo

University College, University of Toronto   *Courtesy University of Toronto*

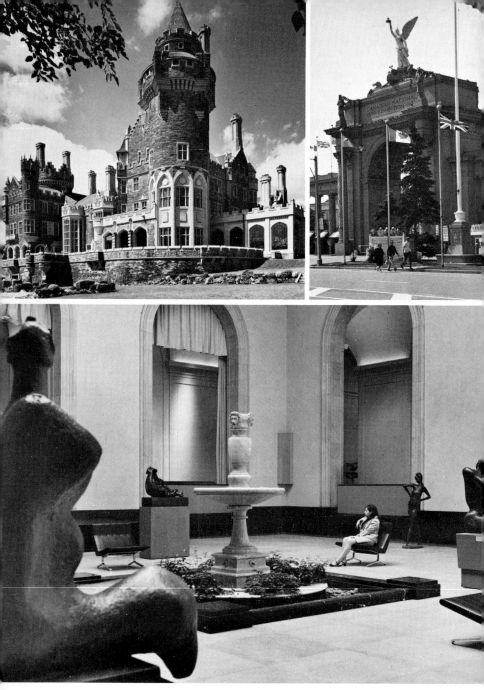

Casa Loma, Toronto

Princes' Gates, Canadian
National Exhibition, Toronto

Art Gallery of Ontario, Toronto

CHAPTER SEVEN

Is It For Knowledge?

Like all other people in the world and perhaps especially in North America the people of Ontario are a little confused between enjoyment and culture. There is still the old Puritan hang-up: If it is good for you it should not be enjoyable. This worrying dichotomy has always been readily discernible in the areas of music and the theatre. Music, for example, in some form or another is usually enjoyable and can be appreciated by most people. In the strictest interpretation of the sober Puritan ethic it is also a credo that music is probably sinful and, if not quite that, certainly profane.

A manifestation of this spirit could be found in certain religious denominations in Ontario in its earliest days. The Presbyterian Kirk, for example, found itself involved in a great internal struggle on this matter. A century ago in the kirk of my forefathers singing was allowed but no musical instruments. The precentor with his tuning-fork would strike the note and would lead the congregation in a hearty singing of the psalms and that was the limit. That congregation like many, many others almost split when it was suggested that an organ be installed in the church. Organs were acceptable in the parlours of God-fearing folk although even there more hymns were played than anything else, but there was considerable doubt as to whether they were holy enough to be played in the church. Ultimately, those who wished organs installed won the day because the impulse to sing whenever one is moved deeply is so basic to human nature that the strictest of dogma could not hold it off forever. The argument of course was further advanced by referring to the harps in heaven and other such evidence to indicate that musical instruments did have holy sanction. Nevertheless, in most of the churches of Ontario even to this day, the only instrument which is considered holy enough to be allowed within the walls of the church is the pipe organ. The old bellows organs have in many instances been supplanted by extremely good and expensive pipe organs as well as a wide range of electronic organs. More than one church organist has run into difficulty when, of a quiet evening, sitting at a great Casavant with all the musical resources at his very fingertips, he has given vent to playing secular music and been caught at it.

The other problem with music is that in a non-religious sense the same contradiction still persists: if it is good for you it is not enjoyable. In secular terms this means that a great number of the people of this province are firmly convinced that the only kind of music which is worth listening to is something which the majority of people do not enjoy. There are a few who have dedicated themselves to the advancement of music and find themselves in very strange waters because of it. One is always hearing it said that the reason most people cannot enjoy "good" music (this is generally defined as opera, symphonic, chamber and the like) is that people are not properly educated musically. This is a somewhat dubious argument. For example, in the roaring twenties the young devotees of syncopation had little time for folk songs. Their counterparts today have turned completely about-face and yet it would be difficult to prove that they have any greater amount of musical education. In the wide range of music which has been created all over the world each generation in its own locale selects that which is best suited to giving vent to his own particular kind of expression in musical terms. At the same time there are still a good number of minority groups who insist on the right to enjoy the kind of music they like. With mass methods of disseminating music of all kinds via records, radio and to a lesser extent television, there has to be a wide range available to satisfy all tastes.

MUSIC AND CONCERTS

The result is as it has always been. In a given community several forms of musical entertainment will be generated. In Ontario there is a wide range. Today, by far the most numerous groups are those whose basic instrument is the electric guitar and whose music is primarily rock. Almost any community of any size in Ontario has at least one and usually many more such groups, all performing publicly when they get a chance and many of them functioning commercially. There may be a profound sociological message here but for our purposes it is merely a fact.

The same community may generate other kinds of music. Singing, regardless of quality, is highly regarded and again the churches have a part to play. Many a singer has got his first training in a church choir. Scattered fairly evenly across the province are churches which have unusually good choirs and which either on feast days of the church calendar or for public entertainment produce excellent concerts. But then we have choirs which take their place amongst the best in the world. The oldest continuing choir organization in Ontario is the famed Mendelssohn Choir which at Eastertime each year still produces the great Handel's "Messiah" for a full audience. A relative newcomer, but one worthy of distinction, is Elmer Eisler's Festival Singers, a magnificent group which is heard in concert throughout Canada and the U.S.A. There have been and are other organizations in various parts of the province, that give choral concerts and are highly popular. One of the oldest of these is the Schneider Choir of Kitchener.

At one time in Ontario a brass band was one of the firmest manifestations of the musical life of the province. All one has to do is to go to almost any public park in any town in Ontario and there he will see a bandstand usually, alas, empty these days. Today, most communities do not have a local band any more and for the most part we have to depend upon the bands of the various sectors of the armed forces. There are two exceptions to this: One is the bands which are sponsored by service clubs in various communities (and some of these are very good) and the other is the pipe band which, despite all its detractors, grows in numbers every year. It must be remembered, however, that band concerts as such (except at such places as the Canadian National Exhibition) are rare occasions these days in Ontario.

Orchestral and local concerts on the other hand are part of the fabric of our lives. In order to perform in concert it is necessary to have a concert hall and our history has fluctuated considerably in this sphere. In the days prior to World War I, the towns developed a fairly high level of local participation and almost every community of respectable size had at least one concert hall. In the small centres these also doubled as theatres. In most of the towns the concert hall was a large auditorium usually on the second storey of a block of stores and often surmounted by a tower or some such ornamented device. Sometimes they were incorporated into the town halls. Mostly they were devoted to concerts prepared within the community itself or to plays also before a local audience. However, in the last decade of the nineteenth century and the first of the twentieth, Ontario was inundated by troupes of travelling players of astonishing mediocrity but with all the glamour of "the stage" attached to them. These made their rounds performing such classics as "Uncle Tom's Cabin" and an assortment of melodramas. They were available in every part of Southern Ontario but by the 1920's their heyday was over. The movies had come. Not only that but the great barnlike concert halls were getting out of repair and were expensive to restore to good order. The inevitable decline made it look as though the concert halls were going out of existence. This was further aggravated during the 1930's by the depression.

But a new manifestation occurred after World War II. As in the other parts of North America, after the war Ontario participated in what was generally known as "The Baby Boom." Children grow up in a hurry and by the time they reach the age of five they have to go to school. The result was that quickly after the end of the war most communities in Ontario found they had to erect new schools to accommodate the ever-increasing influx of young students. For reasons which are still partly obscure to a good many of us it was decided by the architects of almost all new schools that they should include large auditoriums. The contribution of large school auditoriums to educational work may be questioned but they certainly have been a boon to the community. Here, at public expense, was a replacement for the old community concert hall, and since that time schools have been used extensively for this purpose. They were not, however, really designed for the production of concerts; indeed they sometimes were a combination of auditorium and gymnasium giving rise to an execrable word "gymnatorium." They did at least bridge a gap and the fact that they were there and that it was discovered that there were people within the province itself who could come and give most enjoyable concerts substantially increased awareness of the potential of this form of entertainment.

As Canada's centennial year approached a good number of communities decided that the school auditorium was not really good enough for concert purposes and decided to build new concert halls and theatres. The result is that once more in Ontario there are many first-rate outlets for concert performances. They are all being used to a considerable degree. All the small cities for example have a series which is usually called "The Community Concert Series." This is a group of perhaps a half a dozen or eight performances of first-rate musicians, most of whom are Canadian and many of them natives of Ontario. This talent has largely been developed over the past quarter of a century by the Canadian Broadcasting Corporation. The result is that the names are often well known, the level of performance high and the overall level of life in the province has been raised.

In the provincial capital, of course, musical concerts have always been given. For most people, the home of great musical concerts in Ontario is Massey Hall. Now a very old but still very well kept hall, this building for over half a century has been host to most of the great names in music in our time. Every major musical artist has performed in Massey Hall; so have all the great symphony orchestras and indeed the best in all fields of importance in musical entertainment. Massey Hall is to Ontario what Carnegie Hall is to the United States, and it is still going strong.

And a good thing too. Despite the fact that many other cities in the province have excellent concert halls, good old Massey Hall still has to carry most of the burden for the province. For its centennial project, the city envisaged a large centre of the performing arts to be developed adjacent to the restored St. Lawrence Hall which is much too small for a major concert these days. Elaborate plans have been drawn and subsequently reduced more and more. In the meantime the mayor of Toronto, who actively promoted the concept, got soundly beaten at the polls. At the moment it is doubtful just when Toronto will achieve a suitable complex of various-sized auditoriums where all the great musical organizations which are available can perform.

There will be one place in Ontario where this will be achieved and that is Canada's capital city. In Ottawa, costing many millions of dollars more than was originally estimated and a good deal behind construction schedule, a centre for the arts is slowly rising. It will be impressive and magnificent. It too has been and is still being lashed by a barrage of criticism from those who feel that the first place where one should cut expenses when the output of dollars exceeds the intake is in the realm of the performing arts. It would appear that the project is far too advanced for it ever to be scrapped or indeed substantially reduced. Those who feel that there is indeed some value in creating at least one first-rate facility in this province that can rank with the other great ones of the world are gratified that Ottawa's centre of the arts is not likely to suffer what appears to be the unhappy fate of the Toronto project. Indeed, the first performance is now scheduled for early June, 1969.

THEATRES

It will probably always be a matter of debate as to whether or not great concert music is really a civilizing force in our society but it would appear that there are enough people in the province, to say nothing of those who visit us, to indicate that a large number of people believe this to be true. The same thing applies to the theatre. As in most other sections of North America, the live theatre looked as though it might be headed for extinction during the heyday of the movies.

At one time Ontario had several chains of legitimate theatres operating within its boundaries. One of the most important of these was that run by a Toronto entrepreneur called Ambrose Small, and the legend of Ambrose Small persists to this day. He owned theatres from Windsor to Kingston and as the handwriting on the wall became more apparent he gradually began unloading them. One autumn day in Toronto he completed the biggest single transaction of his career, transferring several of the properties for the neat round sum of one million dollars. Having finished his business, he left his office on Queen Street West and proceeded over to Bay Street where he bought an evening paper from the paperboy who had been serving him for many years. That newsie was the last man ever to see Ambrose Small alive. He disappeared completely and to this day there is not a clue as to what happened to Ambrose Small. For several decades the mystery has engrossed many citizens of Ontario.

One day many years ago when I was working as a young producer at the Canadian Broadcasting Corporation an incredible-looking old lady came to my office and solemnly announced that she had psychic powers and that she knew what had happened to Ambrose Small. She told me that one of her "voices" had come to her in the night and instructed her to go to an old hotel in the Parkdale area of Toronto, take a room whose number was specified and spend the night in it. This, according to the old girl, she did. While resting on the bed in the middle of the night she heard a voice coming from the wall calling "Let me out. Let me out." Being familiar with the conversational niceties of such phenomena the lady promptly asked the voice, "Who are you?" And the reply came "I am Ambrose Small. Let me out."

Of course I thought this was a great story and with as much tact as I could muster I managed to get the old gal out of my office. It was not more than two months afterwards that I read in the Toronto papers that the hotel she had mentioned had been demolished and as it was being torn down a human skeleton had been discovered in the debris.

Maybe it was Ambrose Small?

Whatever actually did happen to Mr. Small there is no doubt that he was a shrewd businessman in getting rid of as many of his theatres as he could at that particular time. Between the two great wars legitimate theatre in this province was virtually non-existent. But the impulse for theatres remained strong and it was carried on with great vigour by small groups most of which were formed in the 1930's and were known as "The Little Theatre." In the main, these were highly gifted amateurs, devoted to all forms of the theatre— to writing plays, acting in plays, producing plays, and making sets for productions and designing costumes. They filled a great gap which the departure of most professional performances had left behind. The level of performance which they achieved was more than a little impressive. Many of Canada's best-known actors and producers began in some Little Theatre group or another. There were scores of them in Toronto, and every city had at least one such flourishing organization.

Perhaps the biggest success story in the Little Theatre movement in Ontario was in London. Here a group of devoted people really developed themselves to a point where they were able to buy a legitimate theatre (the Grand Theatre which was once owned by Ambrose Small), hire a full-time manager and producer, and offer a season of at least six plays to London audiences. The London Little Theatre operation still flourishes. The Grand Theatre has been restored and is kept in beautiful order; time and again London Little Theatre productions have won top awards in Canada's drama festivals and, perhaps most important of all, the citizens of London, and for a radius of fifty miles around, continue to support this venture every year with ever-increasing enthusiasm. London is one of the best theatre towns not just in Ontario but in all of Canada and it has contributed more than its quota of playwrights, actors and producers.

Amongst other things experimental theatre flourishes in London, as it has done in various parts of the province. In the thirties with little more to encourage him than eager youth and the auditorium of Central Technical and Vocational School in Toronto, a pioneer of Canadian advanced theatre, Herman Voaden, conducted what has now become a famous play workshop. Here, again, actors who wanted a more rigorous training and a more adventurous opportunity received groundwork which led them to some of the great stages of the world. Herman Voaden produced the first performance in North America of T. S. Eliot's famous "Murder in the Cathedral." It was performed in Toronto's Massey Hall.

Today the tradition still carries on and the man to watch is George Luscombe and his group which are organized under the name of Toronto Workshop Productions. Each year Luscombe's fellows look for a place to perform (never large) and for two years have had a short season adjacent to the famous Stratford Shakespearean Festival Theatre. Like his predecessors he goes his own way, refuses to be trammelled by tradition and is really becoming a force to be reckoned with in the field of drama in North America.

In the more conventional areas of the legitimate stage there has been a renascence. Always one of the major legitimate theatres in Toronto, and for many years a part of the Schubert Brothers chain, the Royal Alexandra in Toronto finally found itself the only remaining legitimate theatre in town. Under the stubborn managership of Ernest Rawley it performed in the face of great odds, getting a little shabbier each year but still gallantly holding its own and for at least three generations the Royal Alex was the only really legitimate theatre in Ontario. A few years ago it looked as if this great old stage would be darkened forever. And then, in the storybook tradition of the romantic theatre, an "angel" came along.

For many people who didn't know him he was an unlikely kind of angel. Most people in Ontario knew him as "Honest Ed", the proprietor of the most spectacular "bargain basement" in Canada. Edwin Mirvish is a true lover of the performing arts. When it looked as if the Royal Alex would probably be torn down, he bought it and in so doing made it quite clear that he was going to respect everything which this great theatre had stood for in Ontario. With loving care he caused the Royal Alexandra to be refurbished. Today it is truly magnificent. Here is theatre in the old grand tradition of elegance, perhaps the finest of its kind to be found anywhere in North America. Any theatre-lover who comes to Ontario should go to Toronto if only to see what a great legitimate theatre looked like at its best. And, in addition to that, he can almost always be assured of excellent theatrical entertainment. The Royal Alex is still "on the circuit" and also houses an ever-increasing number of Canadian productions.

One of the reasons that led many people to believe that the old Royal Alex would never survive was that in the rush of post-World-War-II enthusiasm for concert halls and great theatres, another enterprise had developed in Toronto. This is the O'Keefe Centre. The O'Keefe Centre was and is a controversial counter in Canadian theatrical life. One thing that can be said for sure is that it is an impressive building architecturally and a great big theatre. Having said that, one enters rather troubled waters. Even those who love it best (and there are many) have to admit that this extremely imposing playhouse has always been bedevilled by an assortment of acoustical kinks. The dilemma of the gargantuan O'Keefe is one that has been faced by several recent theatres with extremely large auditoriums.

The problem is simply this: the cost of producing legitimate theatre, let alone the added costs of sending a production out on the road, have risen to such heights that the primary necessity for an economically viable situation is a large audience every night. For a large audience you must have a large auditorium, much larger than in the theatres of the past. Acoustics by no means provide the only problem. Actors complain that the very essence of good theatre is the projection of themselves and the mood they are portraying directly to an audience and that in a huge playhouse the contact is lost or, at best, extremely difficult to achieve. Actors come off stages like that of O'Keefe exhausted and they do not like it. Many of them have reached the point where they refuse to play in such theatres although every electronic device which may help the situation has been installed. I have witnessed performances on the stage of the O'Keefe Centre where micro-phones were used and where as a member of the audience I could actually see players hopping from one mike-zone to another. Of course this intruded in the free flow of a dramatic production. It even affects musicals which, perhaps, would seem at first blush to be more suited to this kind of theatre.

Perhaps some day the dilemma will be solved, or perhaps I and others like me are too hide-bound and too fussy. It is certainly true that, although it has had a continuing record of financial difficulties, the O'Keefe Centre attracts thousands upon thousands of avid theatre-goers every season. Its level of productions is excellent and this in turn leads to frustration. Many people feel that they would like to see a drama, which has won, say, Critics Circle acclaim, before it performs under the most trying circumstances possible rather than the most prime. Nevertheless, if this is the only way we can see this kind of theatre we are very happy to have the O'Keefe Centre in Ontario.

There are some types of productions which do not suffer at all in a large playhouse. One of these is the ballet. Here the spoken word has no place and one looks for visual effects with a large background of music. The O'Keefe is perfect for this kind of show. Before we had a centre, big ballet productions with heavy-drawing power had to be performed in a makeshift atmosphere in our hockey palace, Maple Leaf Gardens. This was far from satisfactory. Lesser productions like our own National Ballet, which has its headquarters in Toronto, or the Royal Winnipeg Ballet, had to perform on the rather circum-scribed stage of the Royal Alex. Now, thanks to the O'Keefe Centre, the people of Ontario can see the great ballet com-panies of the world as well as our own great Canadian ballet companies perform under excellent conditions. The same thing applies to the Canadian Opera Company which has now been operating for twenty years, and for imported operatic per-formances which Torontonians and the people of Ontario enthusiastically support. We had these things before but now we have them under good circumstances in the O'Keefe Centre.

The National Ballet Company and the Canadian Opera Company deserve special kudos. They have struggled hard over many years and have reached a point of excellence which is now beginning to take them into the international realm. Apart from their elaborate productions in the O'Keefe Centre in Toronto and in other large auditoriums, they also mount smaller versions and take them on regular tours throughout the smaller cities in the province. In any given year the people of Ontario and those who are visiting with us can count on an opportunity to see either good opera or good ballet. In this field the O'Keefe Centre came just about in the nick of time. Although well subsidized by both the Canada Council and the Province of Ontario we might not have continued to have opera and ballet readily available to us unless each season a heavy audience had been made possible in the Centre.

And then there is Stratford. After his stint in World War II a young native of Stratford, Ontario, returned, went to the University of Toronto and after acquiring his degree went to work for the great periodical publishing giant of Canada, Maclean-Hunter. Short and slender and balding even in those days, Tom Patterson was a young man almost literally bursting with ideas. Overseas he had seen Britain's Stratford-on-Avon and since he came from Canada's counterpart and had the kind of mind he did, the idea inevitably occurred to him "Why not a Canadian Stratford Shakespearean Festival?"

In retrospect it seems to have been a natural thought. Stratford, Ontario, has always been very conscious of its Shakespearean associations. It has schools named after famous Shakespearean heroes and heroines; streets with Shakespearean characters' names; and a river flowing through it called the Avon. And yet when Tom Patterson began to talk out loud about his idea most people, and particularly the citizens of Stratford itself, thought he was some kind of nut. In those years Tom lived just across the street from me in Toronto and I had access to something which he coveted—a weekly column in one of Toronto's daily newspapers, *The Telegram*. After many a late night session, we almost literally intoxicated ourselves developing grandiose schemes for a Shakespearean Theatre on the banks of the Canadian Stratford's Avon River.

I consented to use a column to give the idea as much publicity as we could. The response amazed not only the two of us but the editors of *The Telegram*. There were people in Ontario after all who did not think this was a crazy scheme and that was all it took for energetic Patterson to go to work. He worked with a will that was prodigious, cajoling, wheedling, bullying and talking, talking, talking until finally the City Council of Stratford—largely to get Patterson off its back— appointed a *pro tem.* committee to investigate the feasibility of some kind of theatre in the city. Most of the members of the committee were sympathetic but many of them timid.

At about that time Sir Laurence Olivier was playing in New York, and Patterson who was never daunted by a great personage, went down to try to convince him to back the embryo Stratford project. Olivier wouldn't even see him. But other people in show business did, practised professionals who were quite willing to take the proposal over on a commercial basis. But this was not what Tom Patterson had envisaged. His dream was not just any theatre operating in Stratford but a theatre that was primarily Canadian, operated by Canadians who believed that the theatre's ultimate goal should not be commercial profit but a high level of artistic achievement. Tempted as he was then and many times thereafter, he never cut corners as he fought to achieve his goal.

The intricate stories of the founding of the Stratford Festival have been told in part many times already and some day the full story will be revealed but no matter how one looks at it Tom Patterson is the Horatio Alger hero of Canadian theatre. Of course all such ventures ultimately become team efforts. The second member of the Stratford team was Sir Tyrone Guthrie of whom, at that time, neither Tom Patterson nor I had ever heard. We learned about him through the great lady of Canadian theatre, Dora Mavor Moore, who told us that he was the one man with brains big enough to grasp the potential and the drive strong enough to force it through. This is exactly what he turned out to be.

Having secured the Stratford Committee's consent to approach Guthrie, but with practically no funds to attract him, Patterson made his first transatlantic telephone call, explained the situation, got an interested response from Guthrie and then asked the key question "How much?" A long pause on the telephone and then Guthrie's booming voice saying, "I will fly into Malton next Tuesday." Later it transpired that the connection had been broken at the critical point, Guthrie had no idea whether or not he would be paid anything except his air fare over but came anyway. As a matter of fact, he did not receive very much money for the trip but he reaped the great reward of having been the key person in the development of a great idea for he looked at Stratford, said it was perfect for the project, scoured the province looking for actors because he insisted that if Ontario was to have a Shakespearean Theatre it must be manned as much as possible by local actors, drew up the plans, worked on the committee and generally provided an essential dynamic to the Stratford development. Even then, things hung in the balance many times.

After Guthrie had left, the Stratford board had time to think and some of them got faint-hearted. I well remember a frantic phone call from Tom Patterson, still largely fighting alone, asking me to accompany him and give him some moral support as he tried to regenerate the enthusiasm which Guthrie had provoked during his visit. We walked into the Council Chamber of the Stratford City Hall to meet a doubtful and skeptical group. They were just on the verge of backing away from the whole project and Tom Patterson was desperate. I shall never forget a moment of sheer anger which overcame me and unleashed a not-very-polite diatribe which both shocked and infuriated the members of the board. But they took another look at the project and decided to carry on and many years afterwards at a recent opening night in Stratford one of that original board came up to me and said, "If you hadn't given us hell that night I don't think any of us would be here tonight."

As most people know, the original theatre was a huge tent erected by the best circus-tent man in North America, Skip Manley. Another memorable day was when the tent was half up and the project had run out of money. Skip was willing to carry on but he couldn't pay his men. We had a weekend to get the money. Once more a desperate phone call. The commercial interests were still keen to get a piece of the Stratford operation and that weekend it looked very much as if the project would have to "go commercial." Happily, due to the efforts of a few prominent Torontonians who had become involved in the project, money was scraped together, the payroll was met and the tent went up.

I doubt if anyone who was in any way associated with the original days of the Stratford Festival will ever experience again quite such a heavy sense of satisfaction as that first night in the summer of 1952 when the now-celebrated Stratford stage was shrouded in darkness, the lights came up and Alec Guinness spoke the first lines of the first play ever to be produced at the Stratford Shakespearean Festival in Ontario —*Richard III.*

These days after opening night there is a great reception for the glittering patrons and their friends who have helped make the Festival a success. Champagne flows, the music plays, the French buffet is a gourmet's delight and, all in all, it is one of the great social events of the Ontario season. After that first night, the reception was held in Tom Patterson's little house not far away from the Festival tent. It was certainly happy, but a little subdued. The critics (and the great critics of New York had come to see this strange creature which had sprung up on the banks of Ontario's Avon River) were yet to be heard from, and there were a great many of us there who could still not quite believe that we had actually done it. Today the Stratford Shakespearean Festival is undoubtedly the best-known and the most successful Canadian theatrical enterprise yet developed in this province and in this nation.

One of the secrets of the Stratford success story lies in the fact that the total operation has never stayed still, never lost its original restless urge to expand and be better and better. The season is now much extended. It runs from mid-June until the middle of October, although the last six weeks are primarily devoted to productions for thousands of high school students who come from every corner of the province to see the play they have to study in the classroom performed on one of the great Shakespearean stages of the world. Very

early, Tyrone Guthrie laid down certain guidelines which
were so obviously right that they have never been changed.
It was largely due to Guthrie's insistence that the theatre was
built the way it is: a theatre in the round, curved about the
ingenious adaptation of an Elizabethan stage created by the
great designer Tanya Moiseiwitsch. Such a theatre has its
own limitations. It is not suitable for many plays which were
written for a proscenium-type production. Guthrie also
insisted that while the Festival should devote itself primarily
to the works of Shakespeare it should also draw from other
great classics of the drama which were suitable in the theatre.
He led the way himself with what became his world-famous
production of *Oedipus Rex*. Since that time the producers at
Stratford have tackled most of the Shakespearean canon and
brought a host of other great plays to Stratford audiences.

It was realized in the early stages that since most of the
audience travelled a considerable distance to Stratford it was
desirable to provide a wider range of cultural entertainment
than just the Shakespearean fare in the main theatre. Early
art exhibitions, book exhibitions, for several years a film festival, and, ultimately, an excellent program of all kinds of
great music have been added. The major addition, however,
is the second theatre. This was originally a fairly large movie
house which has been adapted and is now a beautiful second
theatre, this time with a traditional proscenium stage.

Today, a visitor to Stratford any time during the season
can be assured that during his stay he will have an opportunity
to sample what is just about the best theatrical and musical
package available anywhere in North America.

The Stratford success story has naturally emboldened many
others to seek to follow its example. For example, there is a
Shakespearean Theatre in Stratford, Connecticut, now and,
closer to home, other festivals have been staged in various
parts of Canada and all of them have had some measure of
success. In Ontario itself the second first-rate summer festival
is at the old town of Niagara-on-the-Lake. This is the Shaw
Festival which pretty well sticks to productions of George
Bernard Shaw. While it is far from reaching the proportions
of Stratford, the Shaw Festival, which is held in the fine old

Court House in Niagara-on-the-Lake, does first-rate work. It is largely the brainchild of Brian Doherty, an Ontario lawyer who for most of his life has had an active interest in the theatre.

Immediately after World War II, Doherty was one of the first Canadians to sense that there was a change in the atmosphere from the prewar Little Theatre days. A good number of Canadian performers had established themselves in various types of theatrical and variety shows which were produced to entertain our troops overseas. Doherty not only realized that these people should be encouraged to continue in the theatre in peacetime but he was also convinced that Canadians were ready to pay for shows with perhaps a bit more finish than most of the Little Theatres had provided previously. He also, of course, had the example of the famous Dumbbells travelling show which originated amongst Canadians in World War I and carried on for many years into the 1920's, travelling across Canada and into the U.S.A. Doherty first took a highly successful variety show across the country and then an hilarious production of a Victorian melodrama. From this he moved into more serious ventures and the Shaw Festival at Niagara-on-the-Lake has established him as a major contributor to the world of the theatre in Ontario. Like Stratford, Niagara-on-the-Lake is a picturesque setting, a pleasant town to visit quite apart from the theatrical fare which it offers.

The vitality of native theatre in Ontario is not due only to the daring of producers like Patterson and Doherty. To succeed, it above all had to have a solid body of versatile, experienced and sound actors and actresses. The Little Theatre movement of the thirties provided a good number of these. The "Straw Hat Circuit", which still is lively in Ontario during the summertime, provided still more. But the best source of supply of actors, when ventures like Stratford and Niagara-on-the-Lake were being started, was a group of people who had been attracted to Ontario because the Canadian Broadcasting Corporation's production headquarters for English broadcasts was in Toronto and during the late thirties and forties some of the best radio drama in the world was produced over the CBC.

The guiding spirit behind these productions was Andrew Allen, son of a Presbyterian minister who also had made a name for himself as a broadcaster and who died tragically in the sinking of the *Athenia*. Andrew Allen is generally regarded as one of the best producers of radio drama in the world. His flair and drive attracted remarkable performers from all over the nation to make their headquarters in Toronto and carve out solid careers for themselves. For the first time, via broadcasting, actors in Canada could actually envisage the possibility of making full-time careers for themselves in the theatre. Up to this time Canadian actors either had to go to the United States or Britain or else operate on a part-time basis. Many years ago I was interviewing Winnipeg-born Walter Huston, a great actor both on the legitimate stage and in the movies, in his New York dressing room. I asked the obvious question, "Why did you leave Canada and come to New York, Mr. Huston?" The answer was prompt and accurate "Hell, man, there was no place else to go."

Andrew Allen substantially changed that picture with the result that the core of the early Stratford productions was derived from CBC performers. In the late forties the opportunities for performing on Canadian radio were so great that Lorne Greene, who had become nationally known as the broadcaster of the National News during the war years, opened up a radio school for performing arts right across from the CBC headquarters on Jarvis Street in Toronto. Graduates of Greene's school and Greene himself were also attracted to Stratford and found roles there. Since that time, of course, Mr. Greene has found what is probably the role of his life— Ben Cartwright on the Bonanza show.

Another Ontario name to conjure with in terms of the theatre is Mavor Moore. Son of Dora Mavor Moore, he was brought up with a theatrical background and when I was a student at the University of Toronto he had already established himself as the leading light of the University College Players Guild. (Another pair of leading actors of that era, although not dramatic actors but excellent performers, were classmates of Moore's—Johnny Wayne and Frank Shuster.) From his college days Moore moved into the CBC, worked under Andrew Allen, began producing his own shows and then moved into a bewildering variety of theatrical adventures in many parts of Canada and abroad. He worked with his mother on one of the longest—perhaps the longest—annual theatrical productions in Canada—*Spring Thaw*. Perhaps more than any other producer in Canada, Moore has most successfully mined the local Canadian scene for dramatic and entertainment material. His musical *Anne of Green Gables* was originally conceived and performed in Charlottetown, Prince Edward Island, where the famous story of the little red-headed orphan girl by L. M. Montgomery has its setting.

Anne of Green Gables is perhaps one of the most popular Canadian books ever written. Its dramatic potential was realized, a quarter of a century before Mavor Moore took it on, surprisingly enough by Hollywood. It was made into a movie and had its world première in the Uptown Theatre of Toronto in the mid thirties. As a young lad, I was a friend of L. M. Montgomery's son and attended that (and my very first) opening at his invitation. I had read *Anne of Green Gables* like almost every other Canadian teenager of my vintage, and somehow had an exalted and romantic notion of what great authors had to be like. L. M. Montgomery by this time was a quiet unassuming little lady, whose real name was MacDonald, married to a Presbyterian clergyman living very quietly in a sleepy village called Norval just outside of Guelph. I think I had expected her to turn up at the theatre in Hollywood style, perhaps in a silver-plated Rolls Royce. Actually I do not know how she got to the theatre. She was just there and if it had not been for the most gigantic corsage of orchids I had even seen (provided undoubtedly by a Hollywood publicity man) I would very likely have mistaken her if not for my own at least for someone else's mother. *Anne of Green Gables* was written when she was quite young. She followed it up with several sequels until she got Anne herself married off successfully much in the same way as Mrs. Mac-Donald ultimately found her real career in motherhood.

To come back to Mavor Moore, his *Anne of Green Gables* is still on tour four years after it was originally performed. So too is another production — *Sunshine Town* — this one based on the work of an Ontario writer, Stephen Leacock, whom we shall see more of a little later.

THE PAINTERS

Another aspect of culture in Ontario is its art and artists. Although several of the Ontario cities have art galleries, the major ones are in Toronto and the granddaddy of them is the Toronto Art Gallery which, as was mentioned before, was originally housed in "The Grange" which has been added to substantially. The Toronto Art Gallery has a very solid collection. For some more rambunctious artists it used to be too solid. However, in keeping with the general activist mood of the province as it exists today, the Toronto Art Gallery, like everything else in the province, has shaken off its perhaps original drab respectability and while the breadth and depth of its collection remains impressive it has moved into venturesome and controversial areas including the famous "Hamburg." This has got to be seen to be believed. Rendered by an American sculptor it is a huge and extremely lifelike hamburger done in living colour. Is this art? That is a question which anybody can enjoy debating and "The Hamburg" will certainly spark a debate any day of the week. The Gallery, of course, ought not to be visited just for this reason. A splendid cross-section of Canadian art can be seen here as well as major travelling exhibitions from all parts of the world.

Canadian art was long considered to be the most vital of all cultural pursuits in Canada, largely because a group of artists known as "The Group of Seven" were the first Canadians to achieve international recognition. These young men drew their inspiration from a young "loner" whose name was Tom Thomson. Thomson was the first artist in Ontario to be really moved by the grandeur of our north. He worked up in Algonquin Park where he painted, catching in broad strokes the rock, the pine, the ever-changing sky, all quickened into life and movement by the wind. He died tragically and somewhat mysteriously in a canoe accident in the park but before his death he had activated these seven younger men who understood how he looked at things, how he rendered them on canvas and participated in his excitement. The result was a complete breakaway from all traditional art forms and a Group of Seven painting still strongly bears the mark not only of Tom Thomson's influence but of the vitality of these young painters who experienced the most exciting of all sensations—creating something of integrity, unfettered by taboo or tradition.

One of the seven was rich. This was Lawren Harris, a member of a family which was part of the famous industrial partnership, Massey-Harris (now Massey-Ferguson). One of the great problems of the group was to find suitable places to work and live, and Lawren Harris erected a building in Rosedale Ravine just off Yonge Street in Toronto, known as the Studio Building. It was large and impressive. It was meant to house young painters, not necessarily Group of Seven members, but others like them seeking an opportunity for work and freedom at the same time. Today the best place to see the work of the Group of Seven is at Kleinburg where the McMichael Conservation Collection of Art houses the largest permanent collection of the Group's work.

Perhaps the dean of the group, and certainly one of the most lovable, is A. Y. Jackson, now quite an old man. Jackson canvases hang in major galleries all over the world but he still makes his home in Toronto and still is anchored in Ontario although he has travelled widely, even far into the Arctic regions seeking ever new and stimulating expression in the broad dimensions which constitute his painting. One of the most rambunctious of the group was Fred Varley, a wiry little chap who, despite advancing years, had a puckish youthfulness which could not be subdued. Although a member of the group, Varley was his own man. About twenty years ago my wife got the idea that she would like to have my portrait done and decided to get a young Montreal artist of her acquaintance to do it. He came to our duplex in Toronto, set up a huge canvas and went to work with a will. I "sat" for him on and off for a couple of weeks as he worked on what was going to be an almost life-sized canvas. Our neighbours in the top half of the duplex were a well-known Ontario artist and his wife. Naturally, they made periodic visits downstairs to have a look at the gargantuan project in progress. They, as it turned out, like me, had begun to have some misgivings as to what was emerging on the canvas. One night Fred Varley dropped in for a few rounds of hospitality with our neighbours. In the course of the evening they told him about the project underway downstairs and asked us if it would be all right to let him have a look at it. Varley hopped into our living-room, looked at me, looked at the portrait, looked back at me and said, "That's the goddamndest excuse for a portrait I ever saw in my life. Kick that guy out of here before he eats you out of house and home. And," as an afterthought, "come around to my studio at 4:30 next Tuesday and I'll do a sketch of you the way it ought to be done."

The next Tuesday at 4:30 I was deep in a program conference at the CBC. When I got around to trying to contact Varley to explain what had happened he was out. I tried to track him down in some of his well-known haunts and when I finally saw him he promptly rose, and walked by me without a word or nod of recognition. He never spoke to me again. Perhaps this is what people loosely call "the artistic temperament," but it is one of the major regrets of my life that I didn't duck that program conference and get a sketch done by one of the masters of this particular technique. Fred Varley's sketches are generally recognized as about the most vital and creative of any artist in this country.

There are quite a few Canadians who are under the delusion that Canadian art reached its height with the Group of Seven. Perhaps we have not had as homogeneous and purely identifiable a batch of Ontario painters (or from anywhere else in Canada for that matter) as the great seven. But this province continues to produce a heavy quota of the major painters of Canada. They come in all shapes and sizes. The countryside is littered with weekend painters who go to the innumerable and the endless "scenic spots" for a bit of pretty painting. There is no harm in this and it's great fun. I like to do it myself. In all our major cities there are literally hundreds of young men and women in basements and attics industriously, always hopefully and honestly trying to be painters. A good number of them are very good painters. At the moment there is a particularly vital group in London experimenting and now producing work that is being shown in many of the new galleries which have sprung up especially in Toronto.

One of the measures of the vitality of any region's art is the number of galleries which exist. No matter how much the proprietor of a gallery may be involved in art he still has to eat. Toronto now has at least a dozen galleries which have been in existence for a good number of years which lend encouragement to young artists, have established their reputation and keep their proprietors in food. These galleries are well worth seeing and any art-lover in Ontario ought to seek them out and perhaps he will be amazed and certainly impressed by the calibre of work which is being produced. Most of these galleries are in the Yonge-Bloor St. area of Toronto and there are some others in what is known as Markham Village. This is another project of Honest Ed Mirvish. Markham Street is immediately adjacent to his amazing Bloor Street emporium. His son, David, is a deep devotee of art. Put the two together, along with Honest Ed's genuine love and flair for things cultural, and you get Markham Village, a collection of galleries (one of them run by David Mirvish himself) boutiques, studios, etc.

For me, one of the most astonishing developments of art in Ontario comes from my old friend David Partridge. Dave Partridge was destined for a career in corporate industry. Instead he gave it up to become a painter. For a while he served as the art master of Ridley College, lived in Toronto for a time, and in Ottawa for a while. Somewhere through this period he got busy with his nails. These are large-headed nails 'which Dave drives into planks and then paints them in various hues and colours. Somehow or other he manages to get meaning and vitality into this new dimension of art and today Dave Partridge's nails are included in almost all major collections.

THE R.O.M.

In art as in everything else, we never know what is going to crop up next. One manifestation of the province's cultural life is the one and only Royal Ontario Museum, located at the corner of Bloor and Avenue Road in Toronto. It includes a bit of everything from skeletons of dinosaurs, archeological artifacts from most of the major digs in the world, and what is generally known to be one of the finest Chinese collections to be found in any museum anywhere. The Royal Ontario Museum is a "must" place to visit for anyone who has a bent in this direction. And adjacent to it one can also see the newly-opened McLaughlin Planetarium, donated by the fabulous Sam McLaughlin, son of an Oshawa carriage-maker, who persuaded his father to try putting internal-combustion engines in some of his carriages, eventually made the Mc-Laughlin automobile, and marketed it so successfully that it became the major automotive enterprise in Canada and ultimately the core of General Motors in this country. Mr. Sam, as he is affectionately known to a host of friends and associates, although nearing the centry mark, is still chairman of the board of General Motors of Canada and is in his office every day.

Like a great many other Ontarians, R. S. McLaughlin has made major contributions to many things which enrich the cultural expression of this province. Although the province has benefitted from hundreds of philanthropically-minded citizens Colonel McLaughlin and the Right Honourable Vincent Massey (first native-born Governor General of Canada) are two outstanding examples. Both of them have concentrated very heavily on helping the province's cultural development by giving direct support to several Ontario universities. The Massey philanthropies have been largely directed to the University of Toronto but Colonel McLaughlin has spread a much wider net.

THE UNIVERSITIES

Among other things, the Ontario universities on the whole are tourist attractions. By this I mean they are worth looking at and also that the people of the province take pride in their seats of higher education and like to show them off. It is an Ontario characteristic that we have always and still do place a high value on education although, as far as the universities are concerned, in the beginning the road was rocky and it has continued to be this way more or less ever since.

As early as 1827 the concept of a university for Ontario had been formulated by none other than our old friend Bishop Strachan who, in that year, secured a charter for what was to be King's College, located in Toronto. Controversial as usual, the Bishop was well known for his rigid Anglicanism, and non-Anglican leaders in the province promptly protested the fact that the charter left supreme control of the projected college in the hands of "the Visitor" who, of course, was Dr. Strachan himself. The battle waged hotly for twenty years and it was not until 1842 that the cornerstone for a building was laid, located in the Front Street complex of Legislative Buildings. The next year, twenty-six students were enrolled. In the meantime the Methodists received a Royal Charter for their Upper Canada Academy which was located in Cobourg and which later became Victoria University. In 1842 the Presbyterians received a charter for Queen's College in Kingston and the Roman Catholics a charter for Regiopolis College, also located in Kingston. The battle in Toronto continued and nine years later—in 1851—Bishop Strachan was ready to admit defeat and decided to build his own Anglican college, Trinity College, which was located on Queen Street West in Toronto. The year after that, the Basilian Fathers began a Roman Catholic college in Toronto known as St. Michael's. In the meantime the Presbyterians had also established a college in Toronto called Knox College.

With this welter of fledgling colleges (none of them were either large, prosperous or particularly healthy) the various governments of the province were constantly seeking to get some kind of agreement and consolidation so that at least one single strong university could emerge. In 1851 King's College became University College with the hope that it would be the core around which a University of Toronto would be realized. At this point the University of Toronto was a purely abstract conception. The hope was that students would come from Victoria, Queen's and Regiopolis but none arrived. Finally in 1887 a firm Federation Act was passed in the Legislature which incorporated University College, Victoria University,

St. Michael's College and Trinity College. They did not all move to the Toronto campus at once but ultimately they got there and have been there in force and constantly expanding ever since.

The federation of these four arts colleges provided the nucleus for what is today Canada's largest and greatest university—the University of Toronto. Originally its campus was one hundred and three acres between College Street on the south and Bloor Street on the north, bounded on the east by University Avenue and Queen's Park and on the west by St. George Street. Now it stretches over to Spadina Avenue on the west. In terms of newer campuses, profiting from the congestion experiences of places like Toronto, the U. of T. campus is still small. When it was originally conceived the land was on the outskirts of the small city of Toronto. Today it is in the heart of this metropolis of over two million people.

A tour through its busy grounds reveals almost a microcosm of the macrocosm that is Ontario. In the heart of the campus is the beautiful old Norman building which is University College, erected in 1858. There is no building in Canada which says learning in the traditional sense as beautifully and as emphatically as the University College building. Its front door is probably the most photographed academic entrance in Canada. Indeed, the great door is almost a symbol of the many storms in higher education which have buffeted the Ontario system from 1826 to the present day.

In a lighter vein I recall that when I was an undergraduate of University College the engineers of the university decided to raid it. This was a usual part of the autumn activities on campus but this particular year they seemed to be a little more in earnest and acquired a short telephone pole to use as a battering ram to break down the door. The then principal, beloved Doctor Wallace, would not tolerate this. The door had a meaning far beyond the boundaries of campus high jinks. The principal, wearing his battered old gown, proceeded from his office to the front door just as a somewhat unruly band were ready to mount their attack, stood in front of it and said, "If you are going to break the door down you'll have to batter me first." That year the engineers did not manage to break into University College and perhaps Principal Wallace's example of head-on confrontation at the guts level could be an example for the university administrators who are having a spate of trouble with protestors these days.

University College is not the only magnificent building on the Toronto campus. When Trinity College finally moved up from Queen Street they began an ambitious building carrying out the same basic architecture of their original college, which, in turn, was derived from Trinity College, Dublin. Trinity College today is a magnificent quadrangle of stone incorporating a splendid chapel, the teaching buildings and a residence. Similarly, St. Michael's College on the east side of Queen's Park, is equally imposing. Its neighbour to the north, Victoria College, is a bit of a hodge-podge. On the west side of St. George Street, Knox College, which for a long time now has been only a theological college, is another fine example of college Gothic architecture. The professional schools were originally housed in more utilitarian buildings including "the little red schoolhouse" the original school of practical science (engineering) and the anatomy building of Toronto's famous medical school. Today new concrete and glass high-rise buildings dominate the U. of T. campus and one of the recent colleges—New College—is a model in another mode. So too is Massey College at the corner of Hoskin and Devonshire Place, a gift of the Massey Foundation for the use of graduate students. Its first master was and is Robertson Davies, an Ontarian with a distinguished background in journalism, writing, and other more academic interests.

When taking a stroll through the U. of T. campus it is well to keep an eye out for the remains of an earlier era such as Baldwin House, a large house still kept intact on campus and which for many years housed the entire history department of the university. Simcoe Hall is still the centre of the university's complex administration and the adjoining Convocation Hall still serves the function for which it was built. The campus is dotted with many residences including Whitney Hall, St. Hilda's College and other women's residences which many generations of male Toronto undergraduates have visited frequently.

Among the men's residences is Devonshire House, sandwiched in between Varsity Stadium and Trinity College. A sturdy red sandstone quadrangle made up of North House, East House, and South House, it for many years had the "bad boy" reputation on campus. Life in Devonshire House was vigorous and virile if not always ethereal and academic. In its some sixty years of service on campus it has been a place where male students from all faculties could rub shoulders with each other in a kind of free camaraderie which often produces a vital part of the university experience. Here engineers, meds students, artsmen, and graduate students were able to get together and get into trouble together.

When I was a denizen of East House and one of the spokesmen who had to appear regularly before the university disciplinary body, the Caput, the then president of the university, Dr. Cody, began to recognize me, every time we met on campus, as a long lost friend, "Well Mr. Scott," he would say, "what exuberance is manifesting itself in East House today?" In recent years, life in Devonshire House has been greatly enriched. This is largely due to the efforts made on behalf of this neglected side of the university by Tom Symons who is now president of Trent University in Peterborough. Under Symons, Devonshire House was made to realize the meaning of its many years of service to the university and it has acquired a pride which cannot be equalled by any other institution which makes up the great University of Toronto complex as it stands today. Outside of Dr. Symons himself, the one man who contributed most to Devonshire House is Harold Brown who was originally employed as a houseman and in my day made my bed and took a pass at cleaning up my always untidy room, and eventually became the house porter, serving faithfully for forty years. It is doubtful if the U. of T. ever had anyone who could equal Harold Brown's almost total recall for the thousands of students whom he got to know through the years he served Devonshire House.

One of the great sources of enrichment for male undergraduates passing through Toronto is Hart House, gift of the Massey family and designed to provide a sort of great club for the men students of the university. Hart House is magnificent and has become the prototype for similar student buildings on almost all other Canadian campuses. It is beautifully set off by the Memorial Tower at its west end, erected by the alumni of the university in memory of their fellows who fell in World War I. The tower has a great carillon which, it must be confessed, has not always endeared itself to the students particularly at exam time. In my day at least, the rambunctious scholars of Devonshire House which is not very far away from the tower were wont to become somewhat exersized when the great bells started pealing as we were trying to study. "Shut off those bells!" was the cry from every window from the philistines who obviously were incapable of enjoying the splendid concert.

However, from a varsity man's point of view the real philistines were to the east, in Kingston at Queen's University. The original plan of incorporation in the mid-nineteenth century included, hopefully, Queen's as well as Victoria, Trinity and St. Michael's Colleges. However the independent and rugged Presbyterian founders of Queen's were distrustful of the plan and typically enough decided to continue on their own. It was not always easy going. For many years the denominational university had to make do without any kind of government support but the faithful of the kirk rallied round and kept their university going. Queen's was also fortunate in the calibre of the men who supplied leadership through its trying years. Best remembered of these is the Rev. George Monro Grant who was once described as "a powerful, well-balanced, fervent and good man." This he was and during his long years of tenure Queen's established itself in the role which it continues to play in Ontario higher education today — a great university of unquestioned integrity.

It is a campus which is beautiful to visit. Like Toronto it does not have very much free space any more. Unlike Toronto, there is a greater consistency of architecture on the campus and many splendid buildings both new and old. Queen's has always attracted many individual benefactors although it has long since ceased to be a denominational university and, like almost all other universities presently in Ontario, receives its fair share of government financial support. However many of the province's very rich people have been attracted to this unique university with its continuing unabashed Scottish flavour. Queen's is probably the only university in North America with a Gaelic college yell.

It is also the university which pioneered in extension courses in this country. By now a great number of Canadian universities make it possible for people who, for one reason or another, are unable to take three to four years to gain a college degree, to acquire their sheepskin through summer courses and winter correspondence courses. Queen's was the first to develop a full-fledged program. Perhaps the feeling that Queen's is the kind of university which is really dedicated to helping as many people as possible gain university standard has something to do with the fact that it undoubtedly has the most closely knit, most fiercely partisan alumni of any university in Canada. Today, under the pressures which exist for ever-increasing and expanded university facilities, Queen's University has once more taken a courageous stand. It will not be caught up in the tide of growing for the sake of getting bigger. In the first place, it is severely limited by lack of space but above and beyond this so strong is its drive to retain its peculiar individuality that it is successfully resisting all pressures which might change its intrinsic charater. Queen's has stood in a unique place in Ontario's higher educational system and it intends to remain there.

Of all traditional college rivalries in this country, the rivalry between Toronto and Queen's is the oldest and strongest. Both are old, venerable and respected. Both are progressive, forward-looking and proud of over a century of distinguished scholars who have been members of their faculties and student bodies. Above all, both are strongly aware of their responsibility to higher education. Naturally they would be rivals. Sometimes the rivalry would seem to get out of hand but never past the point of good humour and reasonably civilized conduct.

One of the traditional duties of the freshmen in Devonshire House has been to guard Varsity Stadium, which is next door, on the eve of the Varsity-Queen's football games. The precaution is well-founded, for almost every year the marauding Gaels in the dark of the night will attempt to surmount the high brick walls which surround the stadium and leave some flamboyant mark in Queen's colours. The year I helped guard the stadium we caught such a band and managed to bring one of its members back to East House where we found, concealed in his overcoat pockets, three cans of paint (Queen's colours of course). Retribution was just and speedy. Using a pair of electric clippers we shaved a large T on top of his head, easily visible from quite a long distance away as was proven when it turned out at the football game the next day that he was a member of the band, wore one of the pillbox hats which is part of the Queen's band uniform and which certainly did not cover the large and conspicuous T which he carried on his head.

In 1887, the Baptist Church secured a charter for a university to be called McMaster largely in deference to the Honourable William McMaster who gave the university an endowment of almost a million dollars. Originally, McMaster University was established in a large building on Bloor St. West, adjacent to the University of Toronto. Later McMaster moved to Hamilton and the U. of T. acquired the old holdings in Toronto. The campus which was built in Hamilton was for many years the most beautiful in Ontario. Today, like the other older universities, McMaster is feeling the pinch because of lack of land. Like Toronto it has had to resort to a hodge-podge of architecture but the basic campus is still well worth a visit.

As early as 1849 the capital city of Canada, Ottawa, had an incorporated institution known as the College of Bytown which was founded by the Roman Catholic Bishop Gigues. In 1861 the name was changed to the College of Ottawa and in 1886 it was given university status. This too is in the heart of Ottawa and also suffers from lack of space. It has made a distinguished contribution to higher education but perhaps its most significant attribute is that it was the first and used to be the only bilingual university in Ontario.

The University of Western Ontario in London traces its

origin to the Anglican Huron College which was established by Bishop Cronyn in 1867. Eleven years later under Bishop Hellmuth, the colourful Anglican cleric who was originally of the Jewish faith, a charter was secured which permitted the organization of the University of Western Ontario. Of all the older universities, Western is the only one whose founding fathers had the foresight to secure a large campus, which has been added to since. The result is that with plenty of space for expansion and lots of generous support especially from the so-called London "establishment" and many other friends as well, Western has been able to maintain a pure architectural tradition. The campus of the University of Western Ontario is perhaps the best example of fine college Gothic in North America. This is an unbelievably beautiful campus, rolling, wooded, with stone towers and spires rising to the sky. In recent years, many supporters of Western have felt that the high cost of stone masonry is a luxury which no university can any longer afford but the governors of Western still stick stubbornly to their decision to keep their architectural integrity. It is to be hoped that they can manage to continue this way because this campus stands alone in Canada in this respect. It is justly proud and justly famous for its academic achievements and is a fully rounded university of arts colleges, affiliated colleges of several denominations and professional schools.

Because the campus setting of Western is luxurious and, partly too, because for a period it seemed to concentrate very heavily on athletic achievements, this university often used to be known as "the playboys' college." It is still true that the social calendar at Western is probably fuller than at any other university and that its students certainly can have a good time any evening of the week, but slowly Western is living down its former reputation. It is thoroughly respectable, academically and fiercely proud of its achievements. Western alumni have spread far and wide the fame of their alma mater and particularly its medical and business schools.

These five, all of whom have interesting campuses, all well worth taking time to visit, are the "old" universities of Ontario.

Stephen Leacock's Home, Brewery Bay

"Woodside", boyhood home of William Lyon Mackenzie King,
former Prime Minister of Canada, Kitchener

O'Keefe Centre, Toronto

St. Lawrence Hall, Toronto   *Courtesy Toronto Fire Department*

The province now has a batch of new universities which have developed along two patterns.

Universities, like the University of Windsor in Windsor and Carleton University in Ottawa, derive directly from small arts colleges which were located in their respective cities and which, when the need for expanded university facilities developed some ten to fifteen years ago, were quickly expanded to meet an urgent situation. Both Carleton and Windsor have done this very well. Carleton is an elegant university with a new campus and all new buildings which continue to grow yearly. The same can be said for Windsor and both of them, despite the fact that they are very young, have established firm positions in Ontario's academic life. A visitor to Windsor or to Ottawa should take time out to see just what can be achieved under these circumstances.

If one is in Northern Ontario and in the boisterous town of Sudbury he should take time to go to Laurentian University, Ontario's second bilingual institution of higher learning. Laurentian too is impressively modern and a further indication that the city of Sudbury is a good deal more than just a miners' town on Saturday night.

Metropolitan Toronto obviously required more than one university even though it was a large and well-established institution. The answer has been York University, built on the northern extremities of Toronto on a large acreage where constant building is occurring to house what probably one day will be a university of over thirty thousand students. York began in the old president's house on the University of Toronto campus. It was nurtured by the University of Toronto until it was strong enough to stand on its own feet. Under its first president, Dr. Murray Ross, it then moved to a small estate in North Toronto on Bayview Avenue where Glendale College was opened. Dr. Ross is a man who thinks long and hard about the meaning of higher education and from the beginning York has been attempting to establish several new concepts. Among these is Atkinson College, gift of the Atkinson Foundation, which is Ontario's only full-fledged university college to offer a complete course in the evenings. It is designed to meet the needs of the many people in Toronto who have to hold jobs in the daytime but want to continue work toward their degrees in the evenings. It is a unique experiment matched throughout the whole of Canada in only one other place—Sir George Williams University in Montreal. On its new main campus where York is busily building at a consistent rate the university will achieve its own particular identity. It is already well on the way toward this but it has some time to go yet before the results of Dr. Ross' work can be assessed. In the meantime it has a strong Board of Governors, strong support and will probably achieve its objectives.

Up to this point, of all the new universities the wonder child is the University of Waterloo, located in the twin cities of Kitchener and Waterloo. Starting as a breakaway renegade from a Lutheran college in Waterloo which was known as Waterloo College and affiliated with the University of Western Ontario, the University of Waterloo based its hope for survival and indeed staked its claim for existence on a new concept in education as far as Ontario is concerned. This is the well-known co-operative education scheme which has been in existence in both the United States and England but was not known in Canada until Waterloo began. Under the co-operative plan, students study for four months, go out to work in an allied field for four months and then come back to college, alternating in this way semester by semester until they have achieved a degree. Originally, the co-operative plan at Waterloo was used only in engineering which also happened to be the major faculty of the new university in its early years. Today many other disciplines also use the co-operative plan. At this writing, Waterloo in ten years has grown from about seventy-five students in its first year to almost ten thousand. This is undoubtedly the most spectacular decade of progress ever recorded in Ontario university history. Of the present enrolment, almost half of the students are involved in the co-operative plan.

Waterloo has a campus of a thousand acres of which about three hundred are actually in use at the present time. On this section of the campus there is not a building which is more than ten years old. Naturally Waterloo, like Western but in a very different architectural mode, has consistency amongst its buildings. From a visitor's point of view, the campus of Waterloo provides one of the best examples on the continent of how modern architecture can be rendered for academic purposes.

Even though the pressures of expansion have been tremendous, the administrators of Waterloo have with considerable success managed to maintain a unity of architectural purpose. If one looks closely enough, he will find some flaws and already there are corners of the campus which are far too crowded. The worst example of this is in the engineering section where for a long time it was insisted that the school would never be allowed to get over two thousand students. It is almost three thousand now with the result that the complex of buildings which make up the engineering school do little to add to the beauty of the campus. Another feature at Waterloo is the little theatre which is part of its original arts building. Since Waterloo is only twenty-five miles from Stratford it seemed appropriate when it was building a theatre that it would copy its great neighbour. This was done and the Theatre of the Arts at Waterloo is perhaps the most individual and one of the best university theatres in the province.

All the major universities have some sort of theatre building or buildings incorporated on their campuses. There has always been an active theatre on the campus at Queen's. Hart House Theatre at Toronto was originally tacked on to Hart House by the Massey family in the hope that it would keep one of the members of the family in Toronto — Raymond Massey, who didn't stay at home after all. The University of Western Ontario Alumni Hall is the largest auditorium on any Ontario university campus.

All the universities have full-fledged programs of music, drama, lectures, etc. Anyone in a city or town which has a university would be well advised to check what is going on on the campuses on any given night. The universities of Ontario have always been closely related to the communities in which they find themselves and provide a wide range of opportunity for intellectual and cultural enrichment which is often made available to the general public.

A unique kind of university in the province is that which

is mushrooming into light in the city of Guelph. For many years Guelph was known as the home of the Ontario Agricultural College, especially set up to do research and advanced teaching in agricultural science. As the O.A.C. it was affiliated with the University of Toronto and those who qualified in its degree courses acquired a U. of T. degree. Again to meet the needs of more university accommodation Guelph became chartered in its own right and immediately began a spectacular program of building. This university, like York and Waterloo, will probably be one of the big universities in Ontario— around thirty thousand students or more. At this point it is still struggling to find its own particular personality. Up to now there is nowhere else where advanced agricultural research can be carried on so Guelph must continue this important function. At the same time it must not allow this to drain away from its other academic responsibilities and it is apparently succeeding in melding the objectives of the past with the objectives for the future.

Far up in the great northwestern section of Ontario in the lakehead cities of Fort William and Port Arthur is Lakehead University which suffers from being far away from its sister institutions of higher learning but is managing to develop its own unique characteristics.

And back again in the small city of Waterloo is Waterloo Lutheran University, the only chartered university in the province which still has a denominational character. Operated by the Lutheran Church, W.L.U. has had difficult days. In the early years of the University of Waterloo the rivalry between the two institutions was acute. In the backs of the minds of the administrations of both universities was undoubtedly the hope that the other would capitulate and the two would come together again. Today this is obviously not going to happen and Waterloo Lutheran University is gracefully accepting its own distinctive role. Its supporters feel that there is definitely a place in the province of Ontario for a university which does not depend upon government. While W.L.U. will never be a huge university it has every opportunity to become a distinctive and valuable institution and this is the part it is apparently taking. Its small campus is well built, now well filled and its faculty and students have developed a justifiable pride in their unique situation.

Another young and still small college which considers itself highly distinctive is Trent University in Peterborough. Under its first president, Dr. Thomas Symons, from the time of the granting of its charter it has frankly and perhaps even ambitiously billed itself as a potential Canadian Oxford. It has been the subject of more articles and stories than any of the other new universities and the reactions to Trent, pro and con, are probably more intense than reactions to any other Ontario university.

Some of Trent's fervent admirers have not really helped its cause very much. In actual fact, as its president well knows, Trent is not and is not likely to be another Oxford. It is going to develop its own character but if at all possible, it is going to attempt to remain small enough to use the Oxford and Cambridge tutorial system. At the present time it is doing just this and it is perhaps more significant than most people have noticed that this is the one campus in the province or, for that matter, in the country where there is no unrest on campus itself. Certainly its students have the urge to protest and assert themselves but they are not, up to now at any rate, directing their energies toward the university itself. The reason is quite simple: they like the experience they are having at Trent. It appears to be a good one; the real question is whether or not it can continue to operate this way under the extreme pressures which are applied by both government and citizens in general on universities to be constantly expanding to take more and more students.

Peterborough is in extremely pleasant country as we have already seen. The campus which Trent is building is equally distinctive and pleasant. The visitor ought to talk to a few students, particularly if one feels that students these days cannot be happy about anything. The students at Trent, wearing their gowns, sipping sherry with their tutors, emphatically insisting that learning is a total experience not a trade, seem to have found an environment in which they can flourish happily.

There is another very young university in the Niagara Peninsula just on the edge of the city of St. Catharines. This is Brock, named for the famous general. At the moment Brock has very little identity, is just getting started on its building program, and its future cannot be predicted.

This broad sweep through the theatres, the concert halls, the galleries and the universities of Ontario pretty obviously adds up to one thing—this province is busting with culture. The nature of these cultural expressions is worth taking a look at. To start at the easiest point, Ontario is academically sound. It is doubtful if there is any other province or state in North America which can boast of such a widespread and yet such a uniformly high level of university activities as this province. Although the bill which the Ontario taxpayer foots to support higher education these days is truly astronomical, he complains surprisingly little. The fact is we are proud of our Ontario universities. We like to go out and take a look at them. On a Sunday afternoon, in almost any university city residents will take a drive out to see what is going on "out at the college." It is logical to deduce, then, that as a people we are satisfied with what we have in the way of universities.

Comparatively speaking we have a right to satisfaction but some of us have questions. Put together, and taking a good piece here and another excellent piece there out of all our universities we can be in the major league of academic achievement as it is known on this continent but where is our Harvard or our Yale? Or indeed our M. I. T.? We have colleges which are beautiful to look at, we have colleges which are fun to attend, we have colleges whose degrees will be accepted anywhere.

But where is our great university? Toronto comes closest but it is not quite there. The question that concerns many of the citizens of Ontario is will it ever get there or, alternately, will any other of our universities achieve the distinction of the really great in this field? In other fields we have easily and often proved that there is no limit to what we can achieve. The way we have learned to enjoy ourselves and to share these facilities with other people, the way in which we have expanded our industrial development and the utilization of our natural resources, the way in which our financial corporations operate, all these indicate an intelligence and a drive which makes us feel that "we can do anything." Somehow we don't seem to translate quite this same mood into the area of culture generally, and specifically into our universities. Here we tend to be solid, safe and, yes, even the timid citizens who marked Ontario's development through one phase which has long since past. The Ontarian is culturally inhibited. The one great break we have made so far is the Stratford Festival and in that respect this seems like a miracle which is not too likely to be repeated in the immediate future.

And yet why not? Somehow we have got to find a cultural dynamic which equals the thrust Ontario has manifested in more tangible things. If it is going to come, and I think it will, it will show itself in this group, the horde of young people who are currently attending our universities, colleges, community colleges and high schools. Already they are manifesting a tremendous restlessness which, properly channeled, can be good and the beginning of still another Ontario breakthrough.

CHAPTER EIGHT

Galaxies of Gutenbergs

In spite of the fact that Ontario does not have many really spectacular manifestations of culture, curiously enough the one citizen of the province who is internationally known, highly controversial and a name to be conjured with wherever men and women of intelligence meet anywhere in the world is the famous, and in some people's view notorious, Marshall McLuhan. Actually, McLuhan is an expatriate from Alberta. He came to teach in the English Department at St. Michael's College of the University of Toronto some twenty years ago and from that time has expanded his sphere of influence until he has become virtually the prophet of the electronic age.

As a matter of fact, Marshall McLuhan even in his early days at the University of Toronto was not exactly a quiet man. I knew him in those days, used to get into long discussions with him and when I think back to that time I get a feeling of excitement because McLuhan is and was a man who can generate excitement in those who think. If not widely understood —at least his theories are widely known. McLuhan is a man who has given a new definition to the old words, "hot" and "cold." He is the man who has asserted that "the medium is the message." He is the author of three particularly widely read, widely discussed, deeply profound and violently controversial books: *The Mechanical Bride*; *The Gutenberg Galaxy*; and *Understanding Media: The Extensions of Man.* Very broadly speaking these are books about communications theory.

McLuhan is at present the Director for the Centre for Culture and Technology at the University of Toronto. The aim of this centre is to investigate the psychic and social consequences of technological media, which means that this is a study of communications in a depth not hitherto explored. This isn't the place to talk about McLuhan's theory. The point here is that this guru of the "in" generation found the environment in which he could develop, expand and express his revolutionary views right here in Ontario.

To keep the record straight, however, I must hastily add that Marshall McLuhan would be the first to challenge the entire thesis of this book which is that Ontario is a special, particular and peculiar place. The crux of all the McLuhan arguments is "our extended faculties and senses now constitute a single field of experience which demands that they become collectively conscious." When further expanded and expounded, this root statement leads to the now famous McLuhan pronouncement that we currently live in a "global village." Even if this be so, the individual dwellings of the inhabitants of "the village" manifest at least superficial differentiations of atmosphere and enviroment. If one thinks of Ontario as a house in a global village it emerges as, among other things, a house whose atmosphere has always encouraged free and open discussion utilizing the most effective media available at the time.

THE NEWSPAPERS

It was in Ontario (then Upper Canada) that most of the steam for Canada's only rebellion to date—the Rebellion of 1837—was generated by its fiery little leader, William Lyon Mackenzie, one of our pioneer journalists who fully understood the importance of the mass media of his time — the newspaper. In the columns of his *Colonial Advocate*, Mackenzie got to scores of pockets of unrest scattered throughout the province and hit enough responsive chords to lead him to armed confrontation with the Family Compact. That the rebellion did not succeed in no way diminishes the importance of the press.

From 1837 on, the power of the press has been a major factor in the development of this province. It was used by Egerton Ryerson to smash once and for all the concept of a church-dominated educational system. It was used by George Brown, founder of one of the oldest newspapers in Canada, *The Globe*, in 1844, to establish the Reform (later Liberal) Party in the province and subsequently to influence the citizens to accept Canadian Confederation in 1867. Brown's *Globe* was so powerful it came to be known as the Reformers' Bible. In a later era, John Ross Robertson's *Telegram* became so powerful that for many decades no man could be elected mayor of Toronto without its support. In many other smaller centres both daily and weekly newspapers have been pre-eminent opinion-makers. Among these are publications still flourishing including the *Hamilton Spectator*, the *Kingston Whig-Standard*, the *Peterborough Examiner*, *The London Free Press*, and the *Brantford Expositor*. Scattered throughout the small towns of Ontario there are scores of weeklies which have served their communities and shaped opinion within them for as long as Canada has been in existence or, in several cases, much longer.

Journalism in North America, especially in the past century, has developed its own traditions and character. Great publishers in the U.S.A. such as Pulitzer and Hearst introduced an approach which used to be called "sensationalism." This is nothing more than a kind of two-fisted journalism which created its own definition of what kind of news was fit to print. In Ontario this kind of hard-hitting newspapering is best represented by the *Toronto Star*, founded by one of the toughest and greatest publishers this country has ever seen —the late Joe Atkinson. The old two-fisted journalism of the *Star* is now more suave but still this newspaper which has the largest circulation of any in Canada, punches and pummels, exhorts and often reduces to tears the citizenry of Ontario. Its like cannot be found anywhere else in the province but there is an approximation in another newspaper, also called *The Star*, in Windsor.

Reading a good local newspaper not only helps a visitor understand the territory in which he finds himself but also keeps him in touch with the rest of the world. In Ontario the press fulfils both these functions very well. Either of the two great Metropolitan Toronto evening newspapers—*The Telegram* or *The Star*—is bulky, entertaining and comprehensive. George Brown's *Globe* some thirty years ago became *The Globe and Mail*. It was put together by another fabulous publisher, the late George McCullagh. McCullagh was another Ontario wonder boy in the straight Alger tradition. It is absolutely true that some of his first dollars were earned in his native city of London selling the newspaper which he eventually bought, the old *Globe*. Soon, George McCullagh was making money in another and faster way. A brilliant young man, in his twenties he recognized the financial potential of the gold-mining boom in Northern Ontario and became deeply involved in the buying and selling of stocks, the financing of mining ventures and all the other fascinating facets of risk investment. He was a charmer the like of which this province has rarely seen and this, coupled with his great mental agility, led him to his first million before he was thirty.

From then on he consolidated his financial position. But always restless, always seeking the challenge of new things, McCullagh tired of jousting in the board rooms of Bay Street and decided that he wanted to become immersed and involved in the development of our national life. He fully realized the power of the press in that era and his first step was to acquire a strong and influential newspaper. In order to do this he put together two traditionally great Toronto morning newspapers, *The Globe* and *The Mail and Empire*. Both were in financial difficulties, not uncommon in the depression years. With McCullagh's money, drive and initiative the *Globe and Mail* which emerged was a success from the start. At the corner of King and York Streets McCullagh built the Wright Building, a public recognition of the profitable alliance between McCullagh on Bay Street and Bill Wright, super prospector for gold in Northern Ontario, which had contributed substantially to

McCullagh's first million. In the building he put the finest printing equipment in North America and for many years newspaper publishers from all over the world, printers and journalists, came to Toronto to see what at that time was a true miracle press. It is still a great press today. So too is the newspaper.

Living at the time he did and being the kind of man he was, it was inevitable that George McCullagh would become embroiled with Ontario's fabulous Mitch Hepburn. The *Globe and Mail* began its career as a strong Liberal newspaper. Who knows at this juncture what McCullagh's ultimate dream was? Certainly he saw himself as the *eminence gris* behind the government of the country; perhaps he even saw himself as Prime Minister. Like many another man of ebullience and ambition in that era, McCullagh (and Hepburn too) had reckoned without the toughest and wiliest, the most successful political leader Canada had seen since the days of Sir John A. Macdonald—William Lyon Mackenzie King.

In the thirties the King legend was not nearly so strong as it is now some twenty years after his death. In retrospect one can see that this astonishing man (a native of Ontario) had forged himself into an almost impregnable political figure. No Prime Minister of Canada has ever had more detractors and more enemies than Mackenzie King; no Prime Minister of Canada has held office as long as Mackenzie King. Solitary, suspicious, erudite and incredibly politically agile King used the ambitions of other men but never allowed them to develop to the point where they would threaten his own undoubted control of the Liberal Party and, for most of his political life, of the country itself. There would never be a power behind the Mackenzie King throne. First Mitch Hepburn attempted to tackle King and ultimately his political career was ended, indeed ruined forever. McCullagh tried it too and was stopped dead in his tracks.

It was at this point that the *Globe and Mail* became a Conservative newspaper, the political colouring which it carries to this day. Through its columns its publisher tried all sorts of stratagems to dislodge King including a futile Leadership League. No matter what he did he never even nicked the impregnability of the wily Prime Minister. Though thwarted by King, McCullagh outlived him and continued to increase his control of the press by buying an evening newspaper, *The Telegram.* Yet despite the power that these two newspapers represented it cannot be said that George McCullagh ever realized his ambition of being a decisive opinion-maker in the Province of Ontario. He vastly improved the journalistic standards of the province but he died a comparatively young man in a state of frustration. Yet those who knew McCullagh will never forget him: his bewitching charm, his deep humanity, his infectious enthusiasm and his deep patriotism.

George McCullagh gave me my first job on a newspaper— as book editor of *The Telegram.* While I was still working there my wife was stricken by a sudden and fatal illness. On the desolate morning that she died, within a couple of hours a handwritten note of sympathy and support was delivered by messenger to my home. It was from George McCullagh, the first of many wonderful kindnesses which he did for me in the ensuing difficult months. This was not an unusual gesture; it was part of the man and it is unlikely that the scores and scores of friends whom he had will ever forget the impact of this wonderfully human personality. In less personal terms, his legacy to this province and this nation is one of the finest newspapers in the world. *The Globe and Mail* calls itself "Canada's National Newspaper." Independent critics and observers throughout the world agree that it is entitled to this proud claim.

There is another kind of newspaper in Ontario and it just may be possible that there may be visitors to this province who will respond to the somewhat bizarre and peculiar appeal of these publications. These are weekly tabloids which appear under such names as *Flash, Judge, Tab,* etc. They are almost exclusively devoted to reporting shocking, outrageous or perverted sexual crimes and episodes. Several of them operate large classified advertising sections where "swingers" make contact with each other. Many of our citizens pretend that they do not exist. They do and what is more they flourish. They are widely known throughout North America and undoubtedly they make a good deal of money. Once more we are back to our basic proposition—Ontario is alive and, being fully alive, every facet of active existence (both the good and the bad) is to be found in the province.

There is still one other kind of publishing which, happily, is not widespread but does exist here. In a quiet little village called Flesherton, deep in the rural atmosphere of Grey County, lies the source for the only continuous stream of "hate literature" to be spewed out in this province. In comparison to what is generated in certain states of our neighbour to the south the Ontario output of this scurrilous material is small but, thank heaven, most of us deplore it and wish we did not have it at all. This any self respecting community can well do without.

Our newspapers then, cover the full range of human taste from the depraved to the highly intelligent. We are good in the specialized press too. The *Financial Post* is almost a bible of big business and the business section of the *Globe and Mail* runs it a hard second.

MAGAZINES — LARGE AND SMALL

The *Financial Post* is one of the major publications of Maclean-Hunter, the giant periodical press of Canada. *Maclean's Magazine* is perhaps the best known periodical in Canada. While it is suffering the vicissitudes that are besetting all magazines in all parts of the world, it continues to reflect our national life in a highly readable and intelligent way. It too, originating in Ontario, is one of our national institutions. Most of Canada's English-language periodicals have had their origin in Ontario. As in other parts of the world, the number of our magazines has been declining steadily but in addition to *Maclean's* its publishers also produce *Chatelaine*, Canada's last remaining "woman's magazine," and very good it is. Another periodical which has had an embattled history but still continues on bravely is *Saturday Night*. Under great editors like Hector Charlesworth and B. K. Sandwell, at one time *Saturday Night* was undoubtedly the most potent opinion maker in the country. In the last twenty years it has had a very up-and-down history, changing editors, changing format, changing everything, but most of us who are serious readers are happy that it has continued and are delighted to see what appears to be an upswing for it again. This country still badly needs a serious periodical press. It has always been difficult for magazines in this country, inundated as we have always been by the giants of every era in the United States. The fact that we still have magazines like *Maclean's*, *Chatelaine*, and *Saturday Night* is largely due to the tenacity of their publishers and the support given to them by the people of Ontario and, to a lesser extent, throughout the rest of the country.

In this sphere even the government seems to have conspired against Canadian publications. A few years ago legislation was introduced to protect our native magazines from encroachment from outside the country. The uproar was tremendous and the lobbying pressures immense. The result is that the great magazine giants of the United States still get preferential treatment which may possibly strangle the struggling Canadian magazines. Meanwhile they carry on bravely and are one of the best mirrors of our national posture. And in this field one cannot forget the *Star Weekly*. Published on newsprint, this weekly magazine was for many years the most widely circulated publication in Canada. Produced by the *Toronto Star* it had a multitude of strong and loyal followers.

We have all sorts of other periodicals of course. Again practically all of them are generated in Ontario and include many farm weeklies, a wide range of trade journals and other specialized publications.

Two of our oldest universities produce much respected scholarly journals. These are the *University of Toronto Quarterly* and the *Queen's Quarterly*. In the last twenty-five to thirty years Ontario has seen a spate of "little magazines." One of the earliest and one of the best was *Northern Review*, started and built by the late John Sutherland, victim of cancer at an all too early age. Sutherland was dedicated to attempting to put life and vitality into Canadian writing. He was a rebel and what might well be called a literary provocateur.

Regarded by many at first as a maverick, his iconoclastic but carefully reasoned critiques, his support of young writers, his careful judgments and strong support for certain established older writers, ultimately earned him respect in all literary circles in the nation. *Northern Review* was perhaps the best literary magazine ever produced in Canada. *Tamarack Review*, produced by a group of mostly Toronto literary men and women, is the nearest thing we currently have to John Sutherland's achievement. And over the years there has been a bewildering spate of magazines devoted to unknown writers, mostly poets, giving them a vehicle for publication. Many of these originated in several of our universities. Others just sprang up, almost always driven and forced into life from issue to issue by the dynamic and determination of one man. The pioneer of this field is Raymond Souster, himself a poet, who has been the editor of many poetry publications. Currently I think the toughest of all publications of this type are those produced by the Weed-Flower Press in Toronto.

Like most of these ventures, the Weed-Flower Press is one man. His name is Nelson Ball, a poet of demeanour so quiet and unobtrusive that he would be the last person you would notice in any crowd. Yet this gentle, quiet young man is strong as steel. With no resources whatsoever, with no support except his own vital spirit and a group of enthusiastic but impecunious young friends he has, somehow or another, managed to grind out many publications, mostly of Canadian poetry, steadily and consistently over the past five years. Nelson Ball represents a kind of literary dynamic which most of his fellow citizens do not comprehend but the battle which he wages daily on behalf of the young poets of this country must be a major factor in preventing our ambitious young writers from succumbing to despair and desperation. As in our theatre, as in our painting, so too in our publications is this province happy in that it has always produced men dedicated to the new and the experimental. There is no way of telling how much this kind of activity has contributed to generating the new mood of this province. I suspect a great deal more than any of us has realized up to this point.

BOOKS AND WRITERS

It should not be assumed that the "little magazines" carry the entire burden of publishing and encouraging young Canadian writers. Toronto is the book publishing centre of English-speaking Canada. To the uninitiated, it might seem that a Canadian publisher is one who publishes Canadian books. In most instances, this is a very small and sometimes non-existent part of his operation. Many of our Canadian publishing houses are merely extensions of international companies; a smaller number are publishing houses which have been created and developed by Canadians themselves. In this latter group almost all of them owe their existence to the greatest best seller of all time (The Bible). Almost all the genuinely Canadian publishing houses began either with a church publishing relationship or were started by aggressive young salesmen who got their start peddling Bibles throughout rural Ontario. The phenomenon of the travelling Bible salesman has long since passed; what several of us don't realize is that many of our native publishing houses are the direct legacy of these travelling book salesmen. But whether the house be indigenous or an extension of a world-wide publishing organization the major portion of the business done by them is either in the publication of textbooks or in acting as distributing agents for books published elsewhere, mostly from the U.S.A. or Great Britain. It has long been a complaint of Canadian authors that most of our publishers spend more money publishing and promoting the works of well known international authors than Canadian authors. There is some justification to this charge.

To keep the record straight, however, it should be pointed out that in this century there have been some great Canadian editors and publishers who devoted a large amount of their time and energy to the encouragement of Canadian writing and the publishing of Canadian books. One thinks of Hugh Eayrs of Macmillans, of Lorne Pierce of The Ryerson Press and of Bill Clarke of Clarke-Irwin. Without men such as these and some contemporary publishers and editors with an equal interest in Canadian writing, the authors of Canada would be in a much worse state than they are even now, and they are not exactly thriving at the moment.

Unlike the other areas of the arts, Canadian writing has never achieved international recognition to the extent of, say, the Group of Seven in painting, the Stratford Festival in the theatre or the National Ballet. Actually, we have only produced two writers who achieved and maintained literary recognition on an international scale, and both of them came from Ontario.

One of them was a woman, Mazo de la Roche, author of the famous Jalna Series. Miss de la Roche, a sophisticated cosmopolite, created a legendary family called Whiteoaks, set them down on a pioneer estate on the shores of Lake Ontario called Jalna, and carried them through several generations in a series of international best-selling novels. Until recently it was possible to go into Jalna country, see the Jalna church and absorb the lush rural atmosphere in which the Whiteoaks flourished and from which they went out into their fascinating adventures in many parts of the world. Today most of this countryside is heavily urbanized since it is only some twenty or thirty miles west of Toronto. Miss de la Roche is now dead but her books continue to appear in paperback form at regular intervals. She was one of the most witty, most incisive and most entertaining women I have ever met. She surrounded herself with young people, particularly those interested in the arts. We all loved her and an invitation to one of her scintillating parties was like a royal command. For years she used to send me little bits of doggerel whose content consisted of a commentary on her fellow authors from all parts of the world. I have kept them all and treasured them but most of them are unprintable.

The other international best-seller from Ontario was the late Stephen Leacock. For most of his life he was a professor of economics at McGill University in Montreal but his home was a delightful, rambling structure on the edge of the town of Orillia on the shores of Lake Simcoe. It was built on a cove of the lake which was known as Old Brewery Bay and the house which still stands as Ontario's only literary shrine is known by the same name. In 1910 he published a book called

Literary Lapses, the first of a series which made him one of the prime jesters of the English-speaking world. Best known of all his books is *Sunshine Sketches of a Little Town*, a gentle but penetratingly humorous account of the goings-on in nearby Orillia. Leacock called his fictional town Mariposa but it did not fool any of the inhabitants of Orillia who had been so effectively but so humorously lampooned in his book. But the overall effect is not unpleasant — far from it. *Sunshine Sketches* is a perfect example of how a man can be funny without being destructive. It is a Canadian classic, the kind of book which ought to be read by anyone who seeks both to understand and enjoy Ontario better.

Like Mazo de la Roche, Stephen Leacock is published in paperback editions these days. His lovely old home which was falling into disrepair and might well have been ultimately destroyed was rescued by a group of Ontario citizens, restored and is now open to the public throughout the summer season. Its location is beautiful; Orillia is a charming Ontario town well worth being on the itinerary of every traveller in the province. Today there is a Leacock Society which has an annual dinner somewhere in the vicinity of Orillia every year, an evening of gregarious good fellowship, wit and thorough enjoyment all generated by the pervasive, chuckling humour which was Leacock's gift to his adopted province and, indeed, to the world. With the advent of folk music, devotees chose Orillia to be the centre for a great folk festival which, appropriately enough, is called the Mariposa Festival. Thus the young people whom Stephen Leacock loved so well himself continued the name of the town he created on the pages of *Sunshine Sketches* although the festival is no longer held in Orillia.

It is a curious thing that most of the best known literary names in Ontario are those of people who were not born in the province, but, rather, came here in early youth and in the environment of Ontario developed their literary talent. Another of this ilk was E. J. (Ned) Pratt who up to this point is probably Canada's best known and most widely published poet. Ned Pratt was a native of Newfoundland and, particularly, his earlier poetry reflects his island heritage. However, all of Pratt's adult life was lived in Ontario. He flourished, like Leacock, within the confines of a university campus, in this case, Victoria College of the University of Toronto where Pratt was a professor of English. Although much of his poetry is serious, those of us who knew Ned Pratt well remember him for his bubbling wit and his warm humanity. Ned's "little dinners," usually held at the York Club in Toronto, were famous for several decades. Perhaps less known but even more enjoyable was the group of poker players among whom Ned was a leading spirit. This band usually had dinner at the York Club, and returned later to the library of a well-known Toronto industrialist, and was composed mostly of writers, artists and some highly individualistic but extremely scholarly University of Toronto professors. I think perhaps one of the most satisfying moments of my life was the day when, as a fledgling instructor in English at University College in Toronto, I was asked to become a member of the group. Later, I had some misgivings. Brash as I was, I thought I was pretty good at the game, but found that amongst some of Canada's leading writers, scholars and artists I usually ended up a loser at the poker table!

Perhaps it is because so many of our leading figures, especially in the arts, were not born but rather flourished in Ontario that we have little of the United States variety of "this great figure was born here" spots to be visited. We have a few houses which have been preserved where people lived but virtually none are recognized as the birthplace of a great citizen in any walk of life. In the arts, the only one which comes readily to my mind is in the town of Cobourg where there is a little well-marked cottage on No. 2 Highway which runs through the town and is the birthplace of a famous Hollywood actress of another era—the beloved Marie Dressler.

The lasting memorials of artists are their work. This is probably particularly true of writers. The question then arises for the visitor and the native alike: Where do I find books which have been produced by Ontario writers?

One of the first things which will strike a bibliophile coming into Ontario is the paucity of bookshops in the pure sense of the word. The truth of the matter is there are very few really good bookstores throughout the entire province. There are three or four in Toronto; a good one in Stratford; a couple of fairly good ones in Kitchener and in London; a not bad one in Ottawa and, similarly, one in Kingston. There are probably others but I have yet to find them. Even more rare are used book shops. Perhaps this is indicative of the Ontario mood. Our own past in terms of writing is relatively recent and equally sparse. People who are book collectors in Ontario usually have to go outside the province, or, indeed, outside the country even for Canadiana. The only long established dealers in used books I know of in this province are Britnell's and the Dora Hood Bookroom in Toronto. However, the traveller who is interested in this sort of thing should mosey around the downtown section of any of our cities. In most of them one will find shops which are really more second-hand book stores than dealers in old books, but sometimes they can yield rich rewards. They seem to come and go in a not predictable pattern but they are almost always there. As one might expect, there are more of them in Toronto than anywhere else and some of them are rather interesting because they tend to specialize in unusual but interesting areas. For example, I currently know of one book shop in Toronto which goes in for old comic books going back as far as thirty or thirty-five years. This is a specialized interest but it has a wider range of attraction than one might suspect.

The most common "specialized" interest in terms of books and other forms of publication is pornography. This type of printed material, of course, is available in the province but, although I think I know the area of book-selling very well, I do not know of a single place in Ontario which would be of more than passing interest to collectors of either erotica or the pornographic. What is available is mostly contemporary, mundane and undistinguished. Certainly Ontarians are human enough to provide some sort of market for this kind of printed material but outlets for it do not seem to flourish. I think a reasonable conclusion is that the lack of broad distribution of pornographic material in Ontario is more a reflection of its people than the result of legal censorship. Certainly there are laws against the publication of obscenity; they are incorporated into the Criminal Code of Canada and they have been invoked in this province occasionally. In over fifteen years of close association with writing in Canada I have been called three times as a so-called "expert witness" in what are generally known as "dirty book trials" in Ontario. On two occasions I was called by the defence; on one by the prosecution. On all three occasions, the offensive material had not been printed in Ontario but imported into it. Maybe at one time we had an active puritan ethic but if it ever existed, it is not particularly strong now. One the whole, our attitude seems to be that unless a lot of people raise ructions about it, we are inclined to live and let live.

To get back to less controversial areas, although we are short on book stores in the strict sense of the word we do have many outlets for books. Any city of major size usually has two or three shops which are usually combinations of gift shops and book shops and here one can buy most current books including those which are published in Canada. The range tends to be limited and rather strongly contemporary but current Canadian writing is generally readily available in any part of the province. We also have a wide proliferation of outlets for paper-backed books. The widest range is usually to be found in newsstands. In some cities there are book stores which deal exclusively with paperbacks and range from the highly erudite to the lowest common denominator. In addition, most of the regular book stores have a large paperback section. In relation to the literature of the country and the province, the last decade has seen a significant upsurge of reprints in paperback form of almost all major Canadian books and the majority of the authors of these come from this province. Two or three publishing companies in particular deserve a great deal of credit for making this work available in the economical paperback form and they have done much to encourage and propagate an understanding and appreciation of the literature of our country.

It is certainly fine for the traveller moving into new territory to examine its historic sites, enjoy its recreational facilities, visit its museums and restorations, and participate in its social life but to get the full picture it is equally important to read some of the literature of the region. To get some appreciation in depth of the country through which one is travelling he should go to the nearest outlet and pick up whatever interests him in the way of writing by Ontario authors. If he is historically minded, he can do very well in the area of regional histories. When we in Ontario became interested in our past and started restoring our forts and setting up our musems almost simultaneously we began encouraging the publication of local histories. Some of them are very good and some of them are very dull but all of them are honest in intent. In addition to full-sized, hard-cover books most regions have brochures and pamphlets produced in considerable quantity by local historians. The best place to find these if they are not obviously available in local book-selling outlets is the local weekly newspaper office or at a local museum. It is a happy fact that many travellers and visitors as they roam about the province become so interested in what they see that they want to read more about it and a substantial market has developed for this kind of local historical writing. Usually it is not very expensive to buy and almost always it is well worth taking a chance on it.

For a long time it has been a cliché about Canadian writing that our non-fiction is better than our fiction. Canadians are supposedly an introverted people and the process of introspection and self-examination inevitably leads to the publishing of the results. As a consequence, any reader can go into an Ontario bookstore and find a fairly wide range of material which examines and purports to explain almost any phenomena of Ontario or Canadian life which is readily observable. Studies are continually being done about our voting patterns, our nationhood or lack of it, our industrial and economic development, the potential of our great natural resources, the life stories of our leading citizens, and so on.

Currently, by far the most popular of this type of writing is the Ottawa Exposé. As this book is being written, there are at least a half a dozen new books which have been generated by members of the Ottawa press gallery or frayed-at-the-edges politicians whose purpose is to reveal to all the world the foibles and failings of those who govern us. Some of this is interesting reading. The best examples come from topnotch reporters in the press gallery; the worst examples from former politicians. But all of them are evanescent. They are too subjective and too contemporary to have much historical merit and I would certainly not recommend them to any visitor who would seek to know us better. Neither would I recommend another kind of book which has current vogue in Ontario. This is the kind of book which is written by professional radio or television commentators. By the very nature of their calling the people who write these books are required to make snap judgments, have no time for research and, unfortunately, usually are people with a meagre historical or philosophical background which means that their reputations are based more on agile wits than a capacity for sound judgment. Yet recently, every year, we see a spate of books from these superficial sources which presume to interpret but, with few exceptions, most often merely mouth tired clichés in juvenile generalities. Any one who seriously wants to know this province better would do well to eschew this kind of book.

RADIO AND TELEVISION

Moving away from the Gutenburg-induced linear thinking into McLuhan's bombardment of the electronic age, one has to keep in mind what he will experience in Ontario as a listener of radio or a viewer of television. When I am on my travels I always use the car radio. This can be an education in itself. Instead of listening to one of the high-powered stations which almost blanket the entire province, I tend to take the trouble to listen to a clear local signal as long as it lasts and then move on to the next one and thus keep in contact with the various localities through which I am moving. In this way one can get a closer manifestation of what is really going on in the province. Very often I wonder if it is worth the trouble because this exercise does not yield as much as it probably should. What one finds (and McLuhan predicted this) is that in the mass radio media there is all too much of a sameness.

Wherever you go in Ontario you are likely to hear the same commercials; you will either hit a station which is devoted to rock or a station which is programmed almost exclusively to more traditional popular music or, if you are in an area where the station has to serve both tastes you will get a conglomeration of both types of music and none of it is indigenous to the province or to the country. The one thing one can count on from the radio stations is, at the very minmium, news on the hour which has a basic informational value. You can also depend upon radio to give you the correct time, the temperature and the weather forecast at frequent intervals. Beyond this, the radio fare which is presented to the public of Ontario is so bland that it is almost meaningless. Unless you are vitally interested in the reportage of local disasters and catastrophes, the average impact of the typical Ontario radio station is little more than a purveyor of time, temperature and the possibility of showers tomorrow.

There are a few exceptions and these revolve around radio personalities. One of these is Gordon Sinclair who performs twice daily on one of Ontario's oldest and strongest radio stations — CFRB in Toronto. Sinclair is abrasive, humane, irritatingly illiterate (he murders many proper names and fails miserably in the pronunciation of a good many common words in any man's vocabulary) but he has an almost frightening capacity to know what will interest the mythical and also very real "man on the street." His prejudices are irritating and unpredictable but what he does bring to every broadcast is a beautiful sense of loving and enjoying where the action is. Naturally he has had many imitators but no rivals for those who seek to follow in the same path tend to come out with a preoccupation for presenting themselves as either good guys, reasonable guys, intelligent guys or some other inhibiting characteristic. As much as any man can be, in this medium, Gordon Sinclair is Ontario.

Television is another matter. In Ontario, at least in the southern part, the viewer can see two kinds: the television from the United States or Canadian television which is predominantly that generated by the Canadian Broadcasting Corporation. There is another television network — CTV — which is commercial rather than government-supported but it has few outlets, a confused policy and a resulting presentation which is really neither flesh nor fowl. The CBC takes a considerable amount of understanding for anyone not used to one of our essential characteristics—compromise. The CBC attempts to be all things to all men, a not unnatural aim in view of the fact that the Canadian taxpayers support its existence. The realization of this goal, however, is one not easy to achieve and still maintain integrity.

Integrity is a word which is very high in CBC circles. It is invoked every time the programmers and producers turn out something which produces a public protest. It must be admitted that almost since its founding some thirty-five years ago (then as a radio network only) the CBC has been considered fair game by the average Canadian, as is almost any other government agency. Those of the CBC will insist, quite properly, that this is not a government agency but a rather peculiar Canadian institution called a Crown Corporation. This kind of corporate body is almost independent except for the fact that it depends upon the public purse for finance and its request for money must go through a minister of the Federal Cabinet.

What we are interested in primarily is what the CBC can tell the explorer of Ontario about this province. Almost every motel or hotel room in Ontario now is equipped with television. Certainly for American visitors I would recommend that they give themselves a rest from their own favourite programs and take a sampling of what predominates in this province. Amongst other things they will find that there are slightly fewer commercials; very unbiased and apparently straightforward newscasting; more serious programs—either in the form of documentaries or discussions; some very obviously home-grown corn programs and, surprisingly, a quite heavy proportion of canned importations from the U.S.A. The American visitor must be warned that he is likely to see last year's version of one of his favourite comedy programs, for example, coming over apparently fresh and alive from the CBC network.

One of the stated aims of the Canadian Broadcasting Corporation is to be a communications agent which will help bring together the widely separated regions of Canada. A very simple test can be performed to see if this is so. Let any stranger in our midst spend an evening with the CBC and then tell us just how much he has learned about this land in which he is a visitor. My guess is that he will not have learned very much. Then, just for kicks, ask him how well he was entertained and he will probably say not as well as back home. On the other hand, he may just happen to hit a CBC show which represents its top range of production performance and what he will see then is excellent. The basic problem in broadcasting in this country is not either performance, technique or performers but progamming. It is extremely difficult to meet all the demands required of this particular Crown company which enters most Canadian homes and as yet no one has found a very vibrant formula. Just the same, with patience and selectivity one can find out something about us by looking at our television. Just don't set your hopes too high.

Here then are the media which currently operate in Ontario. And what is the message of the media? Electronic age or not, Gutenberg's linear expression—the printed word—is still the best way to learn something about this province. Issue for issue, day after day our newspapers will tell you more about what we are really like, how we think and how we react than all our radio and television outlets combined. Our books, serious or flippant, fiction or non-fiction, will reveal more of Ontario than a year of documentaries and panel discussions. Indeed, the listener or the viewer should be warned about our panel discussions. In this province most of them are made up of people who have somehow or another (and usually without very much ability) established themselves as "professional" commentators and explainers of the Ontario or the Canadian scene. Much of what they have got to say is so superficial it is painful but one thing you can count on: it is interminable. We have several Mr. Gallagher and Mr. Shean performances jamming our airways every day. They go something like this: "Pierre, I think it is a shame . . ." and "No, Charles, I have to disagree . . .". We have endless open lines on radio where lonely or talkative people release their ill-formed opinions at

the expense of the listening public and where the paid recip-
ient of the calls gets his kicks out of being rude to the callers.
We have university professors who regularly augment their
income by going on the air and talking about anything that
they can sell to some public affairs producer and we have a
small group of good fellows dedicated to the proposition that
the world will be cleansed if you keep throwing dirt into the
pan. So, for the sake of balance and sanity, it is best to
concentrate mostly on the printed word.

Does this mean that Ontario is backward in terms of the
electronic era of communications? Not necessarily, although
it is worth thinking about. I think one of the reasons that our
publications are so strong is that they have had a rather
remarkable history of honest reporting, careful commitment
and responsible writing. We may not always be the most
spectacular or amusing writers in the world but the sum total
of the achievement of the printed word in the province adds
up to something which still remains very meaningful. Until
such media as radio and television can produce the equivalent
of newspaper editors of high standards, exacting the most
from their contributors, the electronic media will not really
reach maturity in Ontario.

Or, on the other hand, it may be that Marshall McLuhan is
dead wrong.

CHAPTER IX

Who Says Who's Lost!

The first time I had a really serious illness when I was a boy, my grandfather, who was a doctor, examined me, sighed, and I still remember what he said: "There is a lot of trouble in the world." This is not a profound philosophical statement; it is a simple fact. From time to time, however, in the recorded history of man a generation seems to occur which is particularly articulate about its "troubles." Perhaps due to increased communications media, or perhaps due to other more subtle influences, we are living in such a time when the cry of the distressed echoes and re-echoes about us, "We are lost, the captain shouted, we are lost!" We had a so-called "lost generation" immediately after World War I. Now, according to the pundits, we are lost again.

Naturally, as a citizen of a province of which I am very proud I am somewhat interested to know whether or not we in Ontario are lost.

Apparently, the signs of "lostness" have in part been identified. They include large groups of young people almost constantly involved in either protest or violence or both; the statistics for those under psychiatric treatment rises sharply; the general population appears to become increasingly frantic in its search for meaningless, escapist diversion; traditional values (especially those of established religions) are subjected to severe questioning; the general population tends to become increasingly inert and more and more inclined to "let George do it." And all these phenomena are analyzed as being symptoms of an all pervading, deep-seated anxiety and doubt.

So what's with Ontario these days? Well, it is certainly true that examples of all the above phenomena can be found in this province as, indeed, they can be found in almost any corner of the world. I have a psychiatrist friend who currently is working in Singapore. She reports that the distressed people she attends to either singly or in groups are much the same as those she used to treat in Toronto. Yet Singapore is the new wonder city of the east. According to expert outside observers, this city has a strong sense of its own identity, is vibrant, vital and exciting and seems to be marching surely to a happy destiny. I think that after a good hard look at Ontario the same can be said about us.

YOUNG REBELS

True enough, we have the full range of varieties of youthful unrest and rebellion. Hippie is the word which usually comes to mind in this context and Ontario certainly has hippies. In Toronto, Yorkville is synonymous with hippies and Yorkville is known throughout North America as one of the centres of the hippie movement. For the uninitiated, the word Yorkville (which has been very widely publicized in the Canadian press) conjures up visions of some sort of monstrous place, usually not clearly defined in the mind. In actuality, Yorkville is one short street in the middle of Toronto, running between Bay Street and Avenue Road, parallel to Bloor Street and two blocks north. In its immediate vicinity are an elegent hostelry, a venerable and fashionable church, the Royal Ontario Museum, a large apartment house which is one of the best addresses in Toronto, and the core of Toronto's luxury shopping area. Yet this short street, with a little spill-over on its immediate boundaries, is the home of the most potent hippy movement we have in Canada with the possible exception of another small core centre in Vancouver, British Columbia.

Originally Yorkville was a little village lying to the north of the capital town of Upper Canada, York—hence the name Yorkville. Today it is an equally small village but with more colourful inhabitants. How this came about is hard to determine. A couple of generations ago when bohemians were yesterday's hippies, their centre was even farther downtown. They lived mostly in an area that was known as "The Village," just west of Yonge Street on Gerrard Street. Here, artists, poets, fine craftsmen, some actors and some people who just didn't want to live their lives within the narrowing confines of accepted respectability lived happily together. They painted their little houses and decrepit shops in bright colours, turned night into day, dressed, ate, slept and talked as they pleased. It was a stimulating and interesting little pocket, refreshing as Toronto burst toward cosmopolitan status. Today, a few stubborn old bohemians and a handful of new recruits still hang on. It is still worth while taking a stroll down Gerrard Street West off Yonge Street. You may pick up an interesting bit of hand-hammered pewter, an avant-garde picture or even a rare old book.

Yorkville is different. It has some little shops and far more coffee houses and other similar places for public entertainment which, throughout the summer, and at least on the weekends during the winter, are packed largely by the curious who are drawn to the area by the titillating lure of nonconformity. Some artists and artisans live in Yorkville but a good proportion of its inhabitants are young people, either in their teens or early twenties, who have what we used to call "run away from home" but which is now known as getting to do your own thing. Perhaps the most significant difference between the old bohemians and the new hippies is a controversial substance known as marijuana. In the old village, escape was facilitated by a bottle of cheap domestic wine or a visit to the village hotel where, before the laws grew more stringent, one could buy a "village bath"—an oversized beaker of beer —for fifteen cents, or a "village tank"—a pitcher of beer— for fifty cents. But even back in those days beer was legal; today marijuana is not. Most of the notoriety which is attached to Yorkville results from the regular raids conducted by the Metropolitan Police of Toronto in their attempt to control the trafficking of this illegal substance. In Yorkville there is little active protest, rare violence, no open immorality and if it were not for the ambiguous position of marijuana one suspects that Yorkville would attract no more attention than the old village. However, since police raids are highly publicized in the Toronto dailies and, indeed, throughout the province, Yorkville amongst other things is a kind of tourist mecca and sightseers' objective. On any fair evening, the little area will be jammed with people, most of whom are sightseers. In fact there is not much to see: a few long-haired, bearded and extremely untidy-looking young men and their female counterparts, and that is about it. Nevertheless, the crowds of sightseers seem to generate their own excitement and Yorkville appears to be high on the list of tourist attractions in Toronto.

There is a fine line between the rabble-rousers in our society and the serious iconoclasts. Only a few blocks west of Yorkville, on Bloor Street, is the newly-erected bastion of those who take protests against the *status quo* seriously. Perhaps naturally enough, it takes the form of an educational institution. It is Rochdale College, an outgrowth of the co-operative student movement which has been in operation in Ontario for nearly forty years and whose original objective was to provide low cost housing for university students. This remains one of the functions of Rochdale College but it extends far beyond that. It is an interesting experiment in the realm of higher education. Those enrolled in Rochdale can be taking courses at the nearby University of Toronto, they can organize their own courses and usually have considerable success in attracting a competent scholar to work with them, or they can just exist and do whatever they are moved to do, hopefully something constructive. It is too early to tell what will emerge from this interesting experiment but the huge massive grey concrete building which stands just west of St. George Street on Bloor Street is an indication that this is no fly-by-night experiment. For anyone interested in new directions in higher education, a visit to Rochdale and an attempt to learn and understand what they are doing is valuable.

It is perhaps significant, or at least understandable, that the much more serious manifestation of nonconformity which is exemplified in Rochdale College does not attract sightseers or interested inquiries while Yorkville which is really not too much of anything, packs them in every night.

The hippie movement and radical action in the field of higher education are both pretty well confined to Metropolitan Toronto. Other manifestations of youthful revolt are more generally distributed. At the one extreme are those who for reasons constantly being investigated by psychologists, sociologists and such give vent to their feelings of frustration in terms of violence. Every epoch in Ontario's history has had its quota of "hard men" or "tough guys" but we more or less took them in our stride. When I was a boy everybody got a good laugh out of a very popular book which was called *Peck's Bad Boy*; today the hero of this book would be called a disturbed young person and labelled a juvenile delinquent. I am rather inclined to think that we are more aware of this disturbing element in society not nearly so much because our understanding and learning have advanced but because the violent ones tend much more to move in gangs than they used to. Even this, of course, is not a completely new phenomenon.

Some thirty-five miles from where I live, just outside a small village called Lucan, is the country of the famous Black Donnellys who have been the subject of two or three somewhat bloodthirsty books. Here was a community terrorized by a gang (in this case all members of the same family) to a point past endurance when other citizens rose up against them, cast aside all considerations of law and order and almost completely massacred the Donnelly clan. Violence there was then; violence there is now. Incidentally, the cemetery where the Black Donnellys who were murdered by vigilantes of the community are buried should not be on a traveller's list. It is closed to the public now. In the eyes of the Roman Catholic Church the cemetery is consecrated ground and idle sightseeing is a profanity. Today, while we have undoubtedly more gang violence than we used to, in sober fact we have yet to produce as shocking an episode as the Donnelly story.

In Ontario we do, however, have a wide proliferation of

black, leather-jacketed motorcycle gangs many of whose members have been prosecuted successfully for such major crimes as rape and murder. To deny the existence of these gangs would be to be looking through rose-coloured glasses indeed. We do have them; we do have rumbles, organized and brutal; we do have potential killers running loose on our highways. But to keep the record straight, on the whole these people tend to fight each other rather than victimize innocents. They are not a happy thing in this happy province and they represent one of our worst social and law enforcement failures up to date. Ninety-nine per cent of us never get closer to them than to encounter them swarming down one of our highways in a pack. We let them pass by and that is all there is to it. Basically this is a remarkably law-abiding province but if anybody is really lost surely it must be the unhappy and disturbed young people who are driven to the extremes of physical violence through frustrations and disenchantment which, fortunately, most of us will never know.

The other young rebels are the student protestors who up to this point at least have not manifested their anger beyond an occasional deliberate disregard sometimes for public and occasionally for private property. These people at least think they know why they are angry and they are constantly making attempts to rationalize their actions. The rationale is not important here; some of the positions will change in a day or a year, and others will remain more constant. The point is that Ontario universities are part of what almost can be called a "brotherhood" of universities around the world where a similar spirit of unrest occurs, in various forms and sparked by various local situations. Maybe the university community of the world is a global village of its own. In any event, the Ontario university student is one of the inhabitants. In the younger generation of Ontario there is no isolationist tendency in thought. Wherever one travels, one encounters our young people—hitchhiking on the road, in service stations or working in restaurants and resorts or just doing what the rest of us on holidays are doing—having fun. A good way to gauge the vitality of any community is to establish communication with its young people. Half the fun of travelling many will say is getting to know people. I think some of the most important new people to get to know are the young. A traveller has missed a whole dimension of challenging and invigorating experience when he stays within his own age group, his own economic bracket or, even worse, carries his own home-grown attitudes, wants and needs with him, with no flexibility for the atmosphere in which he travels.

RULES OF THE ROAD

The question, especially for the motoring traveller, may well arise: Should I pick up young hitchhikers? I do; although from time to time one reads of an unfortunate motorist who has been robbed, and less frequently, suffered from physical violence. This is a personal matter but I would like to write into the record that basically Ontario is a very safe province in which to travel. Perhaps because it is home for me I have no fear about stopping to pick up a hitchhiker in my own territory. I must admit that I am more timid and cautious when I am farther afield. Just the same, I think it is fair enough to say that the motorist is far less likely to encounter difficulties with hitchhikers than he will from the normal hazards of a busy highway. Of course one should use a bit of judgment. I find I have a tendency always to stop to pick up members of the Canadian Armed Forces or students who very obviously seem to be from a college or university. I do not pick up hitchhikers at night. Other than these simple rules, I tend to trust my own judgment and the law-abiding nature of the majority of the citizens of Ontario.

The stranger coming into this province should know a little bit about our laws and how we enforce them. Unlike most other parts of Canada (with the major exception of the province of Quebec) law enforcement outside of major municipalities is not the duty of the Royal Canadian Mounted Police but of a separate police force called the Ontario Provincial Police. Their cars are on every highway, easily identifiable, painted black and white with what today's generation calls "a bubble gum machine on top" i.e., the usual red flashing light. The O.P.P. have stations and sub-stations scattered at frequent intervals along any major highway within the province. The traveller who is in any difficulty at all can easily reach one and be assured that he will find help.

As far as the average traveller is concerned any contact which he may have with the police will be directly related to his activities on the road. There is a speed limit in Ontario usually 60 m.p.h on the main highways unless otherwise marked and on Highway 401 and Highway 400 the limit has recently been raised to 70 m.p.h. on most sections. One word of caution: not all good paved roads in Ontario are provincial highways. Some of them are county roads and the legal speed limit on county roads in Ontario is 50 m.p.h. Almost every motorist has his own standards about speeding and hence has some interest in how alert the police of any given locality are likely to be. In Ontario there are not very many speed traps but radar is used on the provincial highways and in the cities and towns. Of course the neighbourly tradition of blinking one's lights to indicate to oncoming cars that a radar trap lies ahead is practised in the province. One thing which will not be found in Ontario is the kind of speed trap which is only too offensively familiar to Canadians who travel to the southern climates in the winter months. If you receive a ticket for speeding in Ontario you are given a reasonable amount of time to pay the specified fine. You will not find that we practise the iniquitous custom of making you post a bond of $50.00 or more, a bond which you will never retrieve, as happens in some of the southern states of the U.S.A.

On the whole, the law and its enforcement here is methodical, thorough and just. Of course very few people really like policemen but most of our fellows are quite courteous, as friendly as their duties permit and only rarely given to browbeating and other offensive behaviour which sometimes is associated with law enforcement officers. They can be very helpful to those in difficulty on the road. The same thing generally applies to the police forces of a great many of the cities and towns in Ontario. The one exception to the overall law enforcement in the province is on the waterways which are policed by the R.C.M.P.

The fact that in Ontario we accept and respect, even though

we do not passionately love, policemen is a good indicator of one of the moods of the province. Despite manifestations of unrest, an increasing restlessness amongst all levels of the population, an ever-increasing drive to get things done, we still remain very stable.

THE BUSINESS BEAT

But we are certainly not stuffy. The word "change" is the operative word for Ontario today. Change is most easily identified in the physical form of building and rebuilding. Wherever you go in this province it is virtually impossible not to see new roads being pushed through, old buildings being torn down and new buildings being erected in their place or, alternately, a great new urban development pushing out not only from our major cities but from a great number of our towns as well. The urban thrust which really only crystalized some twenty years ago is apparent everywhere. For better or for worse, it is the concrete evidence of a changed economy. We are now a thoroughly industrial province in the south; but still a relatively untouched province in the vastness of our north. Whether we are managing the changeover well or not we are the richest province in Canada and have a more affluent society than a great number of the states in our neighbouring country to the south. The business dynamic of Ontario is tremendous.

The Toronto Stock Exchange is the busiest in Canada. It is located on Bay Street which is Ontario's financial avenue. Along this street in downtown Toronto, and in its immediate environment, are the great financial houses, the huge chartered banks, the brokers and the promoters. To understand us fully one should spend some time in this section of downtown Toronto. Here the pace is fast and the competition hard. At the moment the identifiable focal point is the Toronto-Dominion Bank Tower. Stand in its environs at noon or at five o'clock and one will get some idea and, I think, be surprised by the invigorating, pulsating business life which is epitomized in thousands of well-dressed, intelligent-looking, hurrying people who are literally busy going about their business. The same dynamic on a lesser scale is to be found in any city in the province and, incidentally, if you are taking a flyer in the Canadian market every city boasts at least a branch of one major brokerage house and usually of several.

Another very simple but for us a dramatic symbol of our urbanization is the fact that Toronto was the first city in Canada to have a subway system. For my money it is still the best which up to this point may not be too difficult an achievement since its only rival is a short subway system in the city of Montreal. The Toronto subway can tell the visitor quite a lot about us. It is fast, efficient, clean but extremely utilitarian. Unlike Montreal, or indeed Moscow, the subway stations were not created to have any aesthetic value. They work well and they are astonishingly clean and that is pretty well the way Ontarians want to go about their business.

The industrial life of the province is pretty much the same. It is modern and it is growing at a very rapid pace. Of course the great bogey of Canadian economic life is the domination of American money and American ownership. It is true that a great deal of the industry both in the country and in this province is controlled from the U.S.A. With few exceptions, where this applies the heaviest investment almost always is placed in the province of Ontario. On the other hand, we have kept control of our banking and financial institutions even though from time to time this has been challenged. We also have a very healthy group of insurance companies, investment houses and other forms of holding companies which are almost one hundred per cent Canadian owned. And then there are the truly great Canadian corporations. At the top of the list must stand one of the great mercantile empires of the world, the T. Eaton Co., a hundred-year-old empire with outlets all across Canada and literally owned by one man—John David Eaton, grandson of the founder, Timothy Eaton. This is a unique enterprise in any man's language; that such a gargantuan business should remain in the hands of its founding family is unusual enough, that it should remain in the hands of one member of that family is indeed unique. This country is well

supplied with first rate department store chains and other mercantile chains and most of them began in Ontario including
Eaton's most serious rival the Robert Simpson Company
which now has another affiliate (American controlled) Simp-
son-Sears. The brewing business in Canada is another area
where, despite some most aggressive attempts, ownership
primarily remains Canadian. Of the big three, two of them
are Ontario based—John Labatt Limited of London, Ontario,
and Canadian Breweries, a massive group of well established
brewing operations put together by one of Ontario's wizard
financiers—E. P. Taylor. Several of the great food chains,
such as Loblaws and Dominion Stores, originated in Ontario
and are dominated by Canadian capital.

Regardless of ownership, Ontario is a swinging place to do
business of the expansive, exciting variety. No matter who
owns what, the personnel which provides the drive for the
province's ever expanding economy is almost entirely Canadian. There are a lot of major United States corporations
which still think the executive suite should be occupied by an
American. This is a delusion which merely confirms the acid
comment on our United States cousins in a once popular Canadian review: "You can always tell an American but you can't
tell him much!"

On the whole we have a strong enough sense of identity to
feel this about almost all people other than Canadians. In
Ontario we are prone to think that Englishmen, Germans, and
most certainly Frenchmen, have an over-rated opinion of themselves. At one time this might have been ascribed to an over-
sensitive, defensive provincialism. If it were ever thus, it is not
that way now. We have a long history of outsiders, for one
reason or another, coming in and telling us what to do with
ourselves. Slowly, we have emancipated ourselves from this
kind of position to the point where we have very little regard
for a man's racial origin or the country from which he has
immigrated as long as we can feel that he is genuinely one of
us now. We are not defensive because if we were we would be
aggressive toward visitors. This is an extremely rare thing to
encounter in this province. I don't know how it developed or

where it came from, but we seem to have a built-in courtesy towards strangers within our gates regardless of what part of the province he may be in.

HOW WE LOOK TODAY

There are still definite regional differences in the Ontario character. At the border points, for example, there is so much interchange between our two countries that people in cities like Windsor or towns like Fort Erie are much more Americanized than one will find anywhere else. Eastern Ontario is still predominantly rural in character, and up to this point at least more set in its ways and one would expect to find its inhabitants less outgoing. In actual fact, they are far more friendly than, say, a New England Yankee. Up along the Ottawa Valley where they not only have a distinctive character but a readily recognizable accent, the people are as open-hearted as you will find anywhere. In Southwestern Ontario, the people have often been compared to the inhabitants of the great Midwestern States such as Ohio, Illinois or Michigan. The economic development is similar but the people come out a little differently. We have never had the self-centred and short-sighted isolationism which characterizes so much of the United States middle west. In Western Ontario while we may be very proud of what we are we have always known that there is a great big wide wonderful world around us and we have never attempted to cut ourselves off from it. Up in the north, where man is still fighting to subdue nature and explore its richness, the open-handed, good neighbour pioneer spirit still prevails. The people of northern Ontario have found that being friendly works so well for them that it has become one of their most proudly held virtues.

If all this sounds a little smug it is only because I am writing it. Most of my fellow citizens would never think of expressing in words anything which could be called "tooting one's horn." And yet why not? As a traveller, I have been to many places in the world and certainly know most of North America very well. Just because I happen to be a native of Ontario is surely no reason why I should not assess as best as I can what I have experienced both at home and abroad and say what I think. What I think is that if the people of the world, or of North America are losing their way, we in Ontario are going to be one of the last to lose our bearings.

Certainly there are things we are going to have to do and do quickly if we are to retain the valuable attributes which are our legacy from our ancestors. One of the most important things we have to face in Ontario is the problem of getting back into proper perspective the value of making money and acquiring material possessions. There is no doubt that for two or three generations now we have placed too much emphasis on making money and there is equally no doubt that this has been an important factor in our development and growth. Now that we have reached the point where we have our own identity, our own strong economy and one of the highest standards of living in the world the question arises: "What do we do now?" I think we are generating the answer within ourselves and there are some very optimistic indicators.

As I pointed out before, we are learning to enjoy ourselves more. We can get away from it all, let down our hair, utilize our own great natural resources for enjoyment without feeling guilty. Perhaps even more significant is the attitude of our restive younger generation. Today, a young trainee in a great Ontario corporation looks at the senior executives, growing older, more harassed and more tense as they fly frantically from one branch office to another or else, when they are at home, go away from the office every evening with a bulging briefcase, and say "Those guys must be crazy." For some of the older generation such an attitude is sick and that is when we begin to say that those young people are lost. Are they? Far from it. They are doing exactly what we hoped they would learn to do when we improved our educational system: they are learning to think for themselves. If these young and now generally well educated minds come to different conclusions than their fathers did, it certainly does not necessarily mean that they are sick or lost. On the contrary it may well mean that they are the vanguard of a generation with a capacity to live with more sanity and more enjoyment than any generation that we have yet produced in Ontario.

At Expo 67, the great world's fair held in Montreal in Canada's centennial year, the Ontario Pavilion was one of the best rendered and one of the most popular. In design, it was a tent-like structure of flowing lines, contours suggesting openness, freedom and, above all, a homogeneity achieved by a basic structural integrity rather than by fixed boundaries. I do not know who the architect was and no more do I know whether or not he deliberately built it as a symbol which is appropriate, and indeed so accurate a representation of what the province of Ontario is like today.

Within this building, or perhaps it would be more accurate to say under the umbrella of this structure, there were fixed points of reference, many of them literal in themselves and yet not so literal that different times and modes clashed. Rather they all came together. There was an abundance of rock used throughout the pavilion because the core of Ontario is the Precambrian Shield. This and other devices suggest the still untamed and untrammeled wilderness which makes up such a large proportion of the square mileage of the province. There were static presentations in the form of models and pictures used to illustrate the vitality and range of our industrial and economic development and also our associations with the past. There was also one of the best dining-rooms on the entire Expo grounds, not just a most welcome amenity but also a symbol of a capacity of Ontarians to enjoy good creature comforts. And then there was a movie, one of the most popular features at Expo. This is Ontario's recognition of the importance of communications and this movie was superb of its kind, advanced, technologically sound but fluent, utilizing many new techniques of the modern-day film-maker. It was an award-winning movie which can still be seen and should be exposed more widely yet. Through sight and sound (both magnificent) it says Ontario in every split second of its footage. The theme music is exciting and so was the message carried in the lyrics: A place to stand; a place to grow.

This expresses precisely what is in Ontario today. This is what is happening here. We are sorting out our past, in much the same way in which one goes through an attic or an old trunk, trying to decide what is worth keeping and what should be thrown out. We get carried away by sentiment; sometimes a particular article will carry us back to a moment when we would like to tarry longer than is healthy for us. Sometimes we make the mistake of keeping something merely because it is curious rather than because it has any value. It is not always a pleasant task to have to sort out remembrances of things past. It is also time-consuming. There are other more imperative things to do and we have to force ourselves to leave the attics and get down to ground level and pick up the business of coping with today so that we may look forward to a better tomorrow. If the visitor amongst us keeps in mind that we do have a deep attachment to our past and that we do have a vibrant need to keep moving and to keep growing then perhaps he will understand some of the contradictions and confusions in our character, and maybe he will be a little more tolerant of the areas where we have not yet quite got things sorted out.

The most celebrated municipal building not only in Ontario but in Canada is what is known as the new city hall of Toronto. In an era where architecture is so stereotyped and dull that one could almost call it a contemporary failure, the Toronto City Hall dramatically affirms that current materials can be designed in such a way to make beautiful and thought-inspiring buildings.

The way Toronto achieved its city hall faithfully reproduces the mood of modern Ontario. Not without extreme controversy and harsh debate the city fathers of the day repudiated the approaches of former times. They did not turn to either of the nations which have so dominated Ontario life—Great Britain and the U.S.A. And they certainly did not go to Buffalo. On the other hand, they did not confirm an emancipated but narrow provincialism. In short they committed themselves neither to our mentors of the past nor to our own resources. Instead they instituted a world-wide competition which attracted and stimulated great architectural designers all over the globe.

The result is two slim towering arcs, concave sides facing each other, set on a simple, functional plaza. Here, affirming that in the winter time we can enjoy ourselves, is a skating rink which the citizens of Toronto use enthusiastically. Here too is Henry Moore's great statue, The Archer, and, true to our utilitarian nature, underneath it all is a great subterranean parking lot, well and artfully concealed. With a resolution rare in municipal legislators, especially in a situation where land is so valuable that it is almost sold by the square inch, the city acquired and cleared many blocks of grimy, run-down and outmoded buildings to give its gem of a city hall free space and a fine setting.

As they proceeded with the clearance they soon came to the old city hall. There it stood at a curve in Bay St. where it has dominated downtown Toronto for a long, long time. Like the Legislature, a red sandstone building, now very dirty, a mish-mash of architecture which defies adjectives and yet so much of the Toronto scene, so representative of so many epochs of the past that resolution faltered. Citizens' committees were formed and letters to the editor inundated all the city's dailies. The battle is still being waged, several compromise proposals have been introduced and none of them have won acceptance. Here we have the old battle in the attic and, typically Ontarian, Toronto does not know whether to keep or demolish its old city hall. Meanwhile, only a stone's throw to the west the new one stands, the envy of almost every municipality in North America.

There, at a glance, is my Ontario: new, exciting, enjoyable and forward-looking and, at the same time, contradictory, dowdy, sentimental and stubborn.

Can you keep running and stand still at the same time? Come to Ontario and see how we do it.

Index

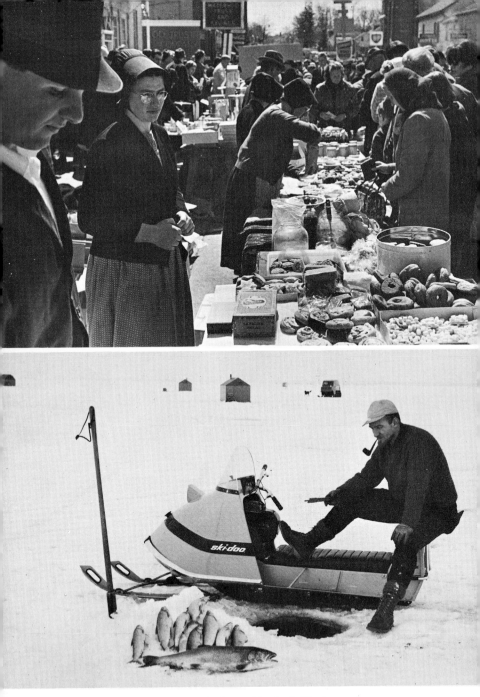

Maple Syrup Festival, Elmira

Ice Fishing, Lake Simcoe

Aerial View of Downtown Toronto

wntown London

The Bruce Trail, Wiarton

McMaster University, Hamilton

City Hall, Toronto

The Mackenzie House, Bond St

Lieutenant-Governor The Honourable Ross Macdonald reading the
Speech from the Throne, Queen's Park, Toronto

Festival Theatre, Stratford